AF530976

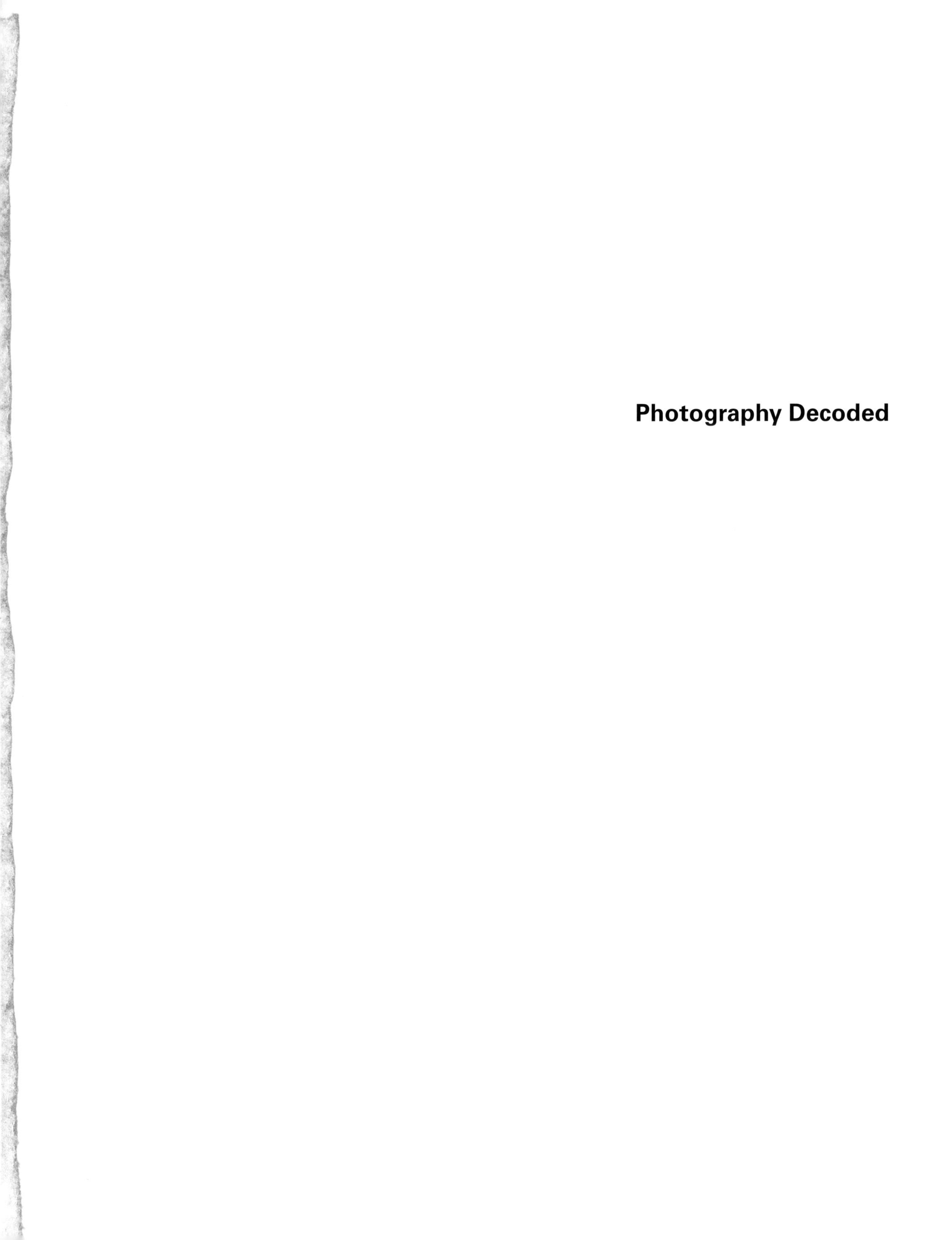

Photography Decoded

Photography Decoded

Susan Bright and Hedy van Erp

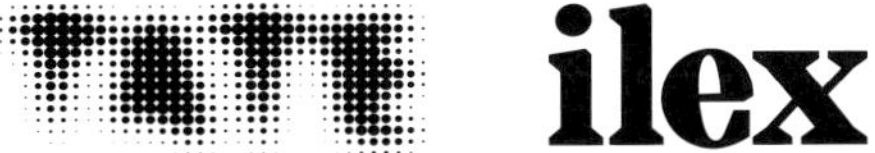

An Hachette UK Company
www.hachette.co.uk

First published in the United Kingdom in 2019
by Ilex, an imprint of Octopus Publishing Group Ltd

Octopus Publishing Group, Carmelite House,
50 Victoria Embankment, London, EC4Y 0DZ
www.octopusbooks.co.uk
www.octopusbooksusa.com

Distributed in the US by Hachette Book Group
1290 Avenue of the Americas, 4th & 5th Floors, New York NY 10104

Distributed in Canada by Canadian Manda Group
664 Annette St., Toronto, Canada M6S 2C8

Publisher: Alison Starling
Commissioner: Frank Gallaugher
Managing Editor: Rachel Silverlight
Art Director: Ben Gardiner
Designer: She Was Only
Picture Research: Giulia Hetherington
Production Controller: Katie Jarvis

Ilex is proud to partner with Tate in our publishing programme; supporting the gallery in its mission to promote public understanding and enjoyment of British, modern and contemporary art.

ISBN 978-1-78157-680-9

A CIP catalogue record for this book is available from the British Library

Printed and bound in China

10 9 8 7 6 5 4 3 2 1

Contents

Introduction

This book aims to guide viewers through the myriad issues concerning photography today. Although photography can appear to be the most accessible form of art and communication – what you see is what you get, in theory – the subjects discussed here show that this is far from the case.

On the one hand, this book will make photographs even more accessible, by suggesting the kinds of clues and approaches we can use to discern their meanings; on the other hand, it will also reveal them to be more complex than we might naturally assume. The ubiquity of photography as a form of note-taking – as it is often experienced via our phones today – means that images may often be seen, but perhaps not really looked at and thought about. Our familiarity with photographs, as a form, makes them approachable, but that familiarity is what often frustrates critical thinking and analytical reflection. In addition, as meanings shift over time, a changed context can throw a photograph into new relief, and new research can unearth stories that may not have been known in the past. How to consider photography – as a means of communication, as art, as advertising, as snapshots – can be unclear.

There are recurring questions pertinent to all types of photography that persist throughout its histories, theories and debates. Here, we identify ten of them. This book asks questions and encourages readers to do the same in order to think about photographs differently and a little more thoroughly, and perhaps to ask 'Why?' whenever a phone is brought out at a meal between friends, or a family photograph is shared online, or a picture disappears from Snapchat. This book does not set out to provide definitive answers, but it can be considered as a toolkit for referring to when sharing, looking at or thinking about photographs. Critical thinking about photography can be approached from a range of positions, such as how an image pertains to reality, privacy, memory or ethics. What following any of these lines of enquiry will do is show that there are no certainties when it comes to considering images. Looking at photographs is a subjective process (both personally and socially), and the different viewpoints are in their own ways each limited. They prescribe directions that are appropriate for different times, applicable to specific pictures and helpful in certain circumstances. There are no single 'correct' meanings or interpretations in art, and the joy of looking often comes from perhaps not liking and understanding it all at once.

Take for example this photograph (right) by the German artist Thomas Ruff (born 1958). What it shows is a young man looking directly into the camera. But what does it tell us? Who is he? And why should we want to examine it? If it is a passport picture, then it has significance to the subject's identity in a very real and relatively straightforward way. If, however, it is an art piece, it becomes more complicated. With an artwork like this, it's okay if we don't 'get it' immediately. We can explore it as one would a piece of music or a poem that might at first seem difficult. Doubt can be a useful position. We explore artworks by asking questions. Answers might not be forthcoming, but the act of asking questions can nevertheless make for a rich experience.

Looking at this photograph, it could be doubted that it took any great skill, and it is unclear who the man might he be. The braces he wears have social connotations: some might think of 1970-era skinhead subcultures (the style of his shirt also suggests this, but his hair does not), while for others, braces are a throwback to gentlemen dressing in three-piece suits. This man does not seem to fit either archetype. Often, we read portraits in the same way we do people – quickly assessing what they are wearing for clues to

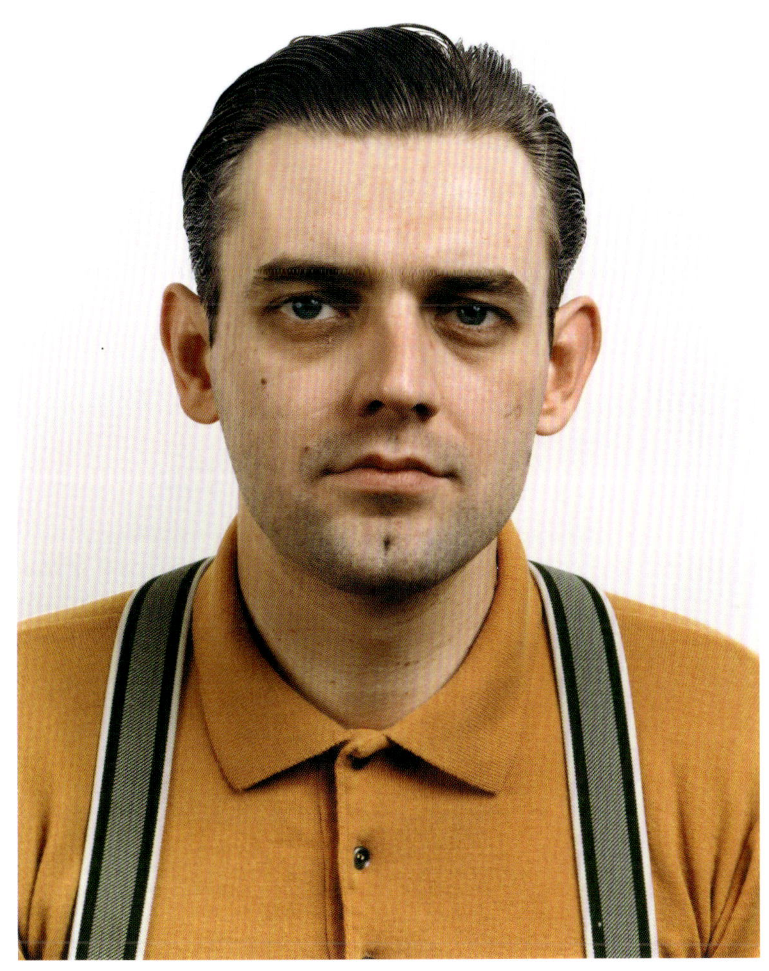

Thomas Ruff, *Portrait (Stoya)* (1986)

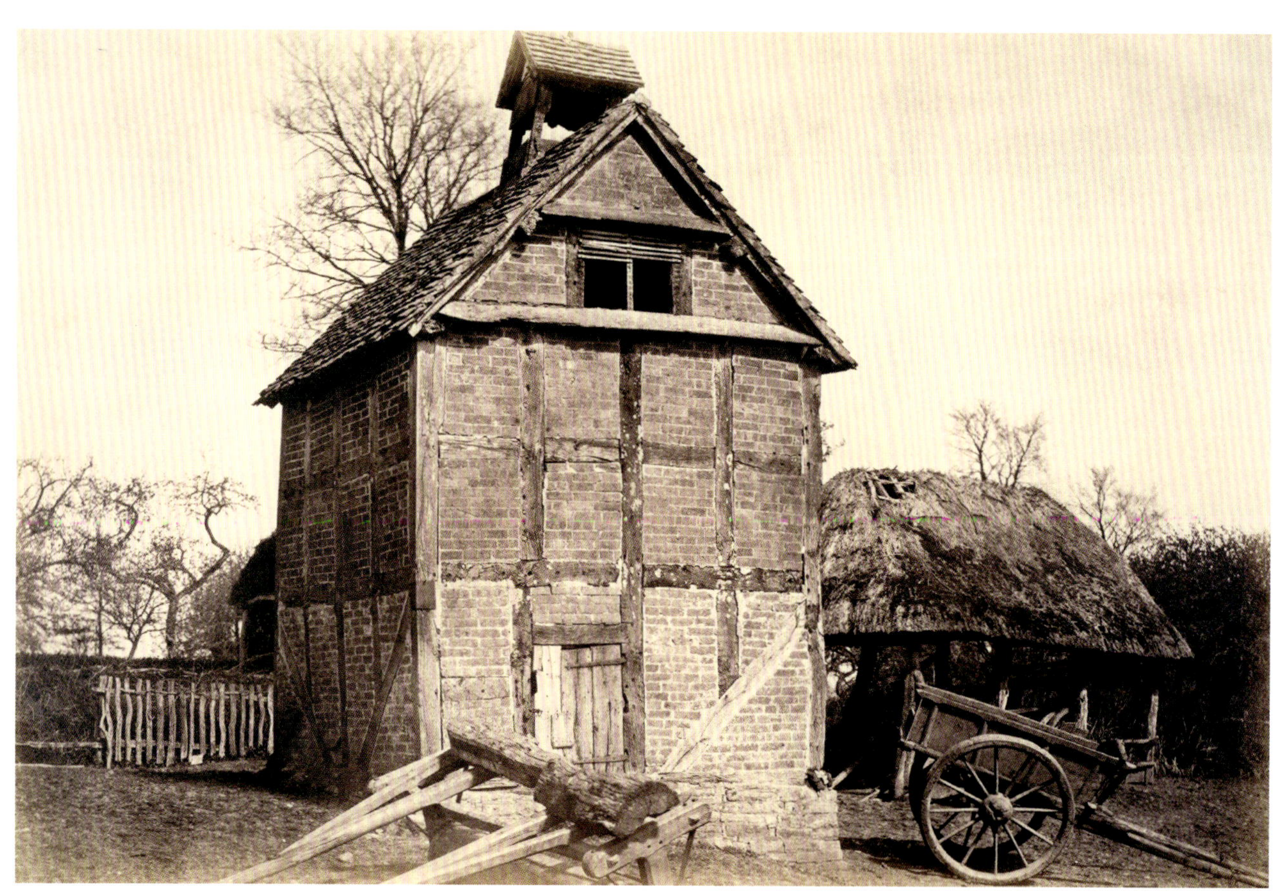

Benjamin Brecknell Turner,
Bredicot, Worcestershire (c.1852–4)

what 'group' they might belong to, what their profession might be or any other affiliation with street styles. These are simplistic assessments, but important ones that help us make quick assumptions about identity. The way we skim these superficial details will be based on our experiences, grounded in our gender, background and other factors that affect how and what we see. This approach can easily lead to erroneous thought and indulgence of prejudices, but we all do it anyway because we need to establish a baseline in order to proceed and process what we are experiencing.

In fact, this portrait is from a series of similar ones that all have the same deadpan style and are printed large for the gallery space (the one shown is 1.6 metres, or 5.2 feet, tall). They give us very little to go on in terms of knowing who the person is, despite being so realistic. The fact that the work may not deliver anything in regard to the questions above is in some respects, the point. Ruff illustrates that any representation of somebody tells us very little about their real identity or character.

Photography is a descriptive medium, a trait that has bothered many since its invention. The 19th-century French poet and critic Charles Baudelaire failed to see its possibilities in terms of seeing past the supposed reality it expresses. He claimed, 'It is useless and tedious to represent what exists, because nothing that exists satisfies me. I prefer the monsters of my fantasy to what is positively trivial.' But just as memoirs communicate the experiences of a real person and history describes real events, their closer relation to objective reality does not make them any less strange and wonderful than fiction. Sometimes the opposite can be said to be true. After all, it is not a camera that takes a picture but a human being, and so the medium is only a tool of expression. A photograph should not be understood merely as a 'trace of real life', as it is commonly understood, but instead as a point of view, a witness or an interpretation. Photography can reveal, communicate, challenge and engage.

The idea of photography as a trace of real life has run parallel to the medium since its invention. When looking at early documentary photography of the 19th century, and comparing the images with the painting of the contemporaneous Pre-Raphaelite Brotherhood, for example, it is easy to see where such notions came from. Those narrative-dense paintings, rich in symbolism and code, seem infinitely more complex than this photograph (left) by Benjamin Brecknell Turner (1815–94), for example. However, this does not mean to say there are not stories, desires, mysteries and puzzles to be gleaned from the latter. Firstly, one must remember that photography at this time was largely a passion for the very few who could afford to practise it. It was laborious, time consuming, cumbersome, relatively unknown and very exciting. What joy it must have brought when it actually worked.

With this in mind, this picture becomes something more precious. It is nostalgic and rather melancholy, and part of a long human tradition of looking to the past through rose-tinted glasses, a habit that can be seen in much of the painting of Turner's time, and indeed of contemporary society today. It's hard to imagine that around this time the Industrial Revolution was in full swing and the Great Exhibition was showcasing all that was new of the modern world. Turner's photographs suggest none of this; instead, his Britain appears as if locked in a dream, lyrical and potent with rural tradition. However, he was using the most modern of artistic mediums, creating scenes as rich in texture and shape as a Cézanne painting. The verticals of the fence and the solid geometric lines of the building contrast richly with the diagonals of the cart and wood-cutting device to give life and dynamism to an otherwise still and silent scene.

Photographs from this era can seem so wholly removed from the medium as we understand it today – photographs are made by default in colour, they can be easily made and created, sometimes they are not even meant to last, but disappear after a certain period of time. For this reason, work from the 19th century can seem hard to interpret, difficult to relate to and unconnected to who we are as people. However, its connections and contrasts to photography today and the different ways we can interpret it according to what we know of history can give it a richness that goes beyond simply documenting 'real life'. We can make parallels with experiments in photography today, as artists return to traditional darkroom techniques in order to explore the potentials of the medium away from the screen. Artists such as Vera Lutter, Meghann Riepenhoff and Adam Fuss breathe contemporary air into practices and sensibilities that might be deemed obsolete, but can in fact still be relevant and vital to our understanding of photography.

The history of photography has been rich in terms of its thinkers, writers and practitioners. With photography changing so quickly, it is time to take stock and consider its identity and presence through the years. Past periods of extensive critical activity include the avant-garde photography practices of the 1920s and 1930s and the experimental period of the late 1960s and early 1970s. These movements resonated not only with exciting innovations that opened up new technical possibilities, but also with debates about photography's status as art – which go back to its inception – changing the terms in which the medium was thought about. Out of these investigations grew the discipline of photo theory. In the 1970s, a major school of thought about photography involved making comparisons with cinema – instead of painting, which had dominated critical writing and thinking about photography previously. A question much considered at this time was, 'Could there be a theory of photographic spectatorship in the same way that there might be a theory of cinematic spectatorship?' Gaining its own identity away from fine art and also cinema (but also in connection with each) allowed photography to be considered on its own terms, at last.

Photography has since developed to a point that is best summarised by Fred Ritchin in his 2009 book *After Photography*: 'The multitudes of photographers now intensely staring not at the surrounding world, nor at their loved ones being wed or graduating, but at their camera backs or cellphones searching for an image on the small screens, or summoning the past as an archival image on these same screens, is symptomatic of the image's primacy over the existence it is supposed to depict.'

Something that makes photography different from many other mediums is that it appears in multiple forms. What, for example, is the difference between looking at a photograph in a magazine, in a themed exhibition in an art gallery, or on an image-sharing site stripped of all contexts? Does it make a difference in which context it appeared first, and how, why and when it was reproduced in another?

Aside from tracing reality, another traditional function of photography has long been to 'capture a moment'. But how to understand what this 'captured moment' is, now that a photograph's role is often performative, intended to be immediately shared far and wide online; and since images can be manipulated to an unprecedented extent? Our ways of understanding and interpreting photographs need to be as mobile and as fluid as photography itself.

This book is for those who are interested in thinking about photography in all its possible forms, and for those who will be participating in its future.

The ten chapters within encourage flexible and engaged ways of thinking. The first chapter, 'Is it real?', demonstrates that photography, as a representative medium, is limited and subjective, and how this apparent contradiction makes it more akin to writing than perhaps one might first think. As mentioned, the reality factor is a stumbling block for many when considering the medium, which is why we address this question first. Writing aims to be precise and realistic, just as photography can be. Photography requires attention to detail equal to that required for an effective use of words, and it covers the same ground as literature, in which genres are not considered static forms but rather as 'open, constantly changing in accordance with the needs and fancies of the community in which they are used to having meaning', as David Bate noted in *Photography: The Key Concepts* (2009). '[I]t is surprising that genre has not been taken up by photography like it has in film theory or the study of literature', he added. A comparison with the genres of literature – be those autobiography, biography, natural or social history, documentary or fiction – may help our understanding of photography, especially in terms of its connection with reality.

From the turn of the 21st century, there has been a rise in what is sometimes referred to as 'post-internet art'. This considers the repurposing and reuse of images from the web in new ways, such as collage, and continues long-held debates in art around the subject of appropriation. In 'Stealing or borrowing?', theories and problems around appropriation are investigated. What is important to consider here is not just the mechanics of using other people's images, but also why such reuse has currency and popularity at certain historical moments. Work by Hannah Höch and John Heartfield was made in turbulent times, when turning contemporary imagery into art was a particular way of making sense of the world. Can the same be said for the plethora of photographers and artists today who use collage in their image-making? The lack of politics in contemporary work is stark, so what does the popularity of this technique say about the state of photography today? Why are so many artists attracted to it? One answer might be that it is an attempt to comment on the very quantity of images out there.

With social networking becoming one of the main ways of experiencing photography, moments captured from private life frequently become uploaded and made public on various platforms. There is a strangeness to seeing colleagues and friends in situations that would traditionally remain private – be those drunken parties or reporting a death with accompanying pictures of the person who has died. This breach of public and private space has more sinister overtones when thinking of the posting of 'revenge' imagery, and what can happen when photographs are out of your ownership and responsibility. Like most of the subjects here, what is considered private and public shifts and changes and depends on context in terms of age or religion, for instance. The chapter 'Public or private?' explores these issues, as well as photographs that have carefully balanced or deliberately conflated the two in order to reveal something to the world that was previously hidden away.

One of the main repositories for photography had traditionally been that of the magazine – now of course much of that has been replaced by the web. Storytelling is vital to how we understand photography. Although it may be a 'realistic' medium, it is also an elliptical one, and narrative either has to be packed into one image or unfolded over many. There are many ways that photography is used to communicate. 'How can you tell a story?' investigates the role of storytelling and photography and how different sites and certain subjects require different methods. For some, a detailed and thorough handling is necessary, which often calls for the multiplicity, open-endedness and fragmentation that the strategy of serialising can afford. In other examples, static images alone are not enough, and words and film have to be brought in to fill in the gaps. Other approaches include cramming an entire story's worth of information into one image, which the viewer must then carefully unpack. The rise of the photobook has encouraged photographers and artists to tell stories again, shifting the proclivity that dominated the art world in the 1990s and 2000s for one-off art gallery 'masterpieces' to more lyrical sequencing, where the viewer has to trust the rhythm and editing of the photographer.

In contrast to the ideas mentioned above, photography has always championed the one famous image. An image might gain notoriety either thanks to its ubiquity, as in the case of Che Guevara's famous portrait, or because of its rareness, as can be seen from Man Ray's *Noire et Blanche* (1926), which sold for €2.6m in November 2017. 'Why is it famous?' examines issues of iconography, popularity and reproduction. From the earliest days of photography, Baudelaire was complaining of its ubiquity. This is a trait that is reflected in the way it is talked about today: the 'river of images', the 'avalanche of pictures', 'bombardment', and similar disaster metaphors all follow a long tradition of distrust. So how, in this world of images, do certain photographs gain a status of individuality and uniqueness? There is, of course, the fact that photography is so often tied to real events and therefore documents those. As with film, moments of social and cultural importance are recorded and remembered by images – be they still or moving. However, with the increase in 'citizen journalism', where anyone can hope to have a photograph or film section reproduced and replayed constantly on Twitter or 24-hour news channels, is it possible any longer to create a truly iconic photograph?

Wrapped up in much of what has been discussed so far is the issue of memory. It seems to cut to the very heart of the medium. 'What do I remember?' considers the different ways in which memory resonates through photographs. The French philosopher and critic Roland Barthes's *Camera Lucida: Reflections on Photography*, first published in 1979, is an idiosyncratic investigation into the potency of a photograph that continues to fascinate scholars and persists in being one of the most influential attempts in articulating what a photograph actually is, what it means and why it matters. The relevance here comes in the second half of Barthes's book, which focuses on a photograph of the author's deceased mother in order to fully investigate photography's links with remembrance and death. Barthes writes, 'The photograph is literally an emanation of the referent. From a real body, which was there, proceed radiations which ultimately touch me [...] a sort of umbilical cord links the body of the photographed thing to my gaze'. With the photograph not reproduced in the book, what remains for the reader is her lingering presence – the memory of her embedded in the identity of her son.

The influence and continued theoretical probing of *Camera Lucida* led photography theorist David Green to state in 2006 that 'the cloying melancholia of a post-Barthes era of photographic theory now haunts not just *Camera Lucida* but critical approaches to "all photography"'. The chapter 'Who do you think you are?' considers ideas that photography is shifting from a medium of memory to one of experience. Image-sharing sites and social networking can be read as encouraging mini autobiographies, in which the role of photography is very much located in the present. The fact that many platforms allow photographs to disappear, and/or to be commented and remarked on, makes photography 'live' and shifts it to a form of communication similar to conversation, rather than one dealing with static, silent objects. Key to photography's new role is the idea of identity, and how this may be explored. By looking in historical terms at how identity has been investigated through photography, one is better placed to understand the fascination with modes of photographic self-identification, such as the selfie.

'Can lying be OK?' and 'What goes where?' explore more issues of manipulation and editing. It can be said that there are three main elements to taking a picture: the taking, the editing and the printing (or sharing). These two chapters show how pictures have always been manipulated to suit the purpose of the publisher or photographer, and the particular stories they want to tell. 'What goes where?' looks at how different editing strategies can conceal or reveal stories that can be open or didactic. In addition, the extreme example of deep fake news – in which computer-generated representations of politicians or celebrities masquerade as reality – may be a hot topic now, but again, by looking back, it can be seen that manipulation has always been a vital component of the medium. When the world was photographed in black and white, was that manipulation? Like the square or rectangular shape of the frame, this was purely a technical restraint, but it bears considering. One can ask where does manipulation start, and where should it stop?

This leads onto more ethical questions, which are discussed in 'What makes it problematic?'. In a climate of renewed conservative values, debates around free speech, live beheadings on Facebook and a proliferation of pornographic imagery, questions about what is acceptable, to whom, where, and why are more relevant than ever. What are the strategies around sensitive material and what is the responsibility of the publisher of such images? The waters are muddy and forever shifting. The camera excels in taking the photographer (and the viewer) into places which are not known – it is one of its very great strengths. The more salacious, forbidden and shocking, the more it can stimulate and encourage the voyeur in us. Who can easily forget a photograph they know they should not have seen? Considering bigger institutional decisions on decency and ethics, this chapter charts a range of images and issues surrounding the role of photography, spectatorship and publication.

Le déjeuner sur l'herbe: Les Trois Femmes Noires (opposite) by Mickalene Thomas (born 1971) finely illustrates some of the issues this book tackles. Drawing on art history, figurative painting and commercial photography, Thomas layers her photographs with symbolic meaning and classical references. Not only is Édouard Manet's iconic painting *Le déjeuner sur l'herbe*, depicting two fully clothed men picnicking with a naked woman (with another woman dressed in a shift behind them), cited in the title as well as the composition of the scene, but the picture also references Greek mythology – in particular the Judgement of Paris, in which an apple presented to the 'fairest one' was claimed by three goddesses, Aphrodite, Athena, and Hera. Thomas replaces the food of Manet's picnic with flowers – a stereotypical symbol of femininity – but the three women with their unflinching gazes, staring fiercely at the viewer, challenge assumptions about beauty and gender.

By knowingly drawing on the traditions of art history and myth, as well as more recent history, including blaxploitation movies and fashion iconography, Thomas's image plays with photography's capacity to mix up fact and authenticity with fiction and artifice. In particular, she uses the medium to shine a light on the way art has treated women, particularly women of colour, throughout history. The photograph serves as a homage, fantasy, and corrective; it challenges who gets represented, and how and why. It does not detract that it is a construct rather than an image of candid reality; in being so Thomas makes a specific point not only about the lives of women of colour, but also about the role the visual arts, including classical painting and advertising, as well as traditional photography, play in the telling of their stories, and how they may be disseminated and understood.

In the same way that *Le déjeuner sur l'herbe: Les Trois Femmes Noires* transcends genres, there are many photographs in this book that could be discussed in more than one chapter. This only illustrates the richness of photography, it underlines the pertinence of the subjects discussed and the connectedness of the questions this book raises, as now, more than ever before, what constitutes a photograph is put into question. 'Photography' is an umbrella term that covers historical material and artworks sold for millions, as well as family albums, fashion spreads and the thousands of snaps held on phones and uploaded and shared over social networking and image sharing sites. How does one compare a Man Ray photograph sold at auction for millions with a picture of a dog wearing glasses found on Facebook? How can they possibly be the same thing? In this book, we take photography in its most expanded form. This can include video, installation pieces, found objects elevated to the status of fine art, and digital works that may not look like photographs at all. It is important to consider photography in its widest terms and not to panic if it all doesn't look like what we expect. A digital image on your phone is as much as a photograph as a one-off daguerreotype made in the 1840s, and with the advent of filters, they may even resemble each other, even if the means of their making bears no similarity.

The medium is nebulous, its results varied, but we hope that the examples given here will give you new ways and tools to consider photography, by encouraging close reading and taking time to ask questions – not only in regard to what you see and what is represented, but about the nature of the medium itself, the culture that surrounds it, and the people who use it.

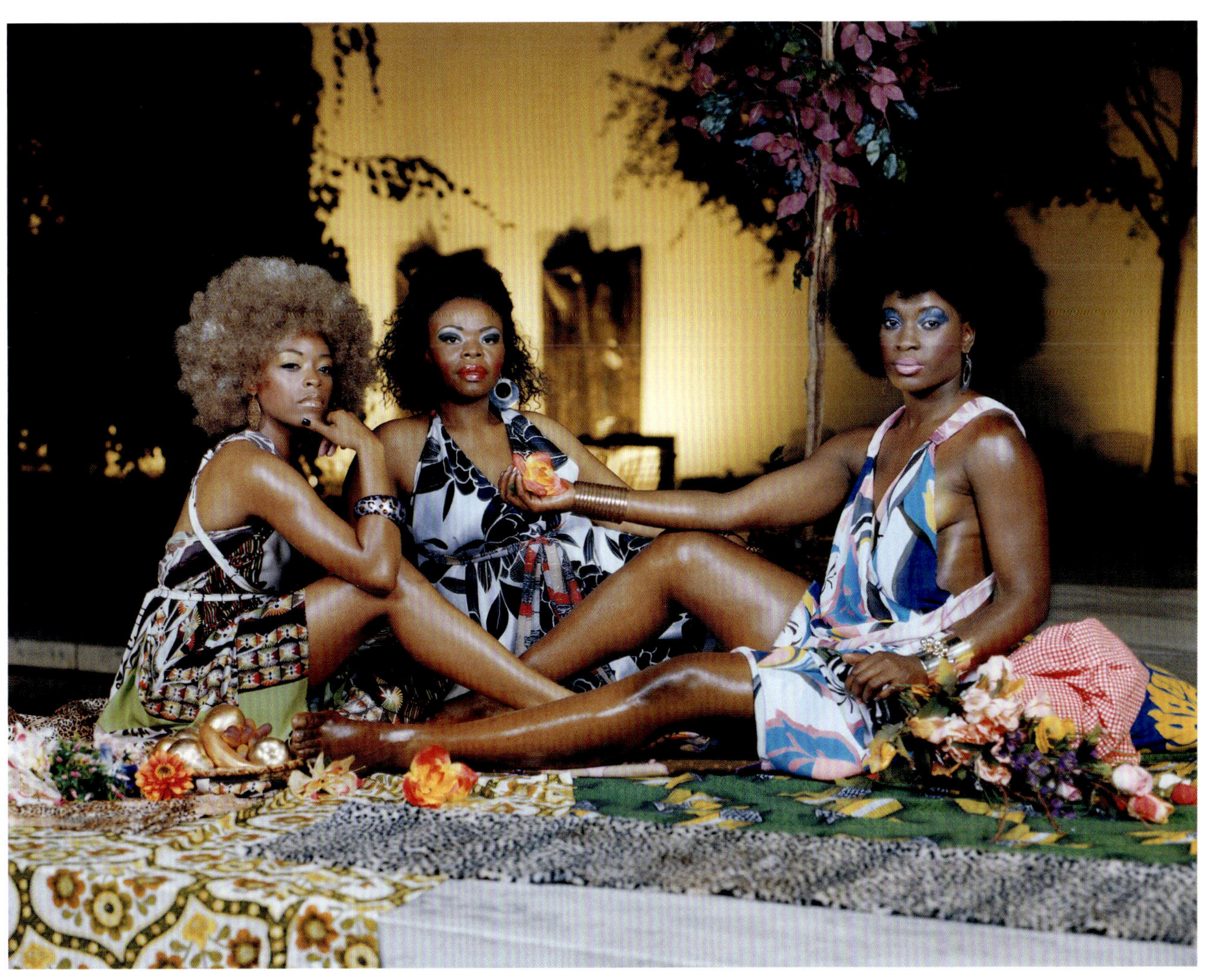

Mickalene Thomas, *Le déjeuner sur l'herbe: Les Trois Femmes Noires* (2010)

Is it real?
Is it real?
Is it real?
Is it real?
Is it real?
Is it real?
Is it real?
Is it real?
Is it real?
Is it real?
Is it real?
Is it real?
Is it real?
Is it real?

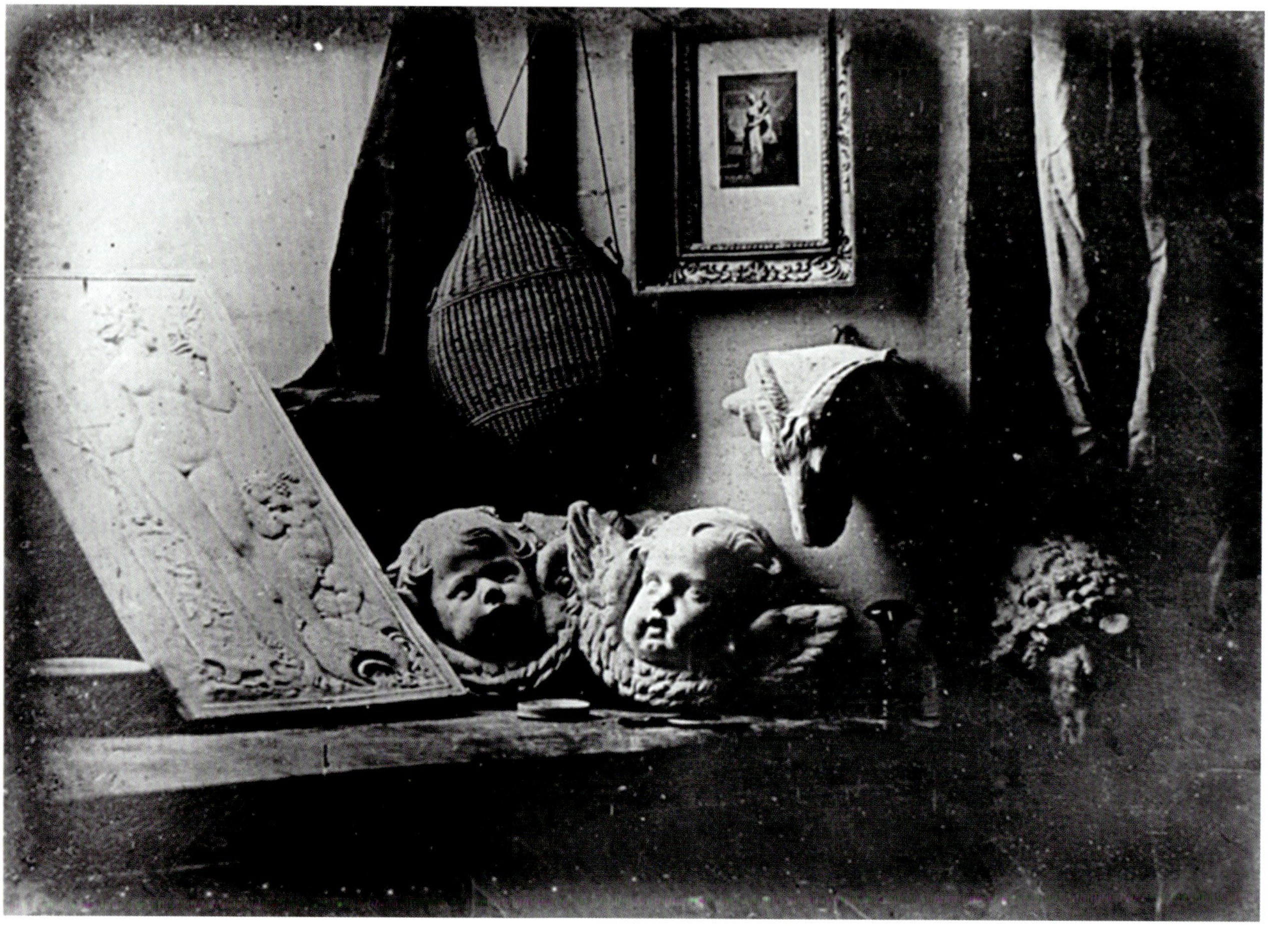

Louis Daguerre, *Interior of a Cabinet of Curiosities* (1837)

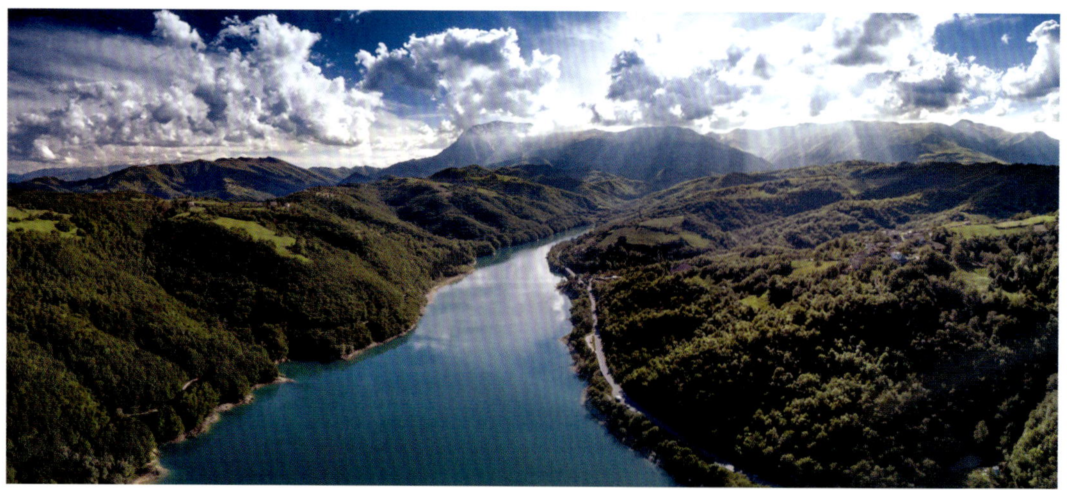

Leonardo Patrizi, Aerial view of a lake in Italy (2017)

Photography emerged into a 19th-century world that was undergoing rapid transformation in almost every aspect, and as such the new medium answered a deep human need to see and explore this changing landscape in unprecedented detail. In January 1839 an announcement by the French Académie des sciences claimed that an image directly taken from life could now be fixed onto a metal plate. The inventor, Louis Daguerre (1787–1851), was both a businessman and a theatre designer. This perhaps helped shape the identity of early photography more than one might think. The drama and tension of Daguerre's new prototype photograph – a 'mirror' image that would soon be kept in a protective case lined with red velvet – illustrates some of photography's mixed identity. The daguerreotype had aspirations to both the realistic and the theatrical, as well as to the commercial. The 'mirror' can serve as a metaphor for reality, whereas the red velvet evokes theatre curtains, within which the beautiful drama would unfold.

One of Daguerre's earliest images is *Interior of a Cabinet of Curiosities* (left, top), which to our eyes might appear as if Photoshopped to look old, so familiar are we now with filter settings that immediately 'age' pictures. This may seem ironic, but at the same time it shows the importance of our frame of reference. The question arises: if manipulation is the first thing someone thinks of in connection to photography, what does that say about the value of the photograph as a reflection of reality? And what does a 'real photograph' even look like: Is it something you can hold? Is it something you can see on a screen and alter?

Daguerre's technique gave a unique image: it could only be copied by being re-photographed – something that already suggests photography's complicated relationship with reality. On the one hand, it is 'realistic': the daguerreotype didn't make up what was in front of the camera, as a mirror doesn't lie. Obviously, this goes for all imagery that is used in daily life, whether in courts of law or for medical purposes; anyone who has ever undergone an X-ray investigation or a full-body scan at airport security knows that there is no denying the 'realness'. Nonetheless, we can still ask ourselves in every single instance: under what circumstances are these images to be trusted as real?

One would assume that this picture (left, bottom) of a sunny landscape is a registration of what the photographer witnessed on a day out. This photograph, however, was not taken by a person with their camera looking down on an Italian lake, deciding when was the right moment to take this picture; it was taken by a drone. One could argue that this actually makes it easier to interpret the degree of reality in this image, for the lack of human subjectivity makes it an example of 'true reality'. But it still doesn't look real. What this picture illustrates is that it is not just photography that is complicated, but the concepts of realism and reality, too. In addition, this belief in objective machine capture does not take into account any post production manipulation done by the photographer.

The process of manipulation starts as soon as we frame a person, a landscape, an object or a scene with our cameras: we choose a portrait or landscape format. What often follows is the addition of non-realistic filters, editing, altering or cropping. The binding principle of photography, however, remains its relationship to reality, especially when at question is documentary photography or a picture in the news media: we are convinced that 'it happened' – that the events they represent were real, that they actually took place.

Documentary and news imagery may seem the most realistic genres in photography, but their realism means nothing independently of how news media apply their ethical codes – if these are stipulated at all. The *New York Times* is known to work with a set of integrity guidelines, which, for instance, say that images in their pages 'must be genuine in every way'. Neither people nor objects may be added or removed from a scene, and adjustments to colour or greyscale should be limited to those minimally necessary for clear and accurate reproduction. If the slightest doubt is possible, captions should acknowledge the newspaper's intervention.

We know that if ten people were asked to take a photograph of the same scene, this would result in ten different photographs, with as many dissimilar points of view. One can then ask: what are the differences between reality and witness and points of view?

The work of the French artist Sophie Calle (born 1953) reveals that reality, witness and point of view can actually blend into one other. Calle uses her artworks to pose questions about approaches to truth and to obscure the lines between fact and fiction. Her work *Suite Venitienne* (right), consisting of a set of 81 black-and-white photographs, came about in an unusual way. As Calle describes it: 'At the end of January, on the streets of Paris, I followed a man whom I lost sight of a few minutes later in the crowd. That very evening, quite by chance, he was introduced to me at an opening. During the course of our conversation, he told me he was planning an imminent trip to Venice. I decided to follow him.'

Calle took a camera, put on a blonde wig as a disguise, and stalked him for several days, photographing him. The man is seen walking away from her down the Venice streets, going about his daily life. The appeal of this work lies in the use of documentary elements in combination with the artist's obsession and the sense of voyeurism that this evokes.

From Daguerre's age to ours, photography has undergone a transformation, not only technologically but conceptually. Initially described as a means of capturing or freezing 'real life', it has gradually taken on an ever more ambiguous, complicated and fraught character as our ability to modify and share images has exponentially increased. At its best, it is a subjective impression that is at the same time both fleeting and enduring – just like any good piece of drama.

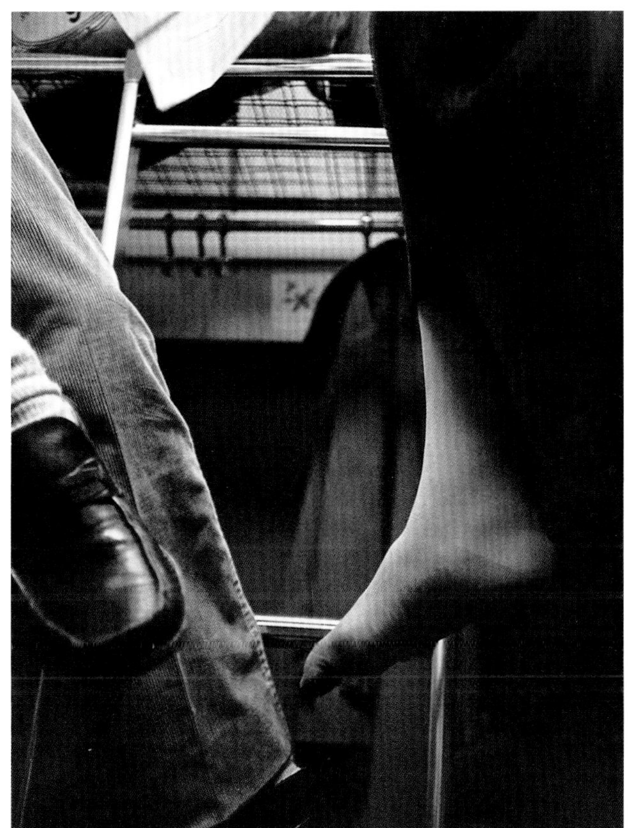

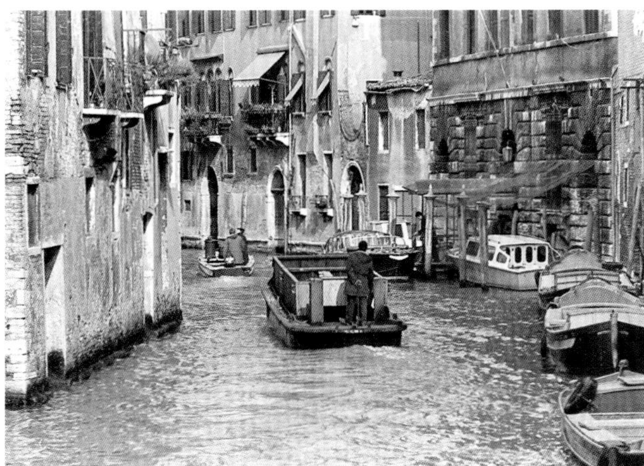

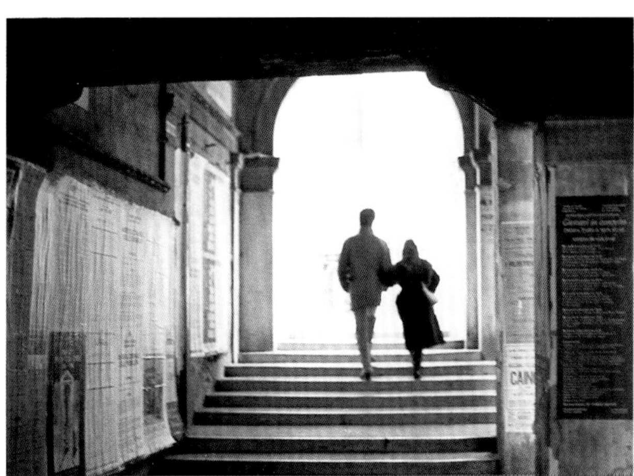

Sophie Calle, from *Suite Venitienne* (1980)

Anna Atkins (1799–1871)
***Polypodium phegopteris* (1853)**

Anna Atkins was a pioneer in photography. She was also the first person to produce a work with photographic illustrations: *Photographs of British Algae: Cyanotype Impressions* (1843). There is an elegance to Atkins's work. She has a forensic eye for the delicacy of plants, based on her experience of making detailed engravings and drawings of botanical specimens. The distinctive blue colour of the photographs is caused by the method of their production, a process known as cyanotype that was invented in 1842 by Sir John Herschel. Atkins knew both Herschel and William Henry Fox Talbot, who is commonly recognised as one of the first inventors of photographic processes. It is not surprising, then, that she would translate her interest and knowledge of illustrating botanical specimens into investigations using these processes.

A cyanotype is made by laying an object onto light-sensitive paper and placing it in the sun in order to create the image. Exposure time depends on how strong the sun is and how defined the maker wants the silhouette to be. The result is a negative image of the object. In a way, it could be said that this is the most realistic of all photographic methods, even though it does not involve a camera. It is literally a trace of the real, similar to that achieved when an object is laid on a scanner. But is it a photograph? Does a photograph need a camera in order to be defined as one? Many contemporary artists are returning to early photographic processes such as this in order to examine and explore the nature of the medium and the forms it takes outside of the stream of digital images we see every day.

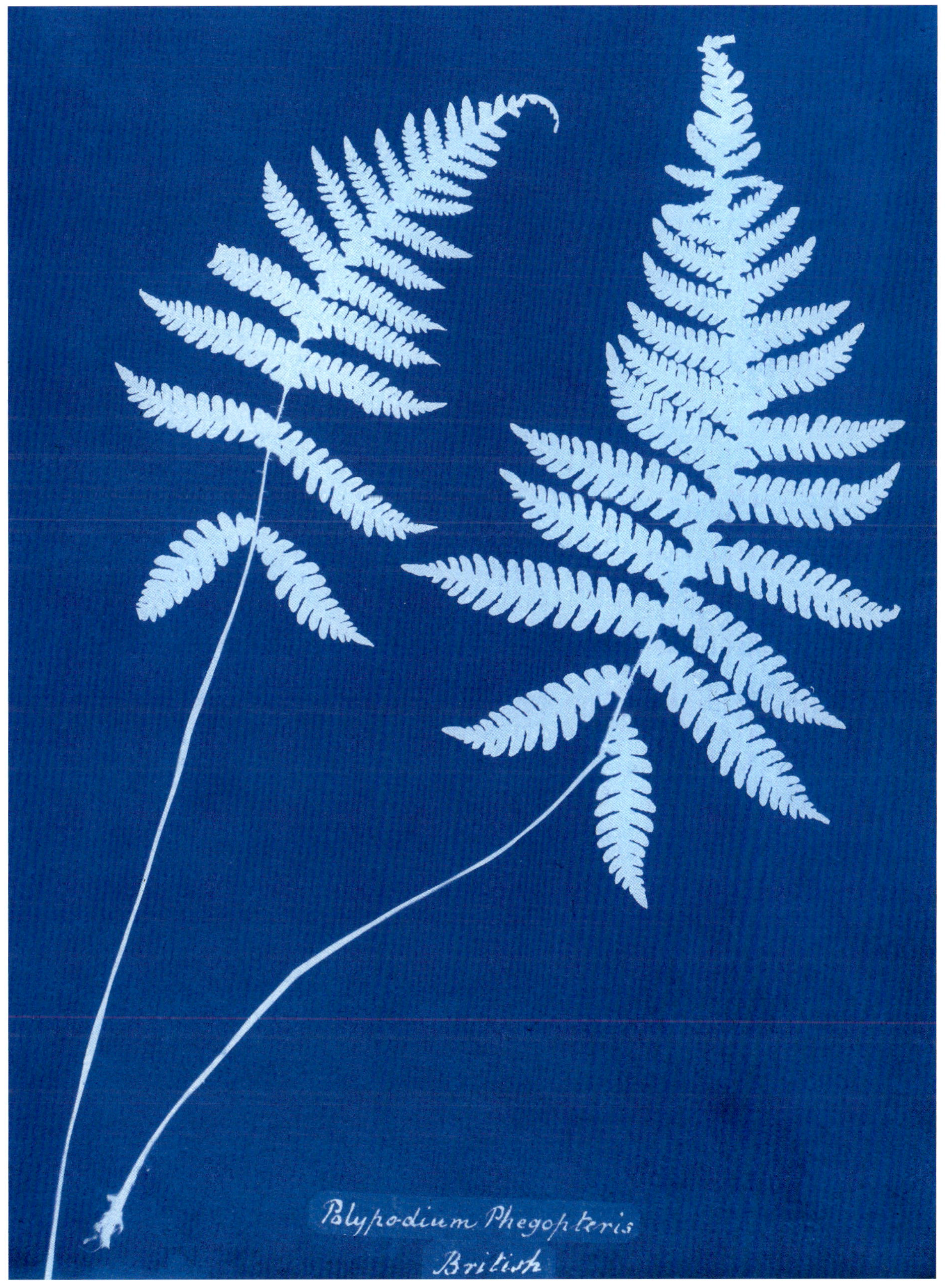
Polypodium Phegopteris
British

**Joan Fontcuberta (born 1955)
and Pere Formiguera (1952–2013)
Fauna (1985–1989)**

Created by conceptual artists Joan Fontcuberta and Pere Formiguera, *Fauna* was conceived as a hoax book and exhibition. It uses the language of an objective document and turns it on its head. Photography has traditionally been used to illustrate and provide evidence for written points and observations in science and botany, and has a long tradition of being used by explorers and ethnographers when documenting foreign lands and people. *Fauna* aims to show that photographs must be questioned even when they are presented in a format such as an exhibition or book, which we typically understand as truthful. By exploring the fine lines between fiction and reality and what is considered neutral, true and objective, the book purports to tell the story of the German zoologist Peter Ameisenhaufen, who mysteriously disappeared in 1955. Effectively, the book masquerades as his notebook featuring field studies, notes, photographs and X-rays.

The meticulous, scientific approach taken by both exhibition and book are superficially convincing. However, the viewer/reader quickly realises that the creatures and plants that Ameisenhaufen is shown as discovering are all fantastical. They include the carefully catalogued *Cercopithecus Icarocornu*, shown here, which is similar in appearance to a small monkey but with a unicorn's horn and wings. The questions the artists ask of photography encourage the reader to do the same – questions such as 'How do I know this is real?' and 'What does a photograph prove?' As such, *Fauna* acts as a useful reminder that the authority of photographs – their claim to the status of fact – must always be interrogated.

Cercopithecus Icarocornu

78

Cercopithecus Icarocornu

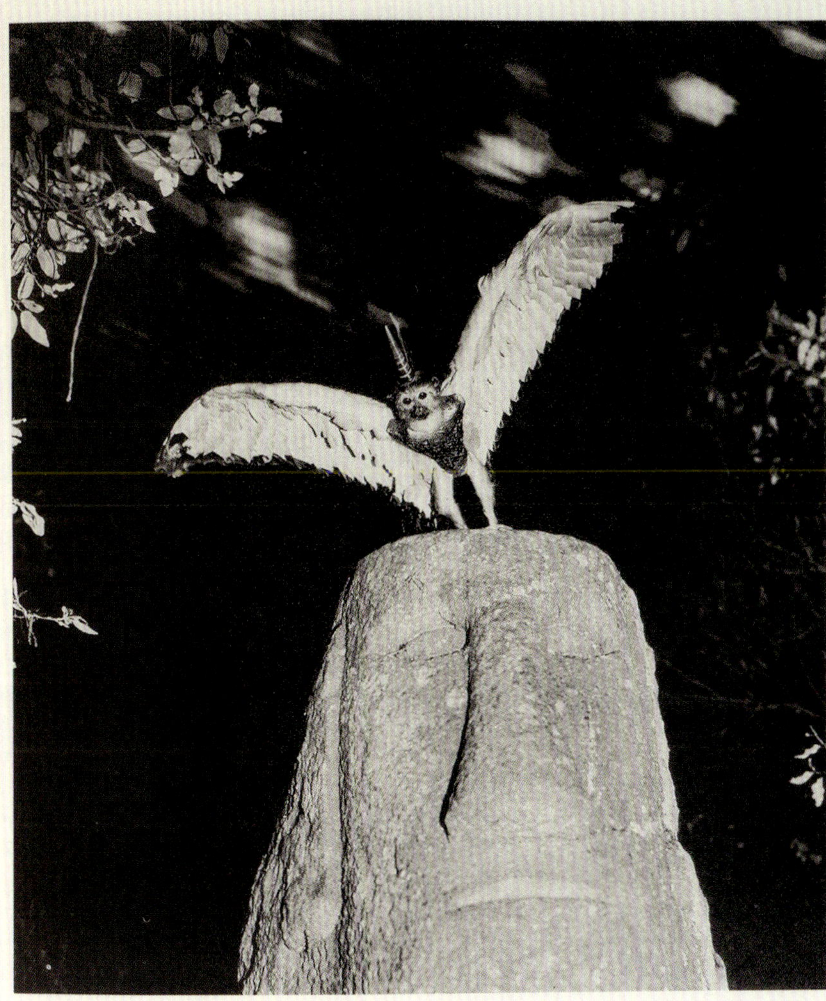

Moment of the magic song over the totem of sacrifices
Beim magischen Gesang über dem Opfer-Totem

79

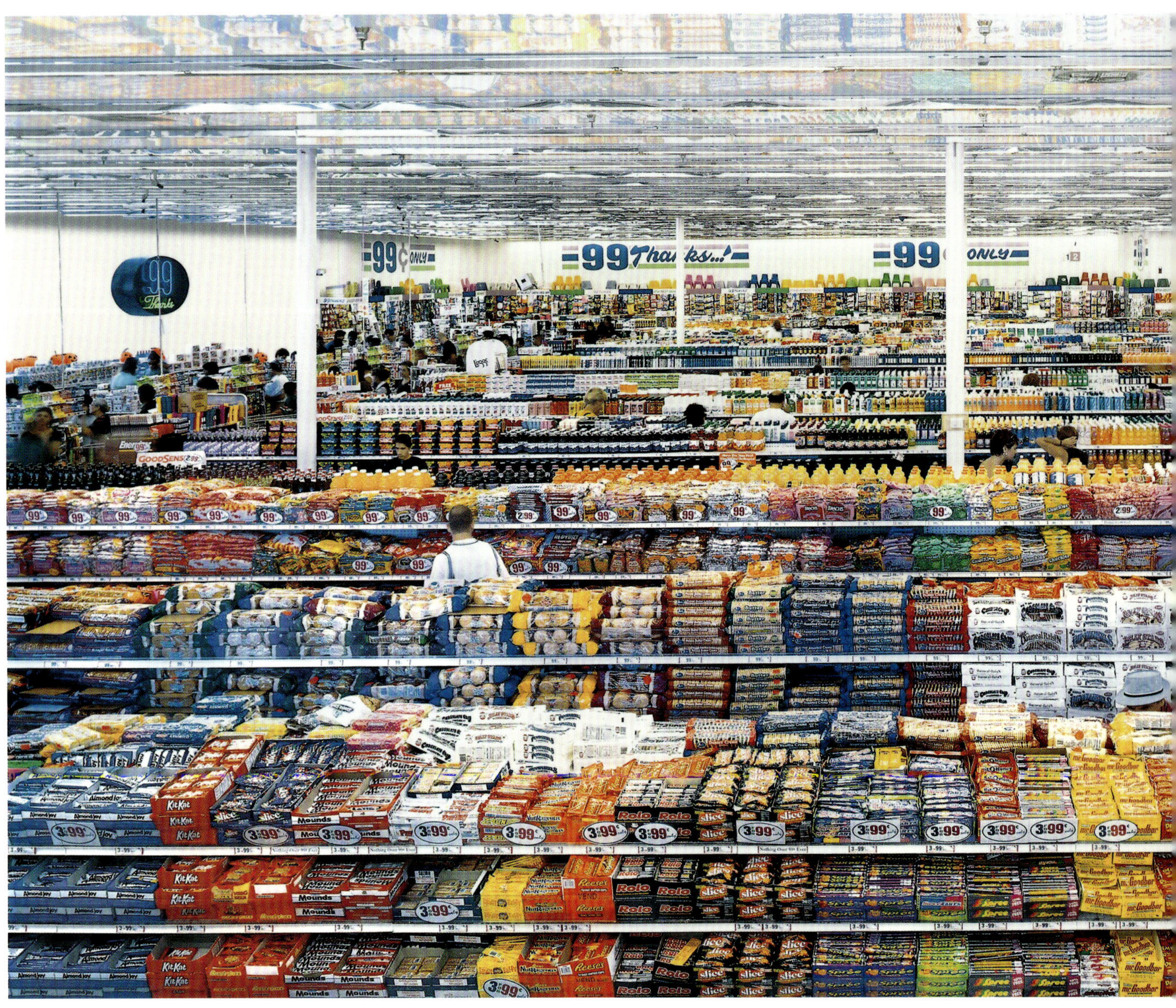
99¢ ONLY
99 Thanks..!
99¢ ONLY

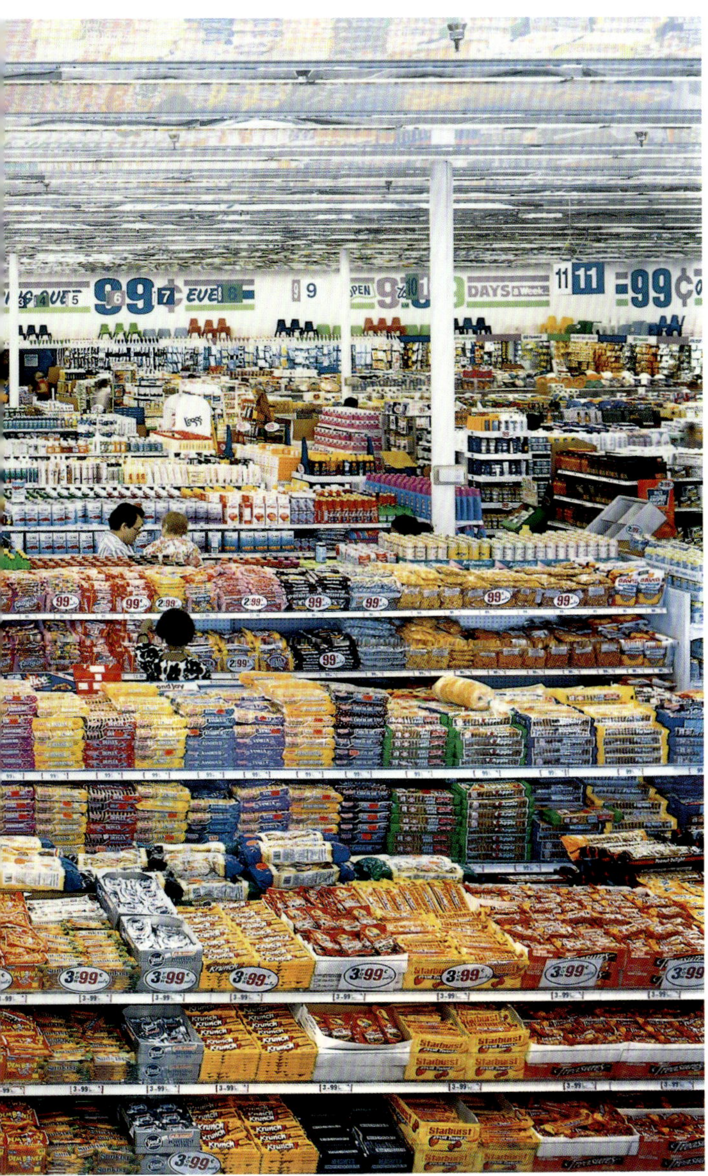

Andreas Gursky (born 1955)
***99 Cent* (1999)**

A good advertising image can suggest a lifestyle, tapping into notions of aspiration and desire. Somewhat perversely, Andreas Gursky turns this on its head by using the seductive tools so readily used by advertising to critique consumerism. *99 Cent* appears to depict the kind of store familiar to high streets around the world. We know that places like this exist, and the photograph looks convincing. We have no reason to doubt it. Gursky, however, does not take 'straight' photographs, but digitally stitches his photographs together from several slightly different views, to create a result that looks real – or hyperreal. On closer inspection, we can see that the goods here are repeated, the patterns are too uniform, and the fakery of the image is revealed.

However, is 'fake' the right word here? Does it in some way devalue the photograph to know that this is not a real 99-cent store, but one created in the artist's mind? When Gursky's photographs were first shown, many of the reviewers expressed their disappointment in the manipulation – wanting the images to be 'real' and feeling cheated somehow that they were not.

The scale of this photograph is very large – it is made for museum walls and the homes of collectors who have space for such an object. By taking the cheapest of goods and making them into art, there is at the heart of this piece a comment on high art versus consumerism. This is a picture with conceptual rigour, but this could easily be overlooked in the spontaneous, superficial encounters we usually have with images, especially where these relate to advertising and consumerism. High and low, art and advertising, realness and fakery, consumerism and collecting: all exist side by side in this photograph, which was once the most expensive ever sold.

Unknown photographer
Neuschwanstein Castle (c.1890)

This photo was taken shortly after the opening of Neuschwanstein Castle to the public. The castle, commissioned by King Ludwig II of Bavaria, was conceived as an imitation and homage to medieval castles, by way of Wagnerian romanticism, and it has always been closely associated with fantasy. Not only has it appeared in many famous films such as *Chitty Chitty Bang Bang* (1968) and *The Great Escape* (1963), but it was also the model for the Sleeping Beauty Castle (1955) in Disneyland. We are so familiar with the silhouette of the Disney castle as it appears before every film made by the company, with fireworks arcing over the turrets, that to see a photograph of the real castle on which it was based seems somehow unbelievable, as if, out of the two of them, this is the made-up castle.

The use of colour in the Photochrom print (a colour photographic lithograph used to make postcards) makes it seem all the more like something out of a fairy tale. We are accustomed to seeing black-and-white pictures from this time, and they somehow feel more authentic, more real, than this one. But isn't colour photography inherently more realistic?

In a time when digitally manipulated images and fake images in the news and on social media timelines are rife, this photograph seems hard to believe – it seems that the castle (which was based on draft sketches by a stage designer) has been artificially inserted into the scene. Our response is probably not too dissimilar to the feelings of the Bavarian people in the 1880s, who saw the folly of their king unfold in this extraordinary Romanesque Revival palace.

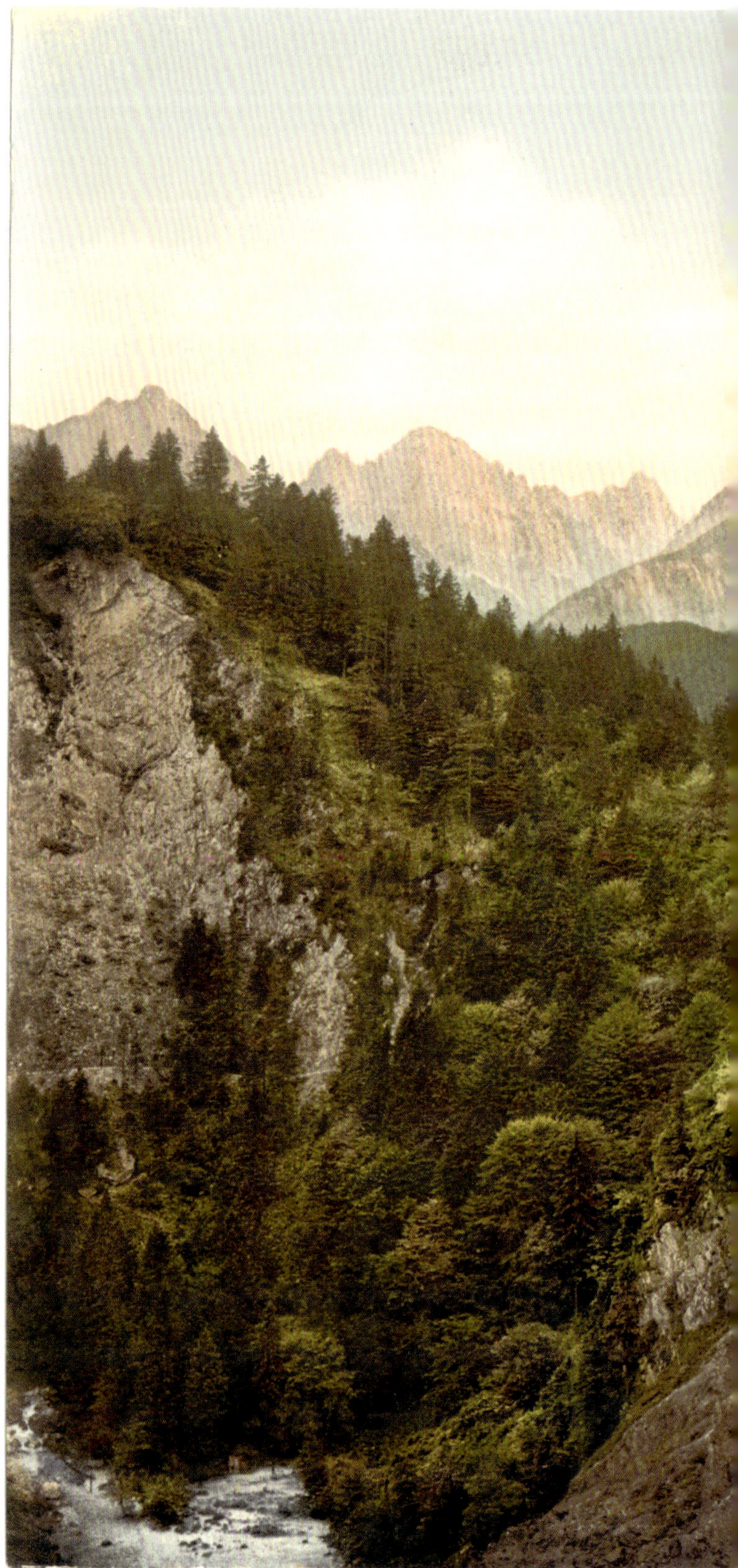

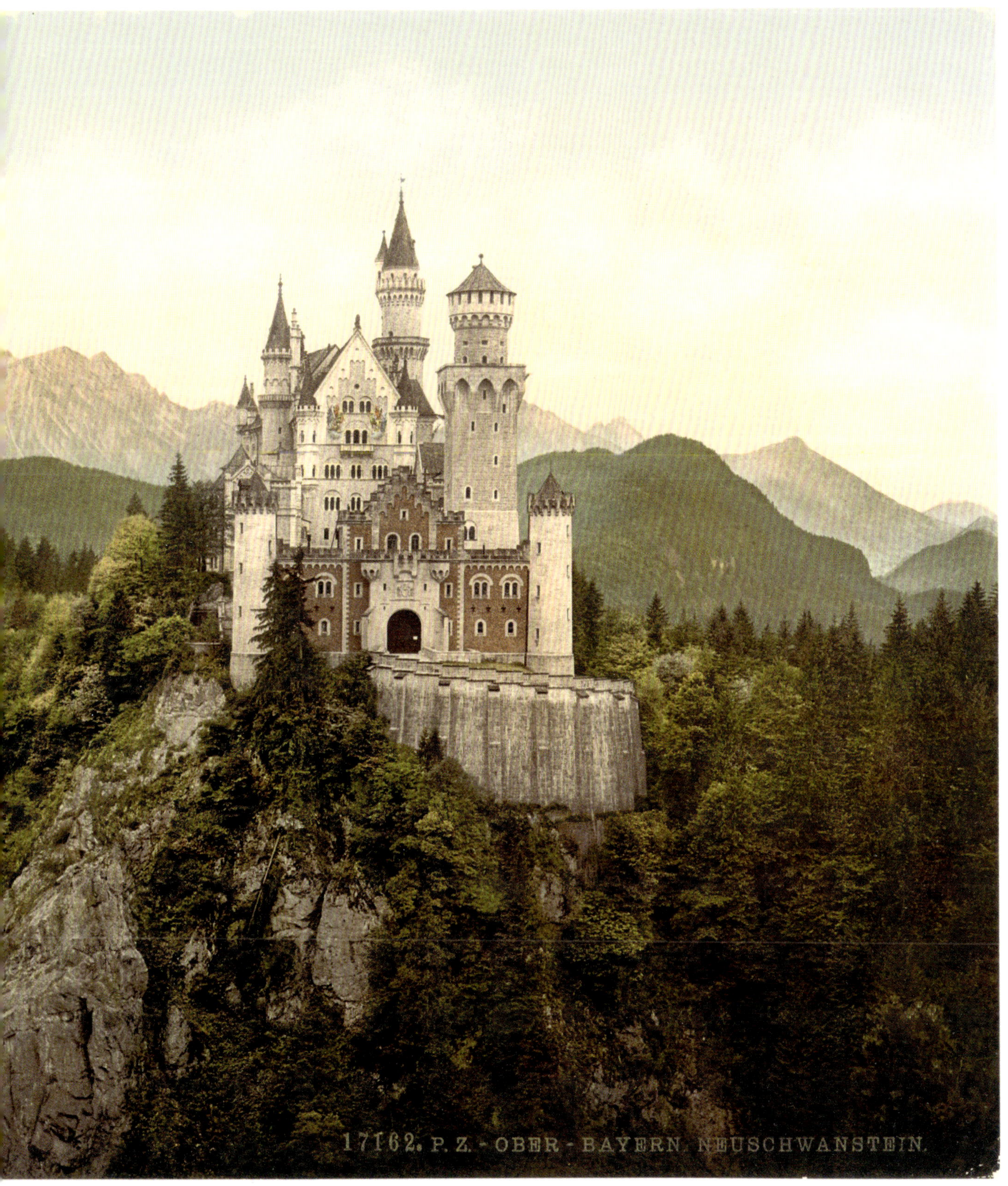
17162. P. Z. - OBER - BAYERN. NEUSCHWANSTEIN.

Gustave Le Gray (1820–1884)
***The Great Wave, Sète* (1857)**

If we look carefully at this seascape, it is obvious that it has been heavily manipulated. Thanks to the filters we can apply in photo apps such as Instagram we are now familiar with vignetting – a technique which darkens the outside edges of a photograph and highlights the middle. Here it looks as though a vignette has been applied for dramatic and expressive effect. But does that make the picture any less realistic? A subjective or artistic touch is not necessarily the opposite of reality, as it attempts to capture an emotional response, which is all part of the experience of viewing. Is it, in fact, more realistic for a picture to try to evoke the emotional excitement that watching the sea can provoke?

Gustave Le Gray was trained as a painter and turned to photography around 1847, quickly establishing himself as a master of the new art. When we examine the picture, it becomes apparent that two negatives have been spliced together to make this picture, so that the clouds meet the horizon in the same way that an eye would view the scene – as opposed to the camera that would flatten it out. It could be argued, therefore, that this picture is a more truthful and realistic representation of how the eye actually views a horizon. Isn't a straight photograph always unrealistic compared with how we really experience a view?

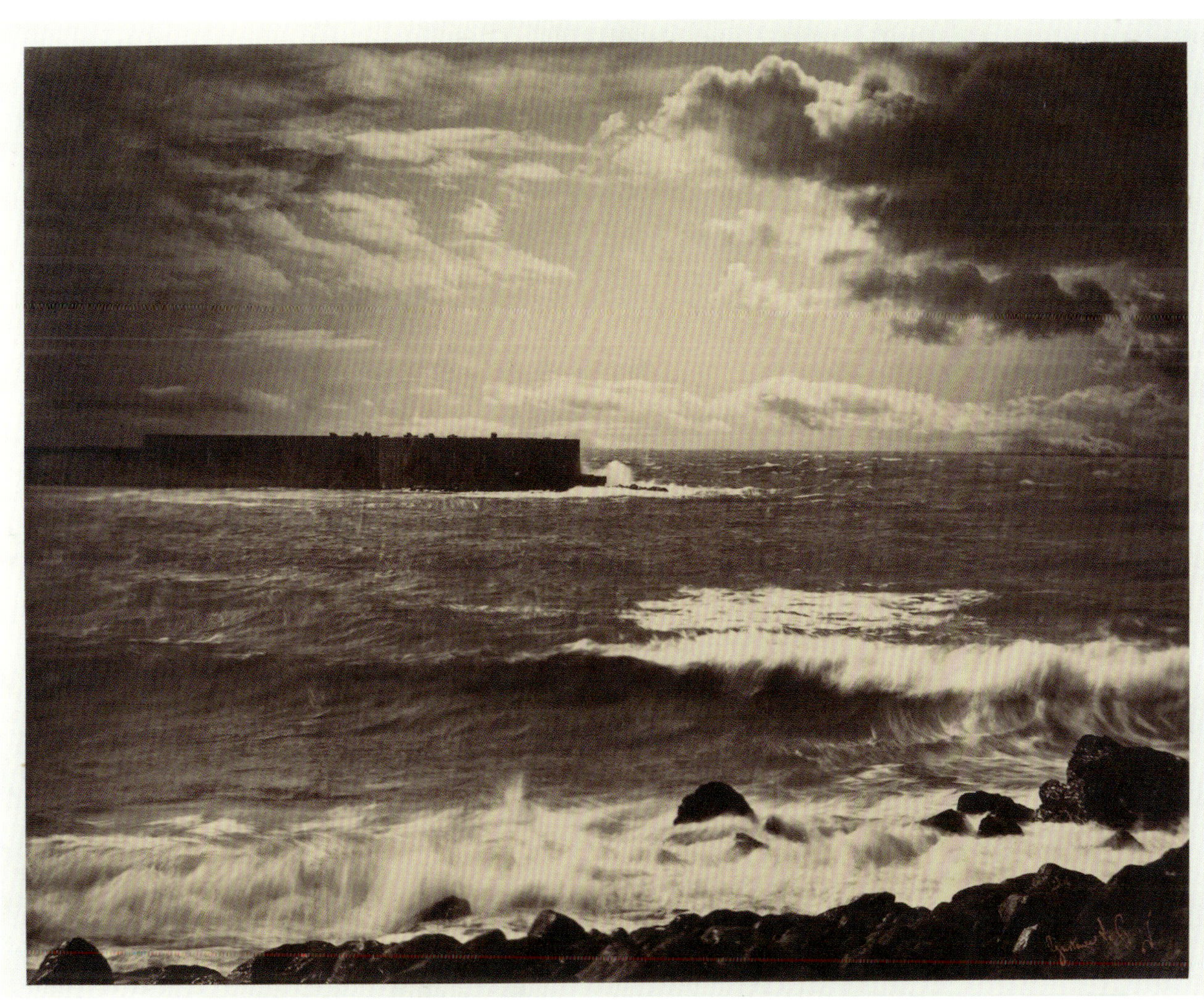

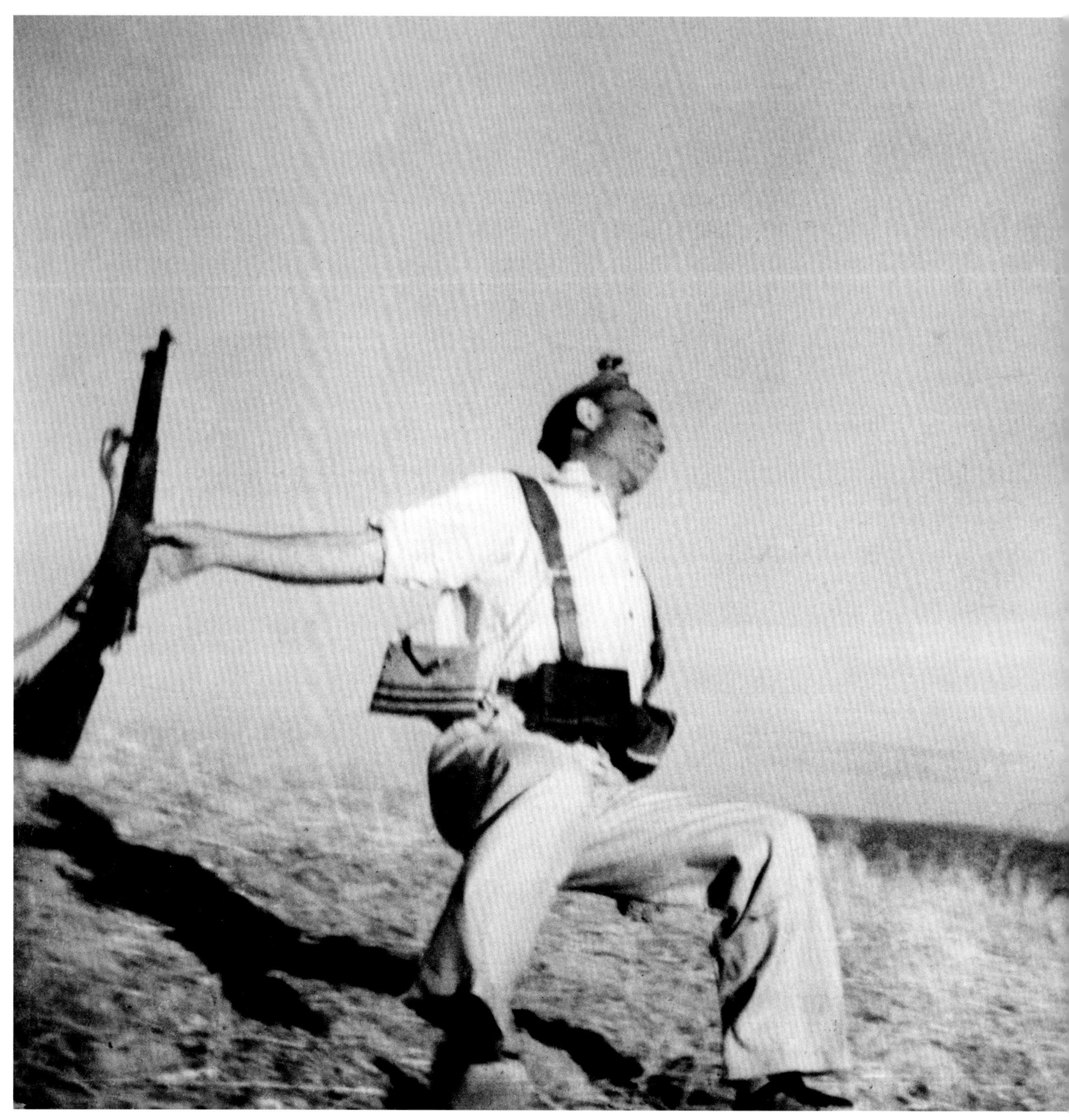

Robert Capa (1913–1954)
***The Falling Soldier* (1936)**

This is probably one of the most written-about images in the history of photography, its authenticity puzzled over by scholars, curators, photographers and historians. Extraordinary lengths have been taken to prove or disprove that it really represents what the photographer claimed (there have been exhibitions, books and a TV programme dedicated to the subject). Robert Capa himself stated that it shows the moment a soldier from the Iberian Federation of Libertarian Youth during the Spanish Civil War (1936–9) was shot and killed in the Battle of Cerro Muriano. However, the identity of the man and the location have repeatedly been brought into question. Even the authorship of Capa himself is unclear as no negative of this actual shot survives. Many believe that it was staged (something that sometimes happens in conflict photography, as it is not always easy for photographers to get close to the action) while others will swear by its authenticity.

In many ways, it is this determination to find out whether this photograph is 'real' or not that is of more interest than what is actually represented. Does it matter which version is true? Owing to its lack of clarity, it becomes a strange object – not quite one thing or the other. It might be a man being shot in the midst of battle or it might be staged. This is an unusual position for a documentary photograph and illustrates that reality is perhaps not the most important issue when making a statement about the role of representation in warfare.

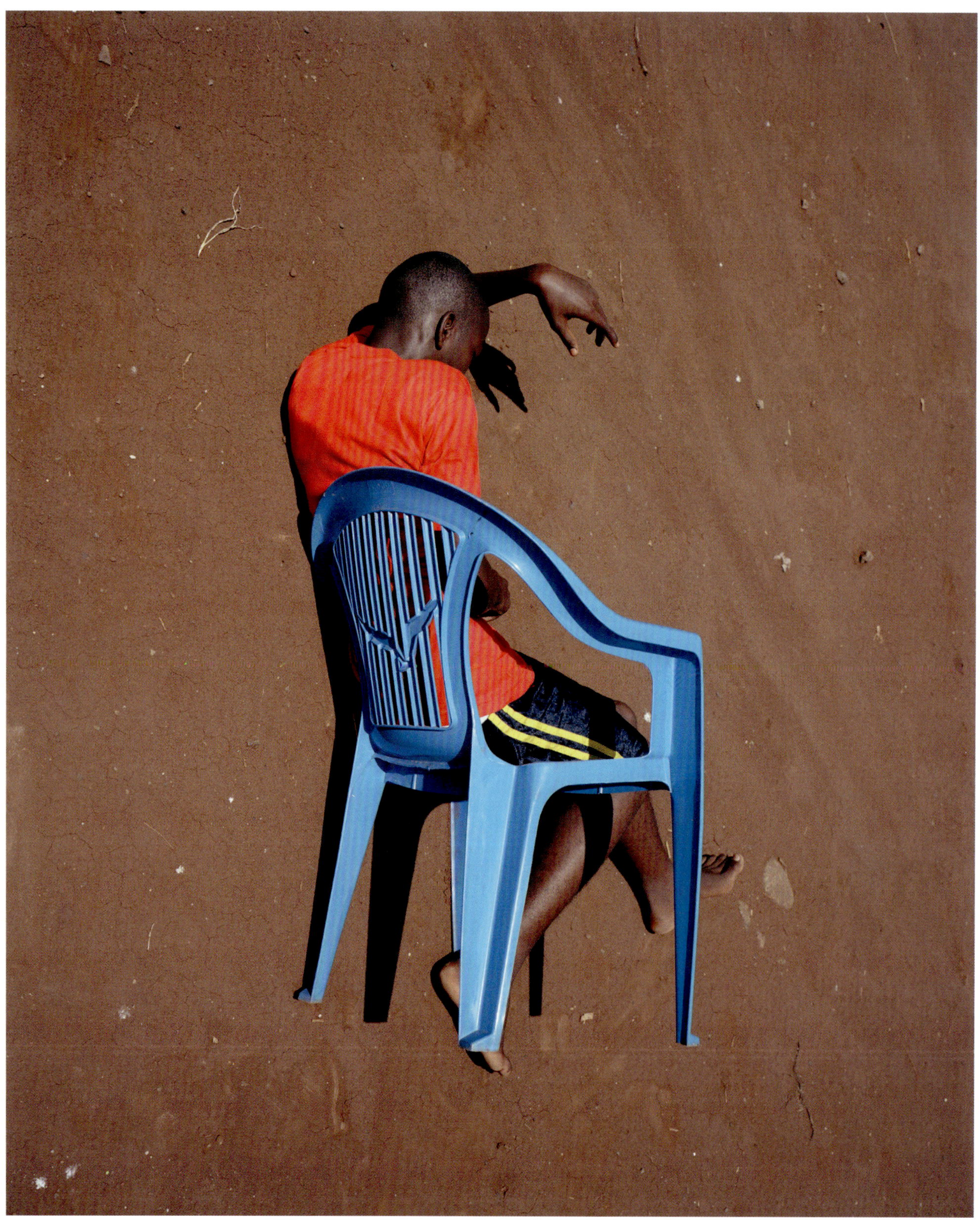

Viviane Sassen (born 1972)
***Parasomnia* (2010)**

The Dutch artist Viviane Sassen grew up in Kenya and returned with her camera as an adult to see how her childhood memories compared to the reality she saw as an adult and an outsider. From this, she created her series *Parasomnia* (also the title of the photograph shown here, from the same series). Trained as a fashion designer and a photographer, Sassen does not depict the stereotypical poverty of Africa, but she lets ordinary people and their surroundings become part of her colourful, captivating yet alienating compositions.

Her images are mostly staged: to Sassen, photography involves a long preliminary process of taking notes, sketching and getting to know her models. The human body is often central, adopting sometimes seemingly impossible poses, camouflage elements, or combined confusingly with another. The body is used as a graphic component within the image, while the face is usually either obscured or turned away. Despite the meticulous preparation, there is ample space for the haphazard, in the light and shadow, as though Sassen has left a space for the uncontrolled world to make its contribution.

Sassen wants to demonstrate that it is impossible to capture the identity of a person or place in one image, and to show the limitations of the medium of photography. Inadvertently, however, she does quite the opposite: her work does not simply show reality, ambiguity, the ordinary, an interpretation, or a mystery; but instead everything at once, in a poetic, otherworldly vision of a certain place. Her view of Africa is as at home in fashion magazines as it is on museum walls. More importantly, perhaps, her images penetrate into the mind of the viewer, inviting them to project and create their own narrative as they seek to enter the world portrayed, or created, by Sassen's photography.

What do I
remember?
What do I
remember?
What do I
remember?
What do I
remember?
What do I
remember?
What do I
remember?
What do I
remember?

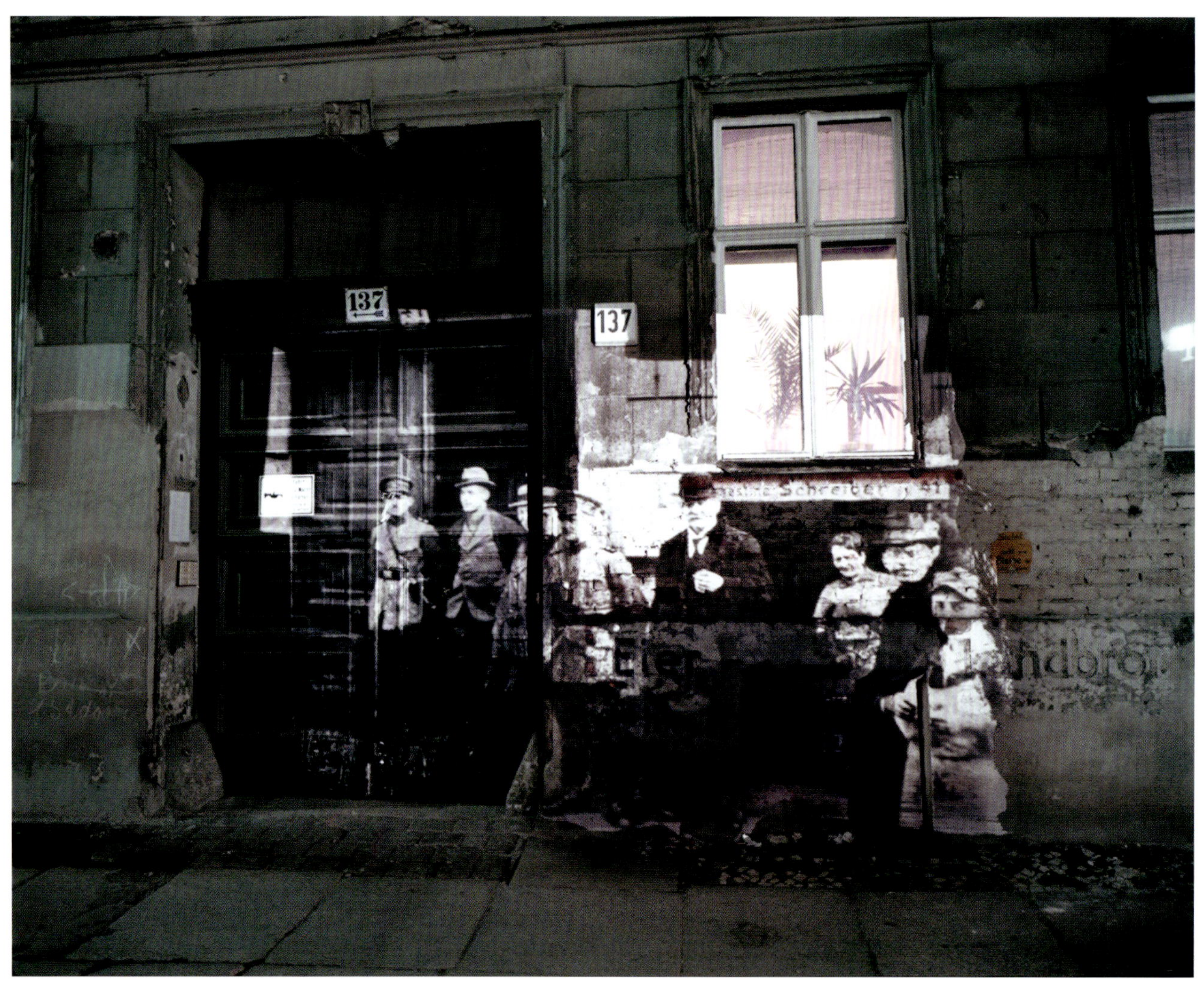

Shimon Attie, *Linienstrasse 137: Slide projection of police raid on former Jewish residents, 1920, Berlin* (1992)

The French cultural theorist Roland Barthes wrote in his book *Camera Lucida* (1980) that, for him, 'The Photograph does not call up the past (nothing Proustian in a photograph) ... The effect it produces upon me is not to restore what has been abolished (by time, by distance) but to attest that what I see has indeed existed.' This approach to thinking about photography – as providing a record of a time gone, never to be repeated – is perhaps the most common way of considering photographs. For most people, looking at a snapshot does not only make one sad for the time or person gone but can also trigger memories of the past, bringing them right back into the present in the mind of the viewer. Photographs, whether happy or sad, and especially family ones, work on both memory and remembrance – at the same time representing a memory and calling us to remember – and they hold a very special and important place in our lives. It has become commonplace for people to claim that of all their possessions, it would be the family photograph album that they would save in a fire. Although of course, this would now be the computer hard drive.

The relationship between photography and memory is more muddled than one may at first think. Do we really remember an event that happened, or do we remember the photograph of it? The majority of our snapshots are taken around happy events such as holidays, birthdays, weddings and parties. Arguments, divorce proceedings, deaths and funerals – these are rarely photographed. Snapshots record and resurrect only a select version of the past. Moreover, family photographs when printed become powerful talismans for the past: they are handed about, viewed and touched, often as part of a warm, shared experience in which stories about the relatives and friends portrayed are retold.

What is strange, then, is that canonical histories of photography have tended to leave out such snapshots, which must surely account for the largest number of photographs taken. Photography as art dominates in the written histories of photography. However, some artists have tried to address this elision by considering memory, and indeed, bring snapshots and other types of vernacular photographs into their artistic practice. *The Writing on the Wall* project (1991–2, see left) by the American visual artist Shimon Attie (born 1957) is an example of this, combining vernacular photographs with large-scale, on-location installations that are then photographed. The artist projected pre-Second World War snapshots of Berlin Jewish life onto buildings (sometimes the same buildings as the ones shown in the snapshot) in the former Jewish quarters of Berlin, the so-called Scheunenviertel. In the case illustrated here, the projection shows a photograph of a police raid on former Jewish residents in 1920. By combining images from past and present, the city becomes one of ghosts. With the knowledge of the Holocaust, these works act as remembrance for the families in the pictures, but also for all Jews everywhere who have suffered persecution. The memories they invoke are then personal, political and cultural.

The combination of these two different types of photograph illustrates how often memory is folded into older images – which can be in the form of mourning, nostalgia, longing or love. In a very different example we can see how the photographic object is used directly as a tool for memorialisation and remembrance. In this mounted portrait designed for display on a cabinet (thus referred to as a cabinet card) of Queen Victoria (opposite) the photographer (perhaps in collaboration with the Queen) has carefully staged every part of it to signify her continued mourning for her husband Prince Albert. This was taken long after his death in 1861 and was commissioned to commemorate the Golden Jubilee. She wears her wedding veil and significantly turns her arm to show a photograph of the Prince Consort incorporated into her bracelet (the inclusion of the then-new art of photography into jewellery, notably lockets, was common in Victorian Britain). This constant reminder of a person, a sense that you must never forget them through both sight and touch, brings significance to the photographic object.

Here a photograph can be seen to offer stability in a changing world, a freezing of memories and the ability to reminisce at will. In terms of memory, photographs are not just visual records but are concerned with very human emotions.

Now, of course, the 'family photo album' mentioned earlier has become the computer's or smartphone's hard drive or cloud archive. Here thousands of snapshots are stored and rarely looked at or printed out. Photo-sharing sites have changed the way we take photographs as well as the subjects. It's not just birthdays and holidays (although they certainly still feature heavily) but also food, painted nails, cats and countless other everyday and banal things and happenings. It could be said that the way we take photographs now, by snapping, sharing, tagging and captioning, has shifted our understanding of photographs away from memory and toward experience. That's a radical change in how we understand a medium, one which has taken place over a very short time.

This shift in how we understand one of the fundamental functions of photography is once again best illustrated in social networking. Photo-sharing sites such as Snapchat, Facebook and Instagram have introduced the ability to present photographs that disappear after viewing. The purpose of these temporary photographs has nothing to do with memory, nor indeed are they the signifier of what has once existed but is now gone, from Barthes's melancholic conception. In fact, their very disappearance can be seen as a counterpoint to the predominant theoretical modes of the medium, that are to do with recording, permanence, witness, proof or 'trace' of life, as outlined by famous writers on the medium including Barthes and Susan Sontag. Once again, this illustrates that photography is a nebulous umbrella term which can encompass a wide range of approaches, media and physical outcomes.

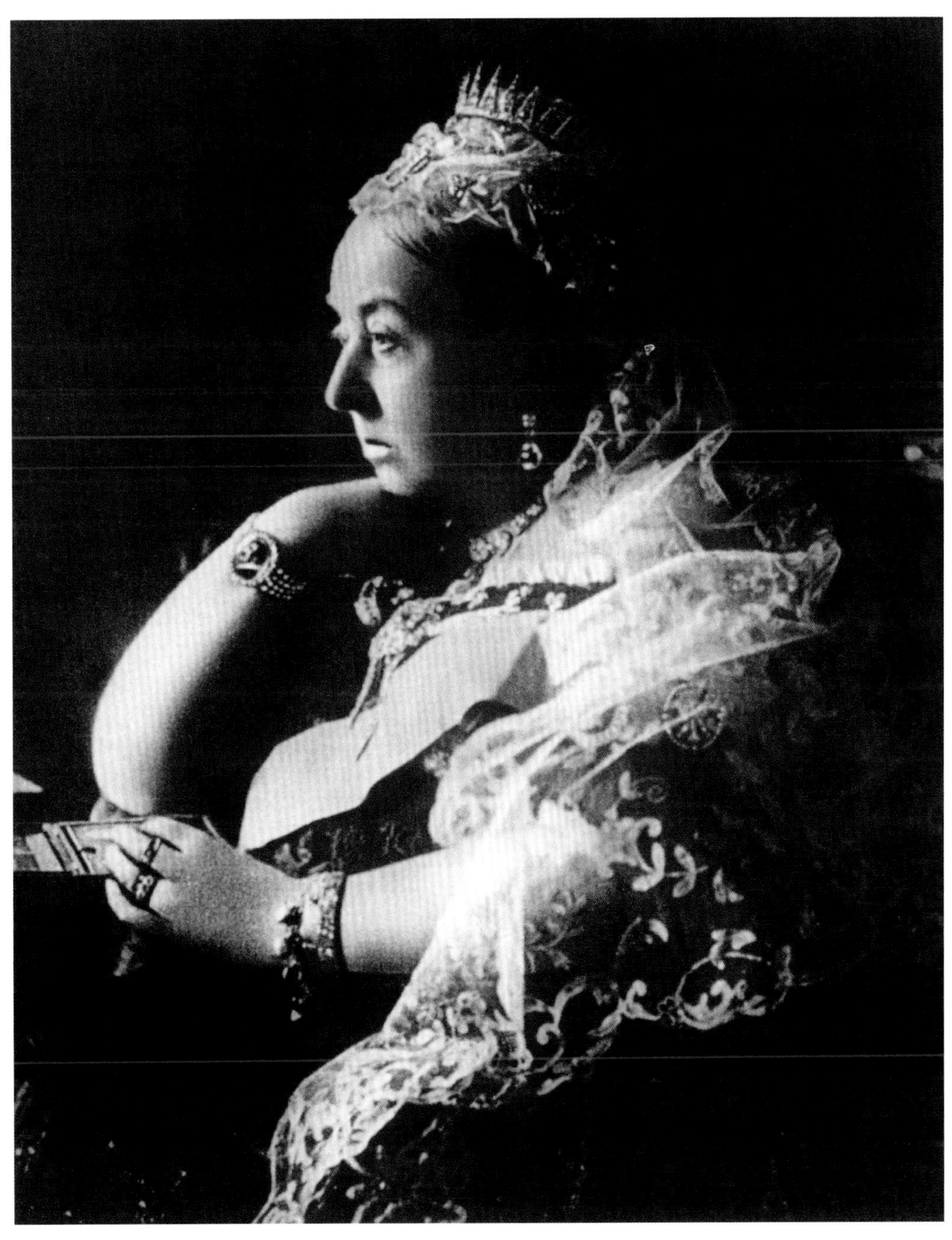

Gunn & Stuart, *Queen Victoria* (1897)

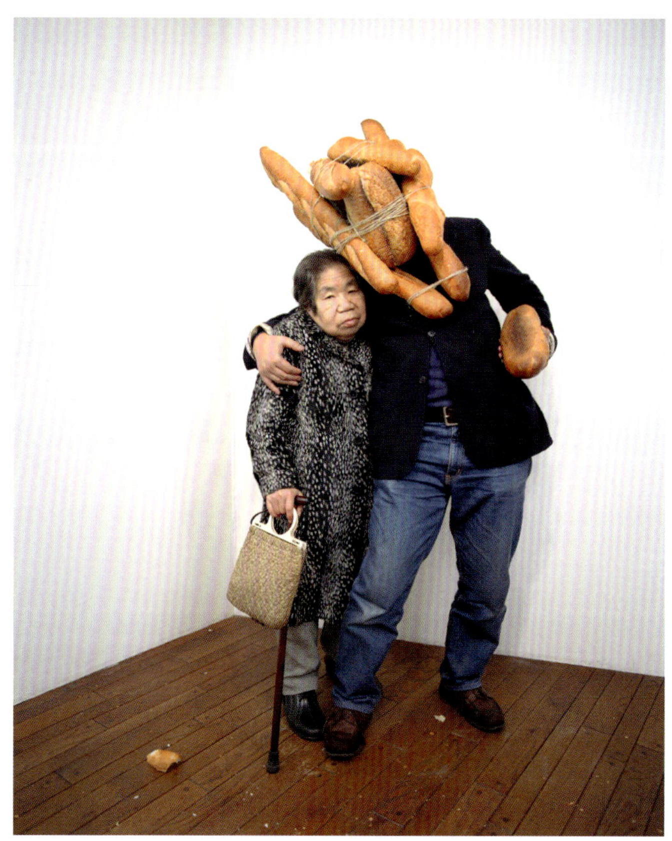

Tatsumi Orimoto (born 1946)
***Breadman Son + Alzheimer Mama* (1996–2007)**

Ishiuchi Miyako (born 1947)
***Mothers* (2000–2005)**

Japanese artist Tatsumi Orimoto is best known as a performance persona whom he calls 'Bread Man' (see *Untitled*, 1996, above). Tying loaves to his face to form a sculpture, he went about mundane activities, while simultaneously looking after his mother who had Alzheimer's disease, until she died in 2017. By blending photography, performance, sculpture and life he created images that, although absurd, are also filled with love, compassion and humanity. His physical difference as Bread Man echoed the alternate reality his mother existed in, engendered by the disease. One is not sure whether his mother was fully aware of what was being undertaken, and although this could be read as exploitative, it isn't. Why is this? As she aged, he also created a series called *Art Mama and Son*, which shows, in a more documentary style, the constant care, and the uncanny resemblance between the photographer and his mother as they both grew older. Memory and remembrance are sewn into Orimoto's work with his mother in all sorts of ways – we can't know what she remembered of their time together and what she did not.

Another Japanese artist, Ishiuchi Miyako, also deals with memory and her mother, although the approach is quite different.

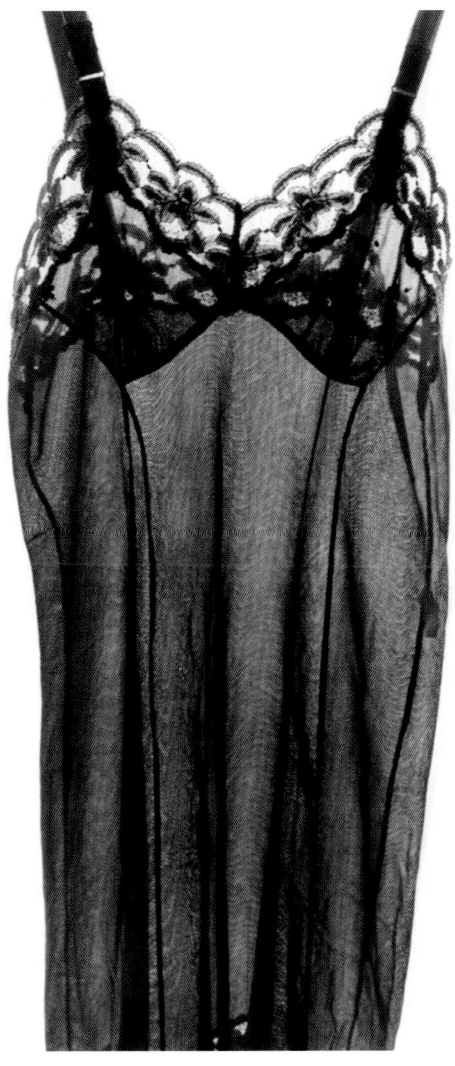

Mother's consists of photographs of the artist's mother's belongings, taken after her unexpected death in 2000. The series reads like a catalogue, simply shot and titled: the 2001 work shown above, for example, is titled *Mothers #5*. The relationship between mother and daughter was conflicted, and had started to heal only just before the mother's death. Ishiuchi states: 'For many years, I was pained by an inability to communicate with my mother, but after my father's death, just when the discord between us was finally beginning to ease, she passed away.' Ishiuchi attempted to come to terms with her loss by photographing her mother's remaining possessions. The objects act both as an extension of the artist's mother's body and as a comment on the fragility and eventual disintegration of the human body. This desire to stay connected means that the objects become suffused with emotion and longing.

For both artists, the urge to document is a way of remembering and immortalising the mother, and becomes an elegiac homage to times past. What both these images show is that memory here is not about recalling appearance or enhancing the quality of a recollection, but instead describes extended acts of anamnesis – 'a state of reverie' – and, as such, explicit gestures of remembrance.

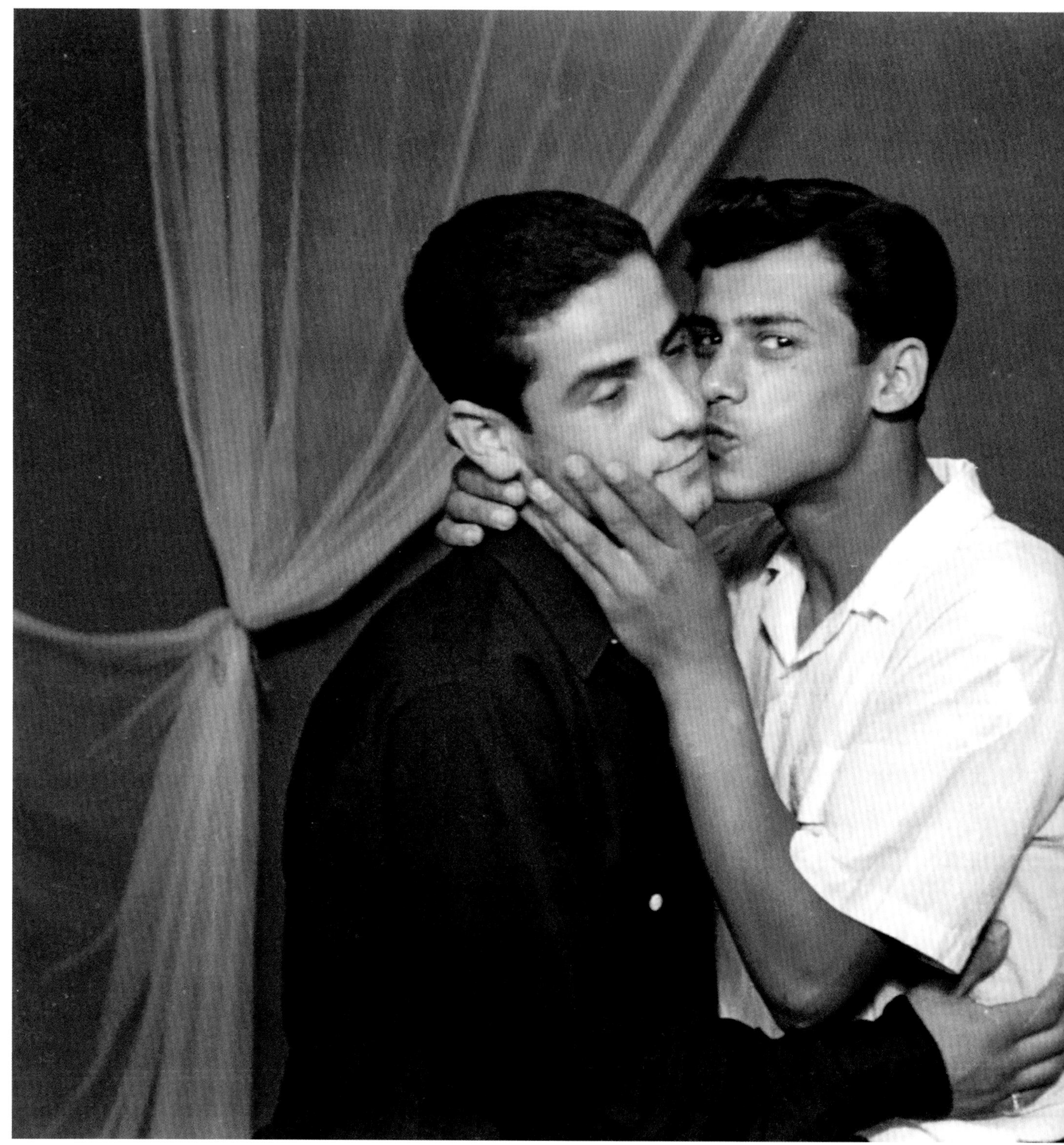

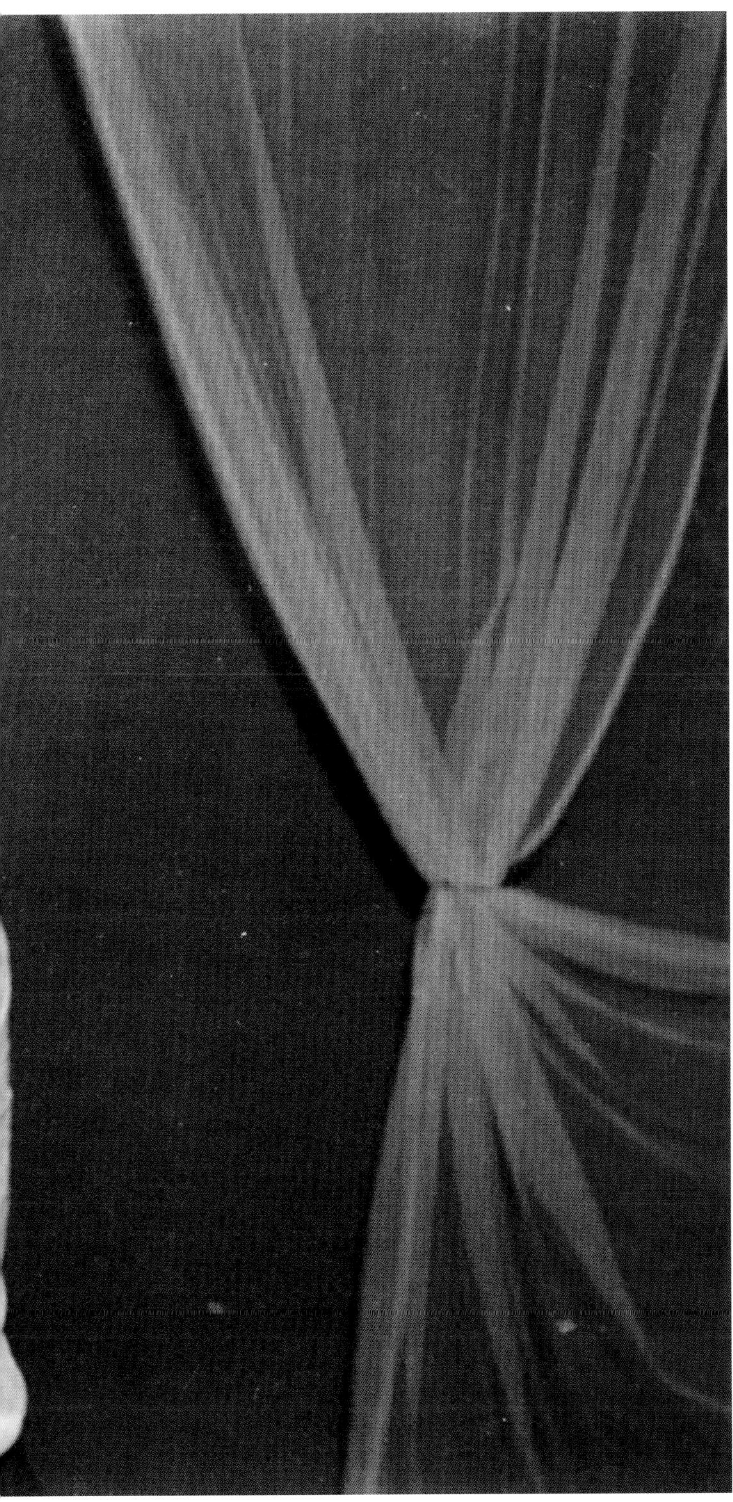

Akram Zaatari (born 1966)
***Tarho and El Masri. Studio Shehrazade, Saida, Lebanon, 1955* (2007)**

Look closely at this portrait of two young men. What can you say about them? This is one of those rare photographs that could easily fit into almost any chapter in this book. First, it deals with remembrance, but it is also about public versus private, identity, reality and ownership.

The Lebanese film-maker and artist Akram Zaatari has secured this image (one of many) from the archive of Studio Shehrazade, run by his compatriot, the studio photographer Hashem el Madani, who was active from 1948 in Zaatari's native city, Saida (Sidon), in Lebanon. By re-contextualising this studio portrait made in 1955, Zaatari has now given this image two 'authors' and two dates, emphasising how a photograph, when removed from its original context, can take on a different meaning in another time and in a different religious culture.

Residents of Saida of all social backgrounds visited El Madani to have their portraits taken in the privacy of his popular studio. The studio became a kind of theatre for men and women to act out various identities. The aspect of performance in this portrait is increased by the curtains hung from the backdrop. Frequently inspired by films, people could select how they wanted to be remembered. Sometimes they allowed El Madani to choose poses for them, and sometimes the customers chose from a book full of images of people in different poses that El Madani provided like a menu. Thus, these two men came to perform embracing and kissing in front of a camera. In conservative Sidon, where a public kiss between a man and a woman was a bridge too far, it seems that two people of the same sex were nevertheless willing to playact a kiss, with one of the young men pretending to be the woman demurely receiving her kiss. Why they did this remains inscrutable. What we do know is that Zaatari makes us rethink our assumptions about hidden homosexuality, and how a picture, once taken to capture and remember a friendship, actually confronts us with ourselves and our immediate judgement.

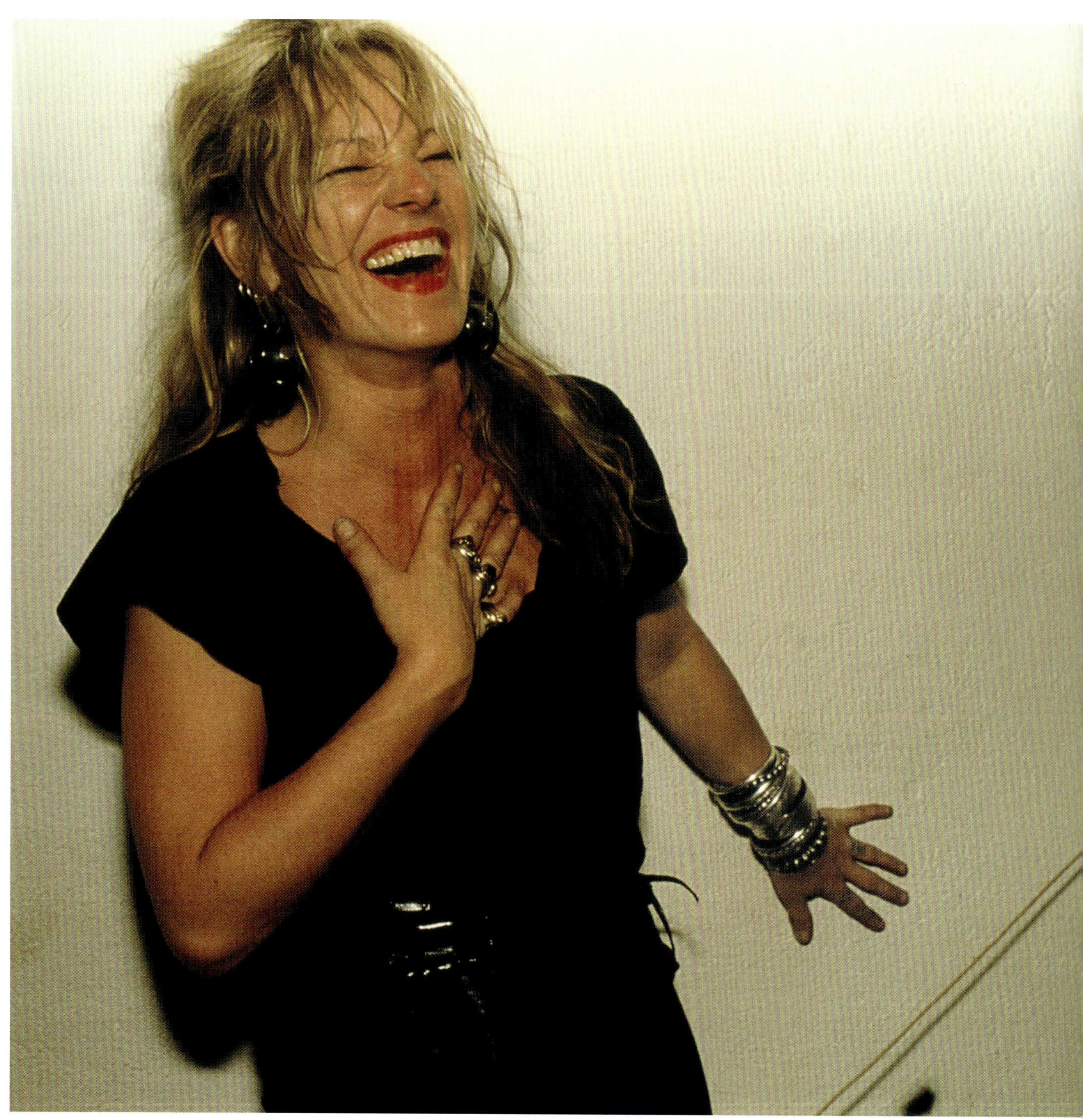

Nan Goldin (born 1953)
***Cookie Laughing, NYC, 1985* (1987)**

The American photographer Nan Goldin famously said she photographed people she loved so that she would never lose them. It's as if she was trying to make her memories stay alive. However, because so many of her friends died during the AIDS crisis of the 1980s and 1990s, the photographs have become totems for how much she really did lose, highlighting the fact that photography cannot preserve or replace a person. Instead of staving off mortality, it crystallises it, recalling Roland Barthes's idea that the essence of photography is the implied message: 'That has been.'

With this in mind, Goldin's photograph of Cookie Mueller has a dual charge: on the one hand it is free and spontaneous, and on the other it is a detailed document of a time that has been and gone. Cookie Mueller was an 'underground' actress who had parts in John Waters movies as well as being a journalist and columnist for New York's *East Village Eye*. She died of an AIDS-related illness when she was 40. This photograph is part of a series or portfolio brought together by Goldin after her friend's death. The limited number of prints and the fact that they exist as physical photographs, as if encased in a time capsule, magnifies their sadness. They have a different sensibility from the images now ubiquitous on social media sites showing friends gathered around a phone for a selfie. Goldin's community seems gloriously unconscious of the camera in a way that today's generation are not. There is no self-consciousness or posing.

As so many people subscribe to at least one social media site today, the way we handle death online is still being worked out. What is appropriate and what is not? Should you disconnect that person's page from yours? Do families still post? There seem to be no definitive answers. Perhaps forming a portfolio of photographs as Goldin did for Mueller might be a good place to start.

Unknown Photographer
Plantation owner with his wife and slaves, Australasia (c.1856)

The problem of collective memory and histories – of who has the right to decide how a story is told and to whom – seethes just beneath the surface of this photograph. It shows a plantation owner, his wife and their indigenous workers, gathered as if they are posing for a family portrait. The ornate frame suggests that this object was treasured with great pride and no doubt was put on display. To contemporary eyes, it is chilling and strange. The patriarch carries a whip, and the young Aboriginal woman sitting at the front looks as though she is wearing a wedding gown – although we might have expected a bride to be positioned in a place of honour, not humbly sitting on the ground.

In addition, Aborigines' relationship to memory is centred in oral practices, in 'songlines', which take cues from the landscape. All this knowledge and history is absent in this photograph which appears as a mere 'blink' in comparison with the rich traditions of Aboriginal memory-making. Just as the workers have been violently severed from their culture and forced to work on the plantations, they are here subjected to a Western form of record-making and the ideology implicit in the technology.

Today, the power balances that historically have been at play between indigenous cultures and Western culture are brought to the fore, and Western ideals of ownership, control and property have been transported to another culture. The horrific oppression and exploitation that was (and in many ways continues to be) dealt against the Australian Aborigines cannot be reversed, but by showing photographs such as these more inclusive histories can be explored, and past actions accounted for.

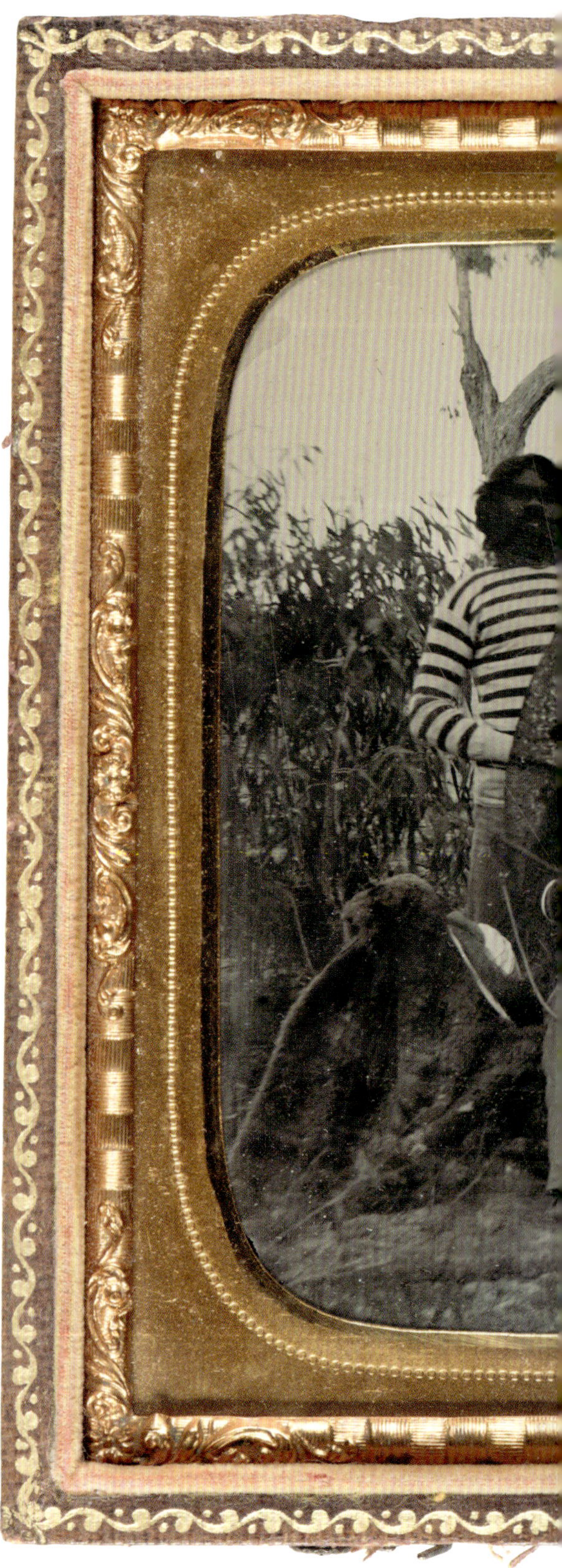

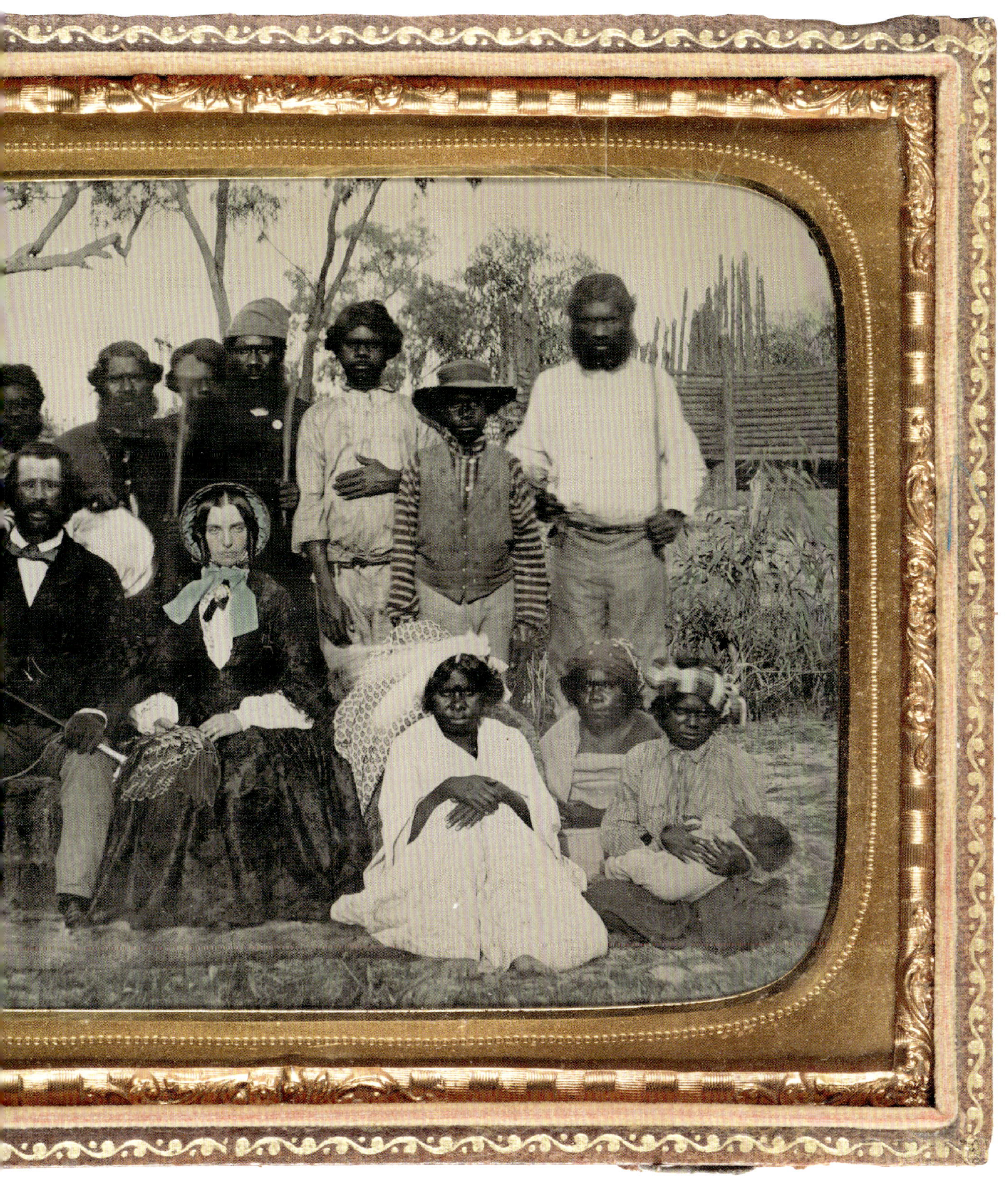

Nickolas Muray (1892–1965)
***Christmas Tree*; cover of *McCall's Homemaking* (1944)**

The Hungarian-born America photographer Nickolas Muray is now remembered not only for his photographs but also for his Olympic fencing achievements and his well-documented love affair with the Mexican painter Frida Kahlo. He arrived in the USA aged 21 having learned the skills of colour photography and printing while working at a publishing house in Germany. The complicated three-colour carbro (carbon-bromide) printing process, of which he was a master, became popular in advertising during the late 1930s and early 1940s, and Muray worked for a range of magazines and advertisers, most notably the monthly women's magazine *McCall's*, where he pioneered the use of full colour on every page.

Muray was adept at creating mythic images for magazines. He understood acutely the need for advertising to create a fantasy, generating images of longing and desire. His commercial photographs represent an America that is over the top, generous and abundant – far from the post-war reality experienced by many. They tap into a collective idea of what a certain event should be like, whether that is Christmas or a Thanksgiving feast. They are the American Dream epitomised – a complex fantasy based on artificial memories, aspirations and ideals. Muray's image for the cover of the December 1944 issue depicts a gorgeous, idealised Christmas, tapping into a nostalgic vision of how Christmas used to be. It stands in for real memory because you really cannot get anything better than the Muray version of an event: his images represent a perfect time that never existed – just like in a Technicolor movie or in a dream.

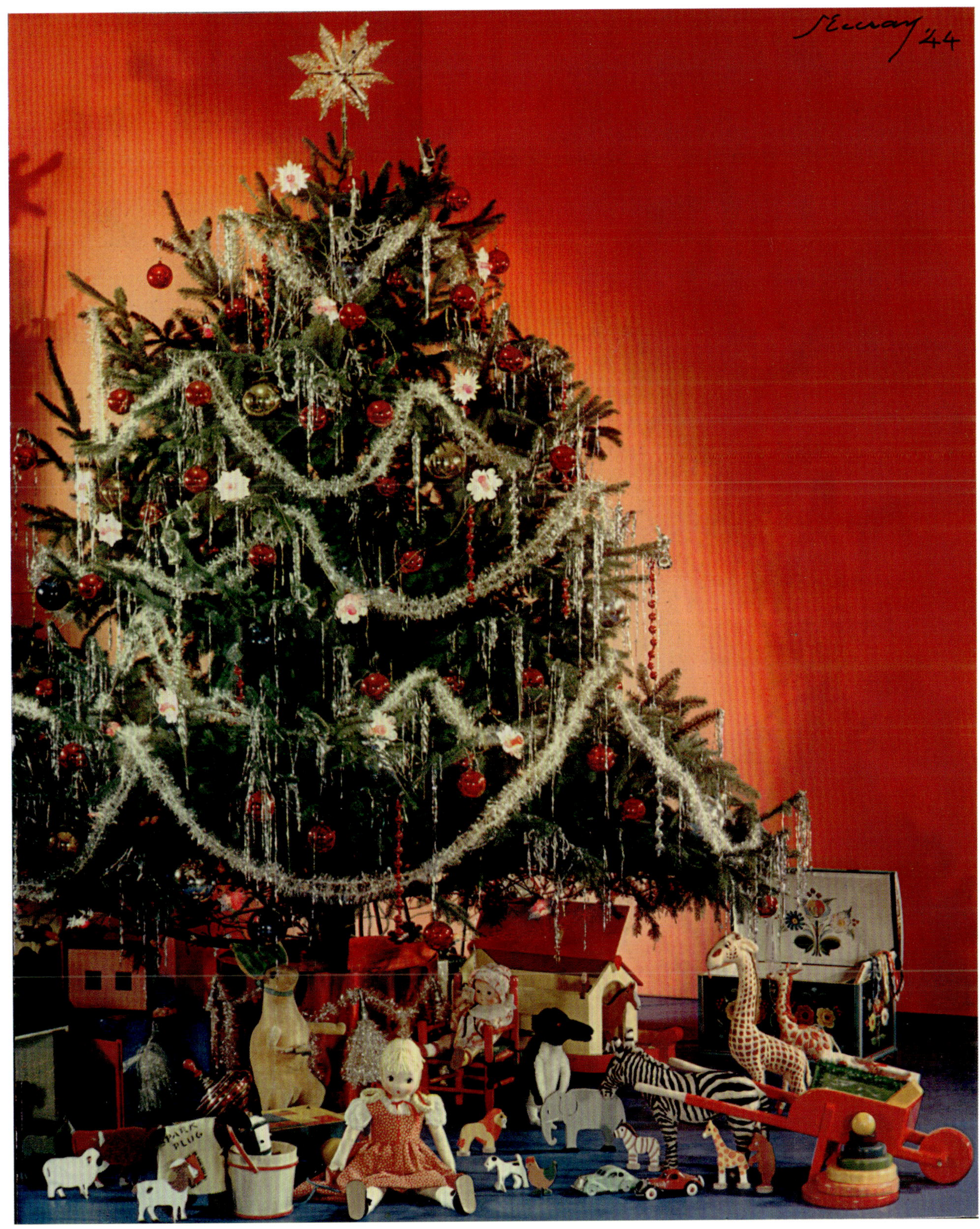

Jeffrey Silverthorne (born 1946)
***Lovers, Accidental Carbon Monoxide Poisoning* (1973)**

This picture was taken in a morgue in Rhode Island, USA, for a series titled *Morgue Work* (1972–91). The American photographer, Jeffrey Silverthorne, has captured a couple who were accidentally killed by carbon monoxide poisoning – keeping his balance by placing one foot on a body-refrigerator door. Silverthorne has placed himself in the picture by showing his leg – a move that seems disrespectful, although perhaps this was the only angle from where he could capture both people in one image. And perhaps, after all, they deserve to be remembered together like this, as they were lovers. However, to imagine a photographer clambering around a morgue as he tries to find the best angle for a shot jars with our ideas of how the dead should be treated.

Silverthorne's portraits of the dead raise a host of ethical questions – not least whether the families gave their permission and had access to the photographs, either through reviewing them or having editorial control. However, his treatment of the theme of death is not driven by voyeuristic desire or morbid fascination, but instead deliberately raises questions of morality, transgression and remembrance. That is a lot to demand of a photograph. This photograph has a charge, as it so directly illustrates a photographer's determination to show the shocking reality of death, usually concealed 'behind closed doors'. The photographer's foot acts as a symbol of interference, preventing the door from being closed and hiding the reality of death, which is ultimately the most shocking thing about this picture, rather than it being a photograph of the dead.

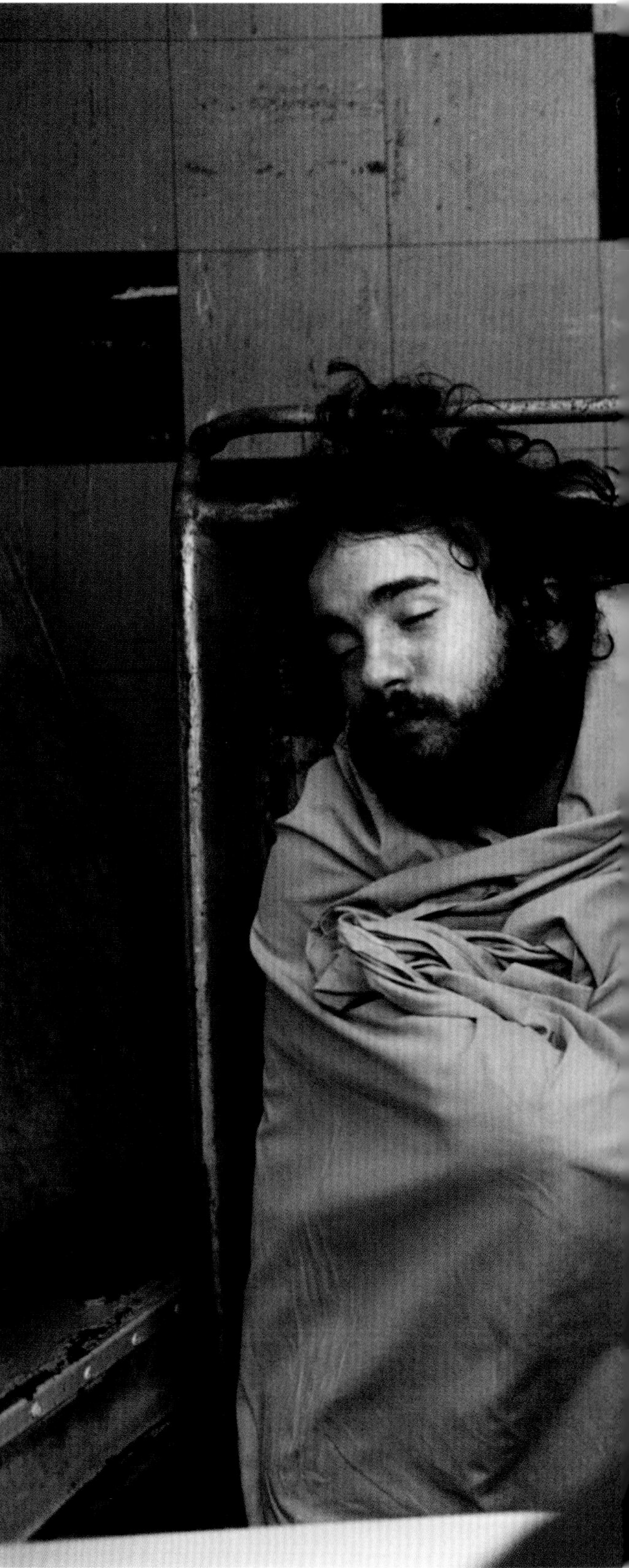

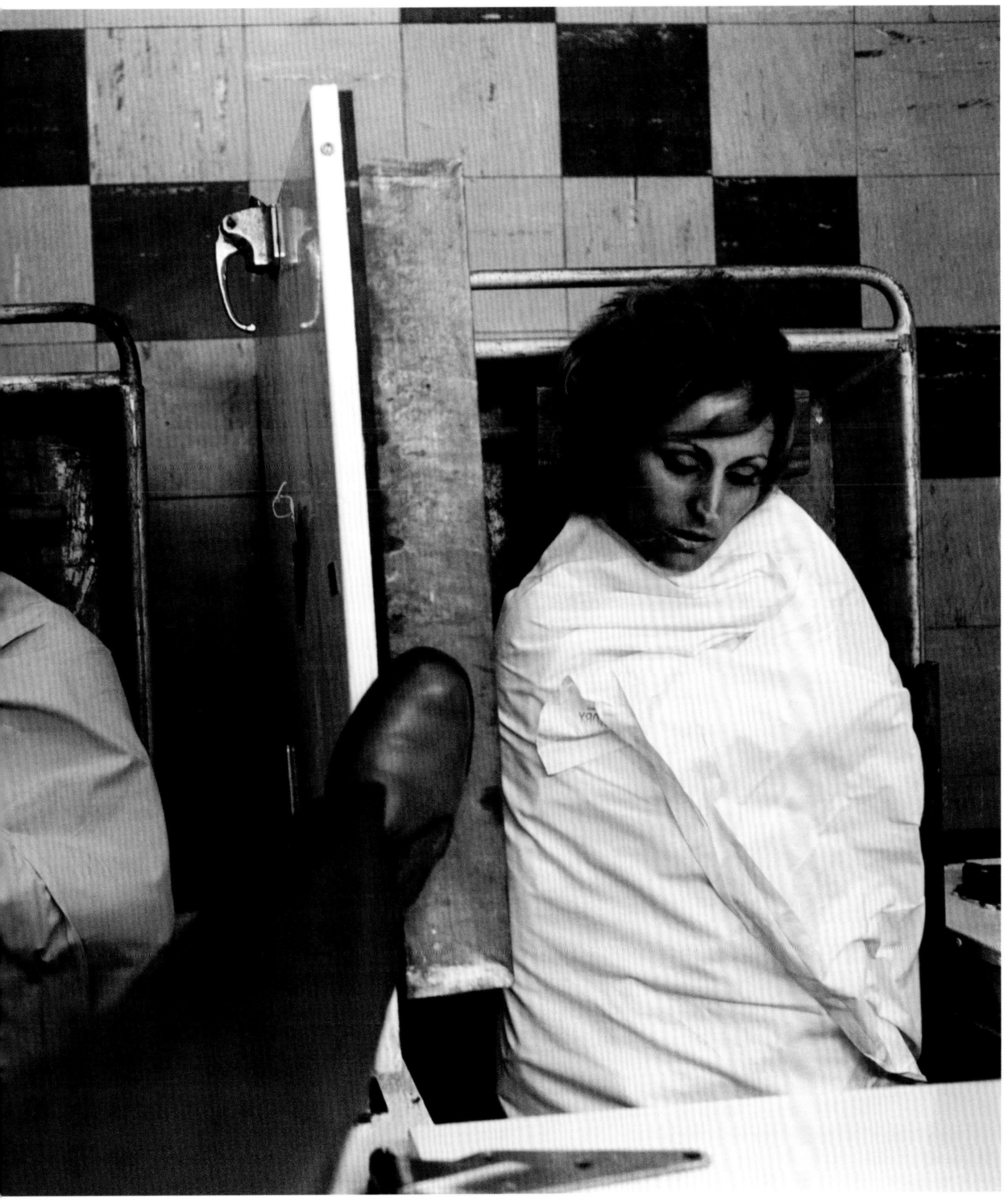

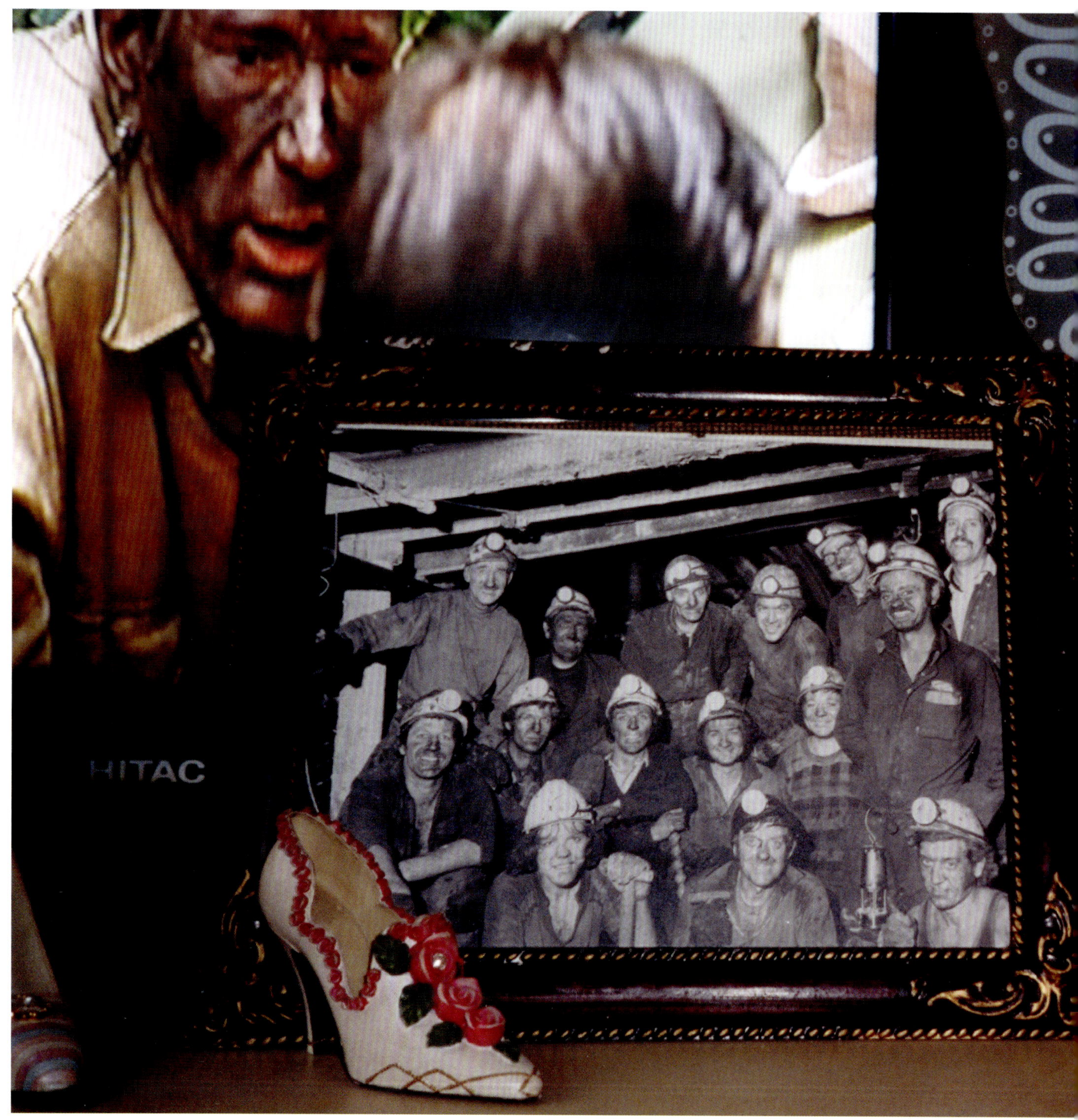
HITAC

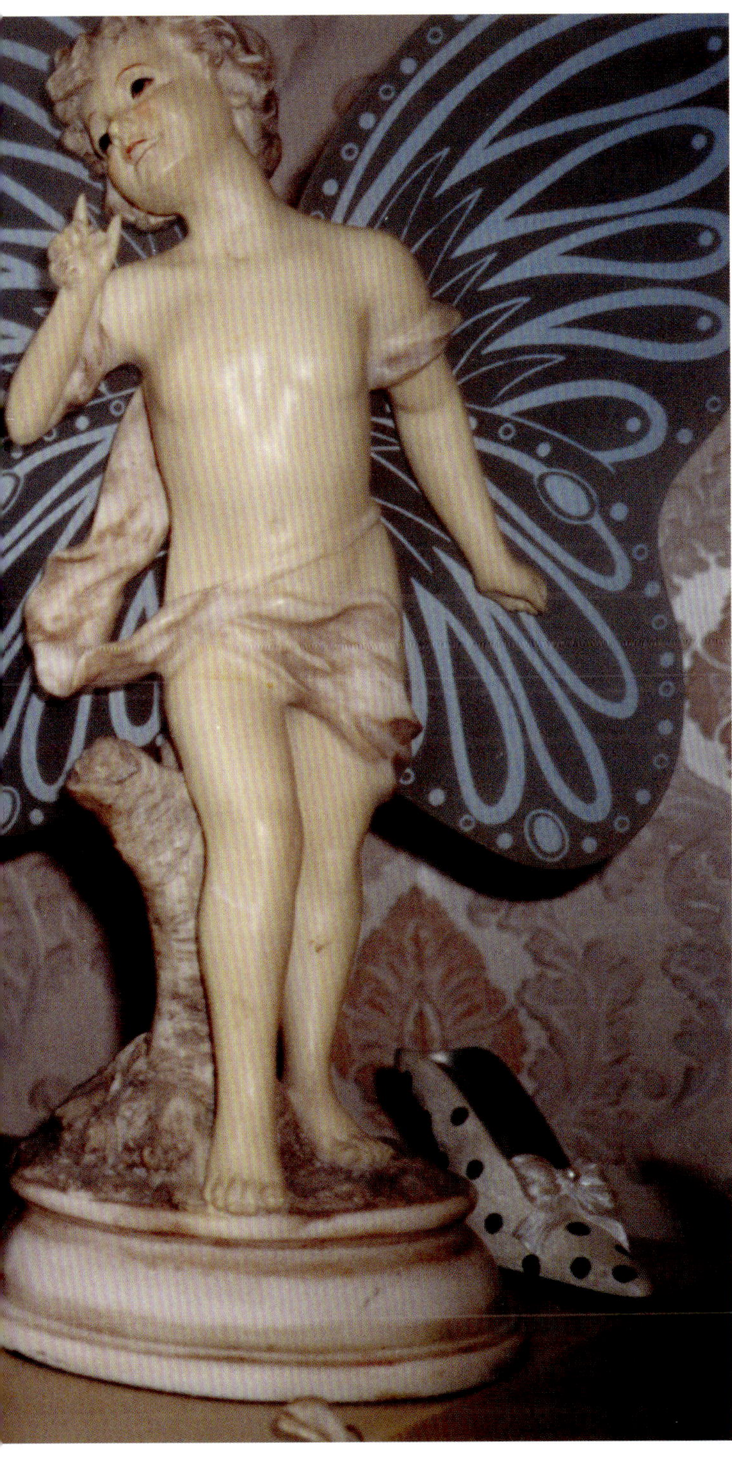

Bertien van Manen (born 1942)
***West Yorkshire, New Sharlston* (2004)**

For her series *Give Me Your Image* (2002–5), the Dutch artist Bertien van Manen visited strangers' homes around Europe and asked to see a precious family photograph. Often people showed her photographs that told an intriguing personal story. On a Greek island she was shown the cherished photo of a murderess who had killed her husband. And a cheerful Moldavian man pulling a face in another picture from 1930 turned out to be one of the many Holocaust victims.

Van Manen then looked for a place in the house where the picture could best be photographed, and re-photographed the memory of an ordinary person, thus recording an intimate snapshot of an ordinary life, enriched by history, memory and emotion. In doing this, Van Manen takes the viewer on a journey across Europe's ragged, impoverished edges as well as to its rich centre, while also presenting many of the great themes from 20th-century history – from the Second World War to the current immigration crisis. In Budapest, she visited the new rich, and in a Parisian suburb, she met immigrants who kept their photographs in shoeboxes.

In West Yorkshire, the photographer visited a mining family, whose community had been shattered by mine closures. Here, she placed a framed picture of a group of smiling miners on a sideboard topped with the family's ornaments. The miniature high-heeled shoes and the figurine of a fairy contrast strongly with the miners' rugged appearance and their tough working conditions. When Van Manen looked through the lens, she had all the luck a photographer could hope for: the television in the background that had been on since she entered the house showed a miner with a blackened face, reinforcing the memorial function of the photograph while catapulting the scene into the present.

Van Manen's photograph clearly speaks of a desire to remember the person in the group portrait, which shows a world that no longer exists, and people who are no longer alive. The private photo showing the eternal connection to those they left behind functions as a talisman of remembrance of both people and objects. Just like Van Manen's photograph.

How can you
tell a story?
How can you
tell a story?
How can you
tell a story?
How can you
tell a story?
How can you
tell a story?
How can you
tell a story?
How can you
tell a story?

The camera is a tool that allows people to express themselves artistically, politically, socially, critically and comedically. In this respect, photography can be used to tell a story in as many ways as literature or film can tell a story. However, because a photographic camera can take only one picture at a time – as opposed to the flowing narrative possible in the mediums of writing, film and video – photography has to work harder to get meanings across and utilises a series of different strategies in order to do this. Perhaps the word 'snapshot' best explains this characteristic of photography: we never get the whole story, just a slice of it, and it is up to the viewer to 'fill in the blanks' and make the story understandable.

This elliptical nature is one of photography's strengths, but it can also be a source of ambiguity, mystery and even frustration. Because so much of photography works on a documentary level, story can be crucial. But how can a sense of sequence be expressed in just one image? The easiest and most common way around this lack of context is to accompany a photograph with a caption. The seesaw effect of reading and looking is essential for providing context.

In the 19th century, some pioneers of photography were adroit at layering images with metaphor and symbolism in order to tell a story, in the same manner as painting had traditionally done. By doing this, they expanded the ability of the medium to tell more of the story; to do more than present a straight documentary 'slice' or a trace from life. To achieve this wider narrative, photographs were commonly staged. By having the subjects act out a scene for the camera (as one would in a play or film), the subsequent viewer knows that the scene has not been taken from life and that a story is at the heart of the meaning. In staged or constructed (art) photography, the fictional qualities are pushed to the fore. A clear example of this can be seen in *The Two Ways of Life* (right) by the Swedish-born Victorian art photographer Oscar Gustave Rejlander (1813–75). For this photograph, Rejlander layered as many as 30 negatives to create a dense tableau depicting vice and virtue that to contemporary eyes seems melodramatic and over the top, but which to the eyes of the Victorians would have been fully aligned to fashionable academic painting. This method of layering negatives (or files, as is done today) has continued to be a popular device, and one used by several artists in this book, including Jeff Wall, who creates similarly fantastical scenes, albeit with very different meanings.

Another, contrasting method of storytelling in photography is through the use of a large number of sequenced images. This was a device used in early

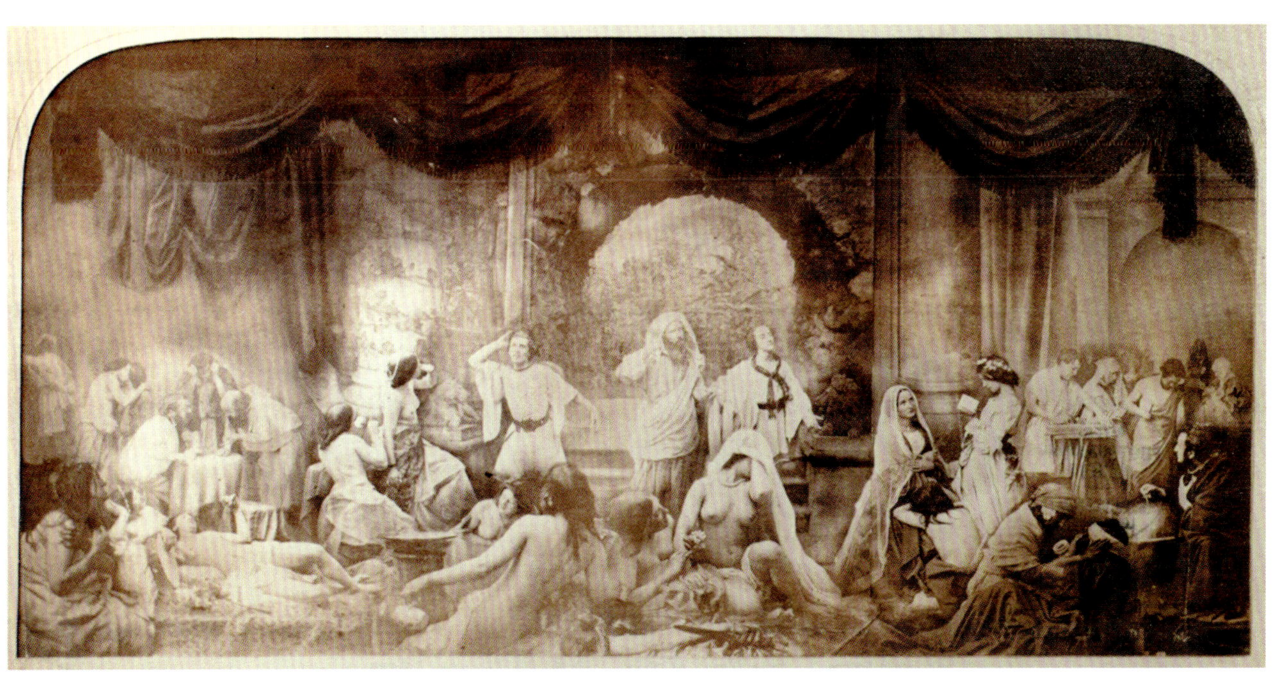

Oscar Gustave Rejlander, *The Two Ways of Life* (1857)

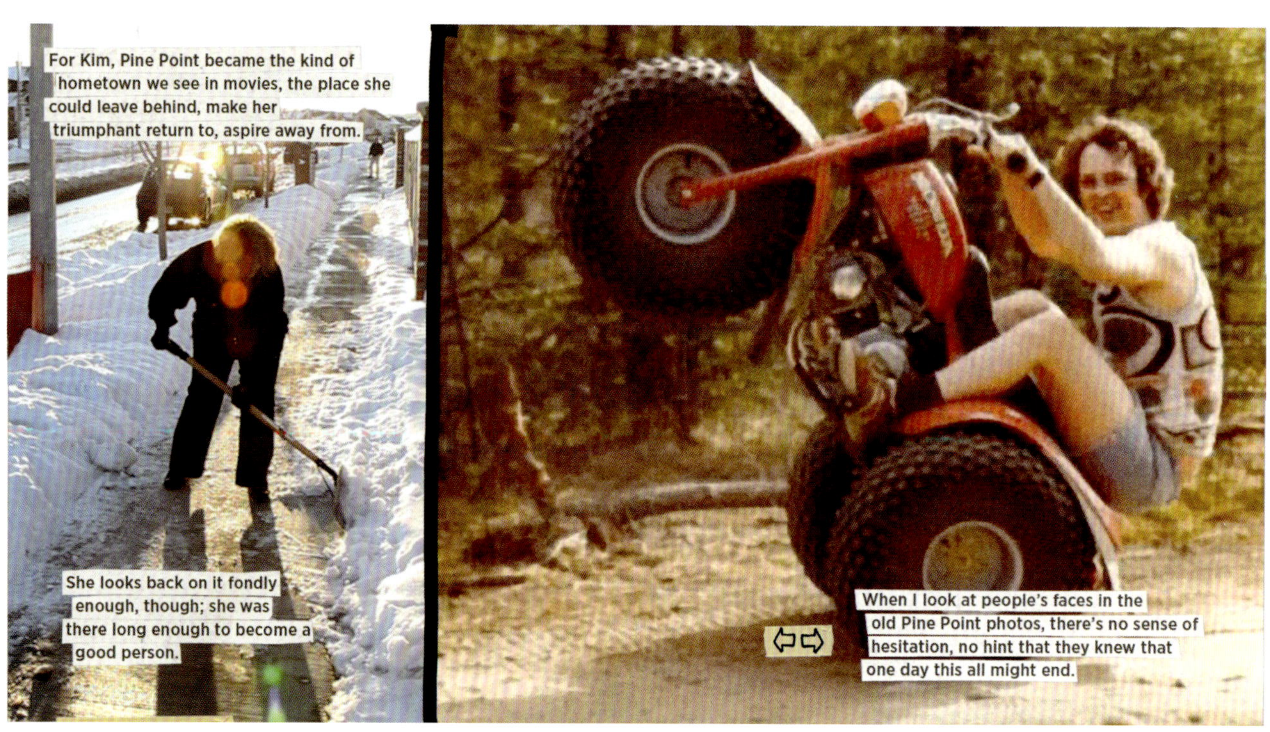

Michael Simons and Paul Shoebridge, *Welcome to Pine Point* (2011)

photography – such as Eadweard Muybridge's *The Horse in Motion*, which tells the basic story of how a horse gallops – and one that has developed in line with technology ever since. The technique has, for example, advanced with the 'slide show' as a popular way of viewing stories on the web, and over the past decade, as technology has developed, the rise of multimedia storytelling has gained in popularity, initially in documentary circles. This method employs photographic stills, sound and video clips, voice-over, music, interviews, graphic design and illustrations, in any combination, to give as much context to a story as possible. An early and significant example of this is *Welcome to Pine Point* (left), an interactive web documentary by the Canadians Michael Simons and Paul Shoebridge. The pair set out to make a book about the death of the photo album as a way to keep memories, but they eventually developed a multimedia piece that turned out to be a rich alternative to both the photo album and the traditional notion of documentary. Equally important is its exploration of how we remember the past and how memory proves to be an unreliable source for distinguishing between truth and fiction.

Using cameras as well as narratives as their tools, photographers tell stories about themselves and others. Narrative, however, is something broader than photography. Narrative and oral history are characteristics of humanity, storytelling being an important way in which we transmit knowledge, data and opinions. In photography, narratives are built by both photographers and viewers, because a narrative is inextricably linked with context on the one hand and interpretation on the other. If the maker/photographer provides no context – for example through captions – the interpretation of a photograph will inevitably be steered by the viewer's own experiences, background and education. As a result, without at least some context already in place, concepts such as fact and truth (as conceived by the maker) immediately lose their value. On the other hand, where context is abundantly provided, as in a multimedia piece, the opinion of the maker may be foregrounded, leaving the viewer with less room for personal interpretation. So a good use of narrative might seek to provide room for and balance both authorial intention and the viewer's interpretation.

In multimedia storytelling, the photograph offers an array of alternatives to the classical structure of linear narrative – a story with a beginning, middle and end, and with one or more characters. Multimedia non-linear storytelling can be more easily enriched by the use of flashbacks, memories and digressions, for instance. Whether linear or non-linear, and whether the stories provide a dénouement or are open-ended, a photographer developing a visual story will usually ask themselves the following questions: What is the audience am I trying to reach? What is the theme of the story I want to tell? What is the context? What will be the events? Do I need a character to personify the issue I am raising?

Character-driven storytelling is a way of making the narrative personal, in fact employing a cinematographic storytelling technique. On a vernacular level, this can also be seen in the rise in popularity of 'stories' across image-sharing sites that allow users to create mini-films using photographs and video that can also be written on, or to which music and sound can be added. Regardless of how the result relates to truth or fiction, everyone's life can now be turned into a Hollywood-style production, to be viewed once rather than treasured forever.

Henk Wildschut (born 1967)
***Monday, 14 December 2015 10:14* (2015)**

'Business flourished in the shopping street.' This sentence evokes images of shining shop fronts, luxury products in beautifully illuminated shop windows and excited people doing their Christmas shopping. The line is from the book *Ville de Calais* (2017) by the Dutch photographer Henk Wildschut, and the shop we see (pictured here) is in fact made of waste wood, plastic and cardboard. The street has a mud floor, no pavements. The word 'flourished' refers to an extension that had been constructed by using some more waste wood and plastic, two months after Wildschut first photographed the shop.

From 2006 to 2016, the photographer documented the rise and fall of the Calais Jungle, a 'village' consisting of makeshift dwellings created by refugees and illegal immigrants who were hoping to make their way from France to the United Kingdom. They were not welcome in either place. To survive the period during which they waited for a chance to make the dangerous crossing by smuggling themselves onto boats or through the Channel Tunnel, they built temporary shelters. The way in which the basic need for shelter takes shape became a theme for Wildschut, resulting in the publication *Shelter* (2010) as well as *Ville de Calais*. In these books, he shows us the ways in which people who are looking for a better life can build a community even in the harshest conditions. Without ever depicting the 'village' from close to, and only rarely showing its inhabitants as recognisable individuals, Wildschut is nonetheless able to depict a humanitarian crisis down to the smallest details, and without visual clichés. The shelters symbolise the larger, underlying story of poverty, fear, sorrow, exclusion, violence, courage and hope.

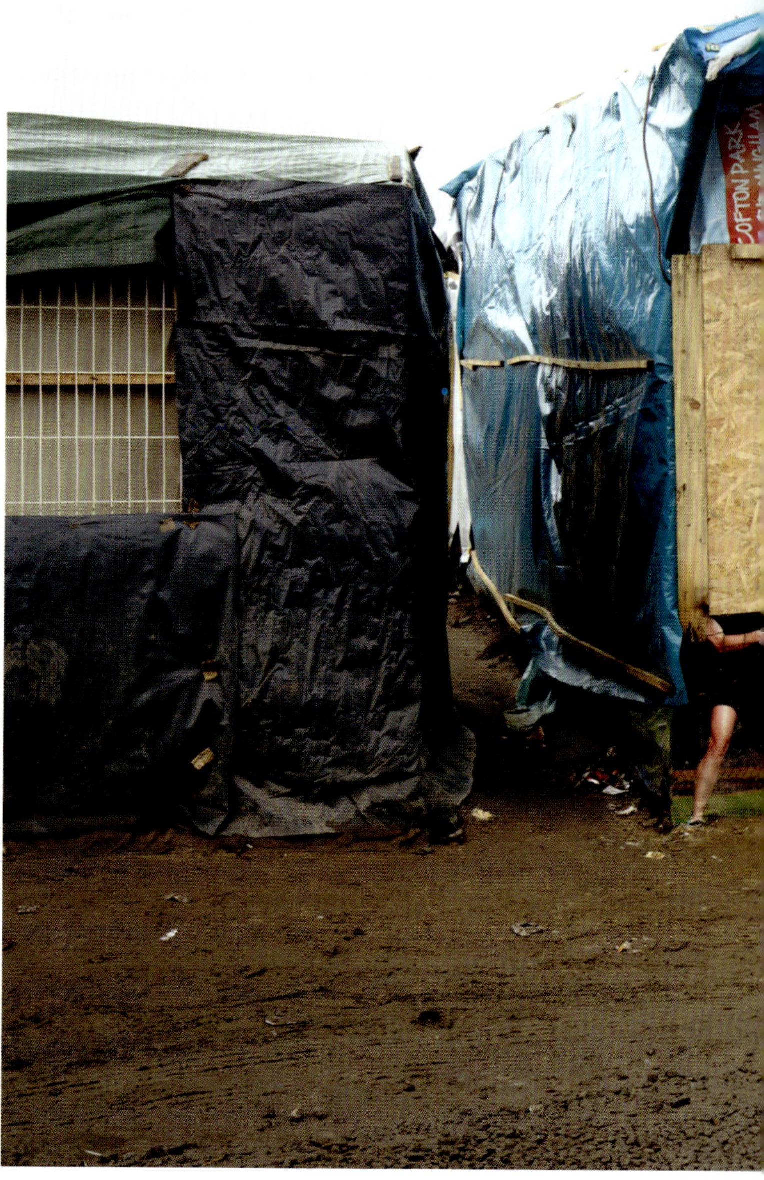

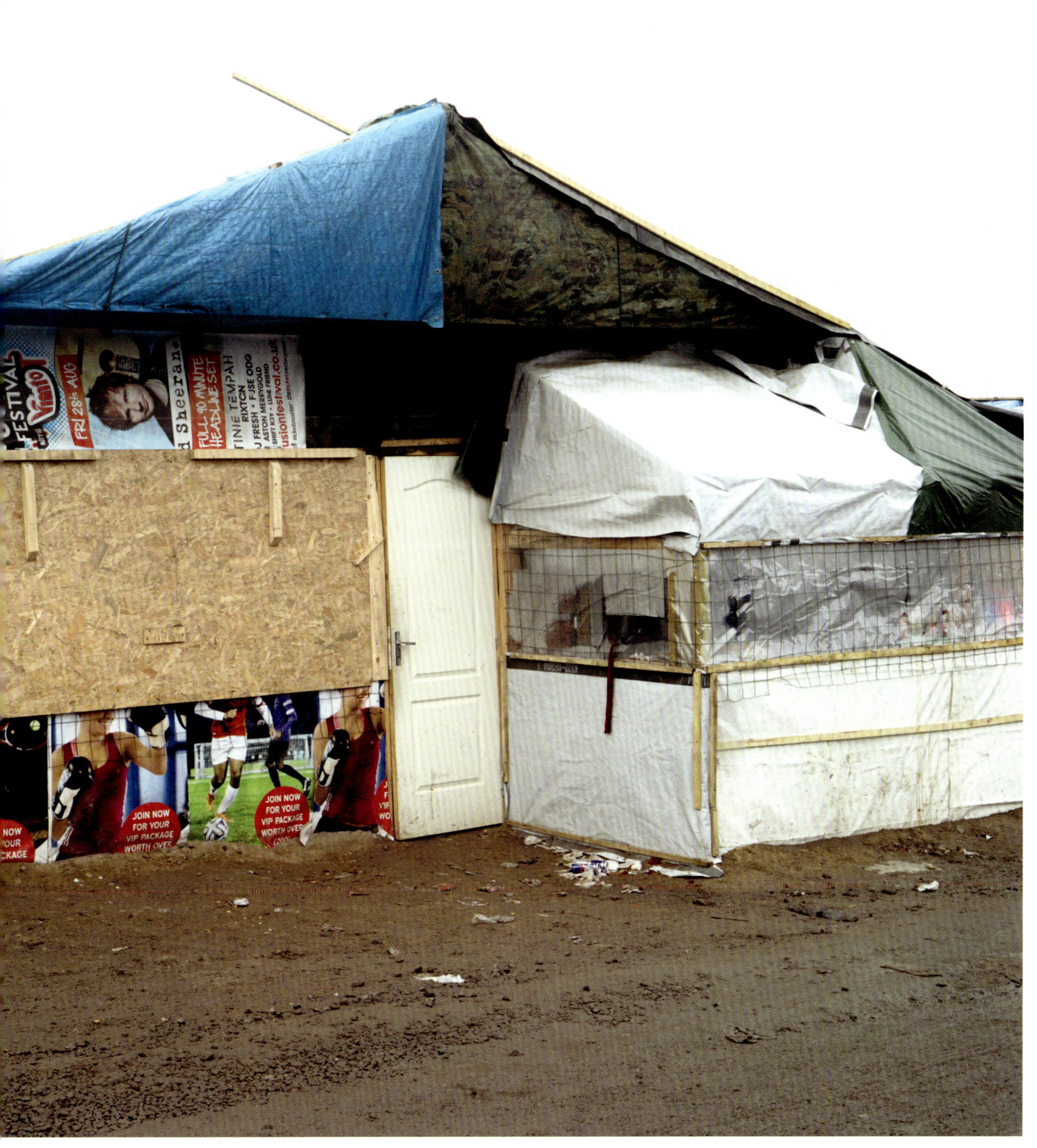
FESTIVAL
FRI 28th AUG
FULL 90 MINUTE HEADLINE SET
TINIE TEMPAH
JOIN NOW
FOR YOUR
VIP PACKAGE
WORTH OVER

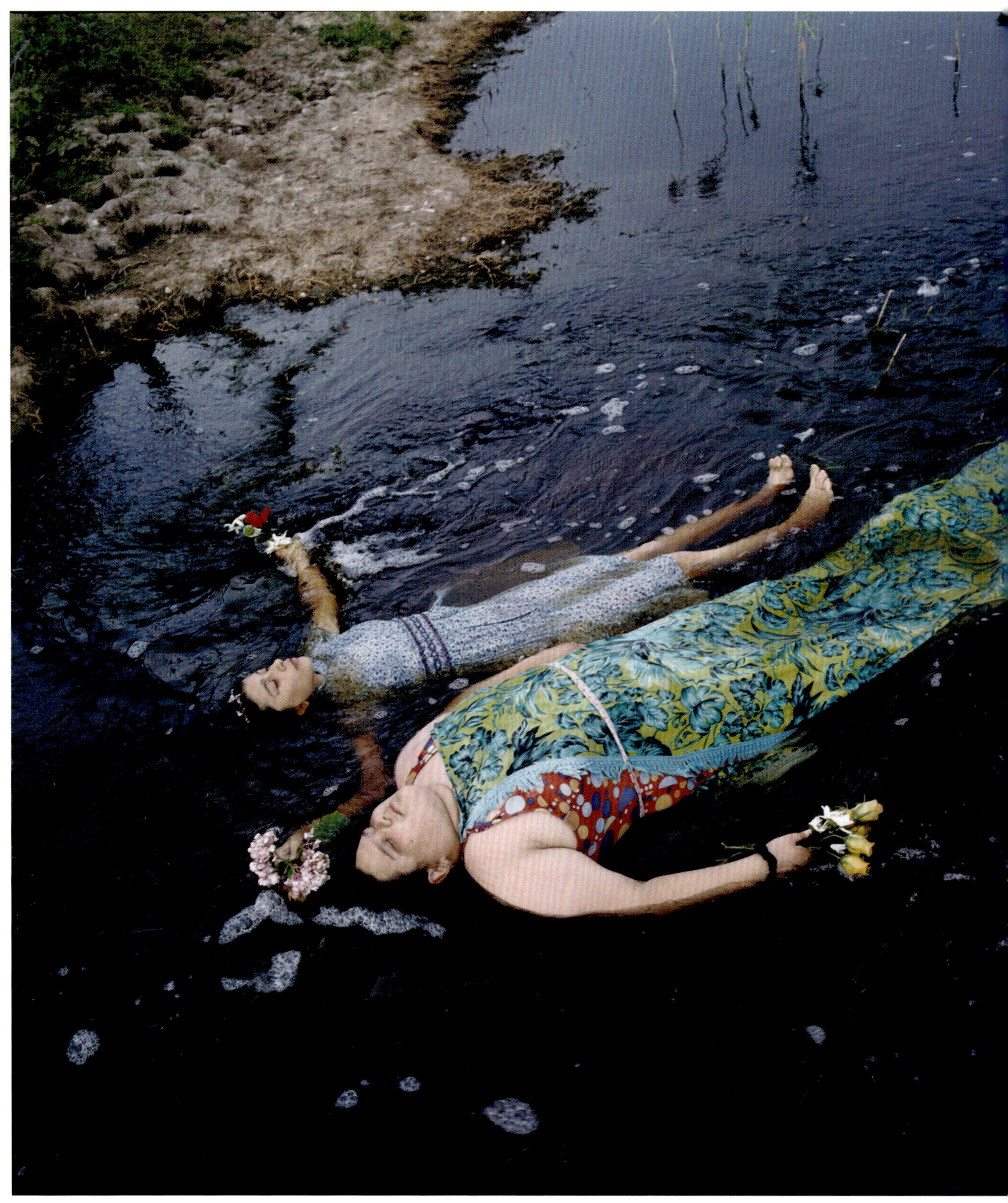

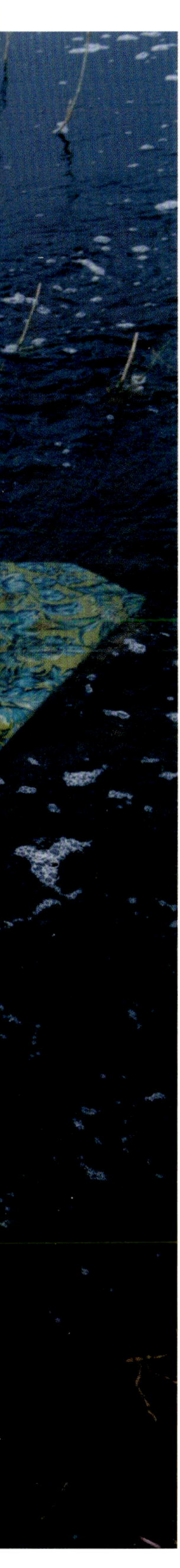

Alessandra Sanguinetti (born 1968)
***The Adventures of Guille and Belinda and the Enigmatic Meaning of Their Dreams* (2009)**

Alessandra Sanguinetti works in a documentary tradition; however, the photographs in this series do not form a linear narrative, but are instead a dreamy interlacing of interconnected stories that weave in and out of focus. The two young girls, aged nine and ten when the project started, create a world for themselves and invite the photographer in. The pace is slow, the mood is quiet and the viewer is reminded of the long-forgotten games of childhood. In *Argentina, Buenos Aires. Ophelias* (2001) shown here, the doomed Ophelia from Shakespeare's *Hamlet*, and perhaps more specifically the John Everett Millais painting (1851–2), is referenced as the two girls float in the stream. What do you think their game involves? What's the story?

The series is best understood as a book where the pace and rhythm of the story unfolds in a flowing narrative. We learn that the girls are often on a farm – their relationship with the animals is a natural and easy one. But the most important thread of the story relates to their friendship. They share an intimacy that is by turns serious and light-hearted. They dress up in various costumes, and their physical difference makes for both comedy and pathos. This push and pull of difference and fantasy is what makes the project so compelling. It is as if Sanguinetti has captured something wholly universal about childhood, something which seems strange to adults, but utterly right to children. The line between real and make-believe need not be so distinct. In the innocence and charm of the girls' relationship, there is also a hint of melancholy, as we know that this chapter of their lives will close and the story will take another route – sadly one more rooted in reality, as stories of growing up often are.

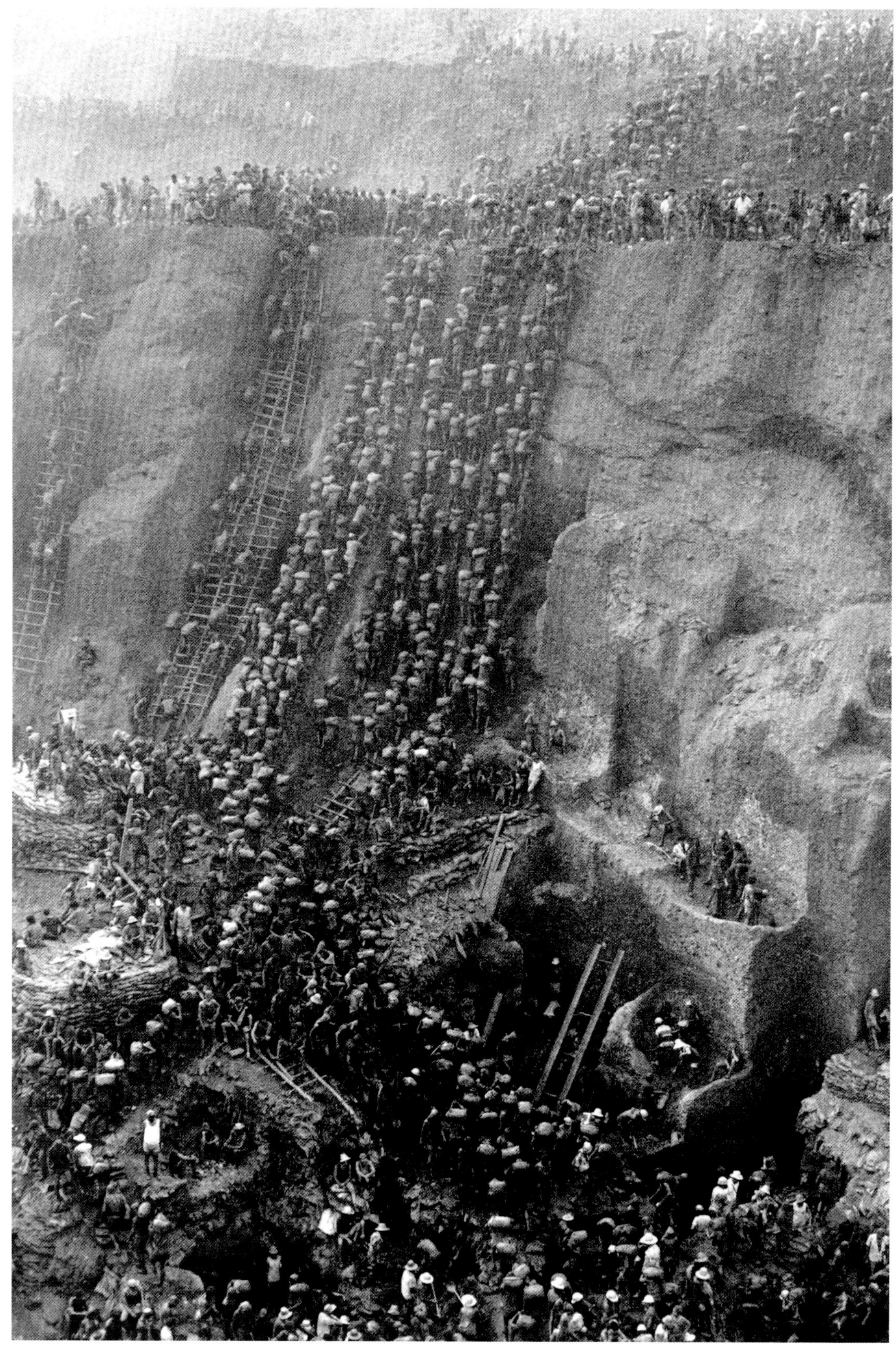

Sebastião Salgado (born 1944)
***Gold Mine, Brazil* (1986)**

Trained as an economist, Sebastião Salgado became a photographer around the age of 30, dedicating his life to showing inconvenient truths about human intervention and its impact on the environment. His most famous pictures are of the Serra Pelada gold mine in Brazil, some 270 miles (430 kilometres) south of the mouth of the Amazon River. The dark power of this image lies in Salgado's distant point of view: the mine has an unnerving resemblance to Dante's Inferno, with the portrait format further emphasising the depth of the open mine and the epic scale of the miners' descent into its abyss. From this distance, the miners appear not as individual human beings, but as a herd of muddy human animals brought together by their restless search for a better, more prosperous future.

The gold rush began at Serra Pelada soon after a child found a nugget of gold on the banks of a local river in around 1980. The news about the discovery spread fast: tens of thousands of men sped to the site, which would soon become the world's biggest open-air gold mine. The gold fever brought out the worst in people, spreading violence and abjection. The nearby town became a place where murders took place daily and where teenage girls prostituted themselves for a flake of gold. At its peak, some 100,000 gold diggers worked in Serra Pelada under appalling conditions. Miners were paid 20 cents on average for digging and carrying up one sack of ore. When Salgado saw the mine for the first time, it reminded him of the time before Christ when the Egyptian pyramids were built: 'the history of mankind unfolded'.

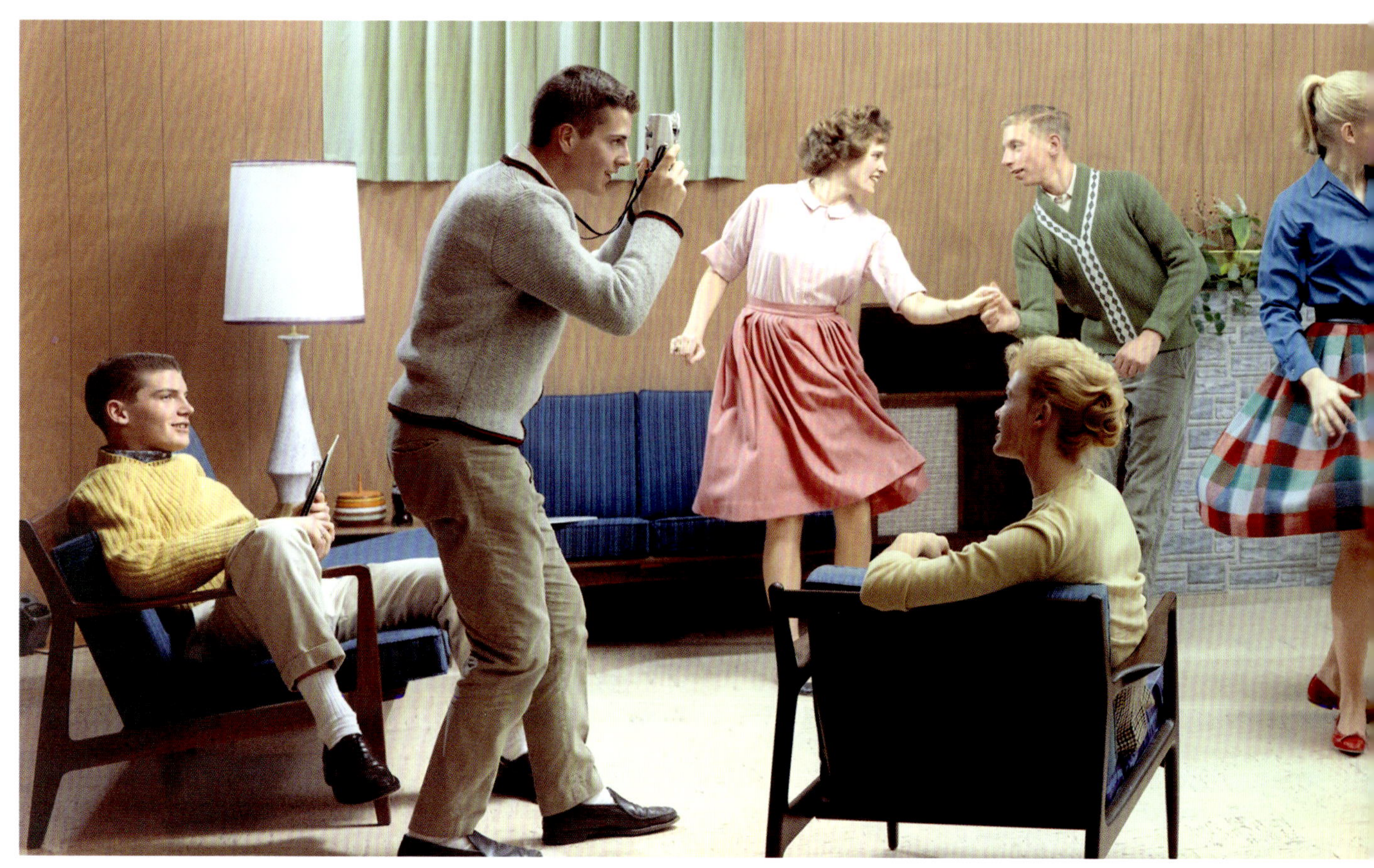

Lee Howick (1928–2009) and Neil Montanus (born 1927),
***Colorama #193 (Teenage Dance)* (1961)**

What a party! In a time when the term 'teenager' was new, this scene is trying to recreate what adults thought young adults did when they got together. Or, more accurately, hoped they did. Frozen in a suburban recreation room, the image shows a melange of activities from dancing to guitar playing to gazing at a man taking a photograph. This picture is one of the many vast 60-foot-tall back-lit transparencies called Coloramas installed by Kodak in Grand Central Station in New York City from 1950 to 1990 that together told a story of American values and aspirations, focusing on travel, leisure and family. Looking at these, it seems that all uplifting events are real only if captured by a camera. Sound familiar? Although the fashions and pastimes may be different, and the context is one of advertising and promotion, the attitude summed up in the phrase 'It's only real if it's on Facebook' seems to have its roots in these strange, all-too-perfect American tableaux, which even at the time thrived on and exploited people's propensity for nostalgia.

Continuing a desire for a nostalgic past, Instagram, for example, originally provided for only square-format images,

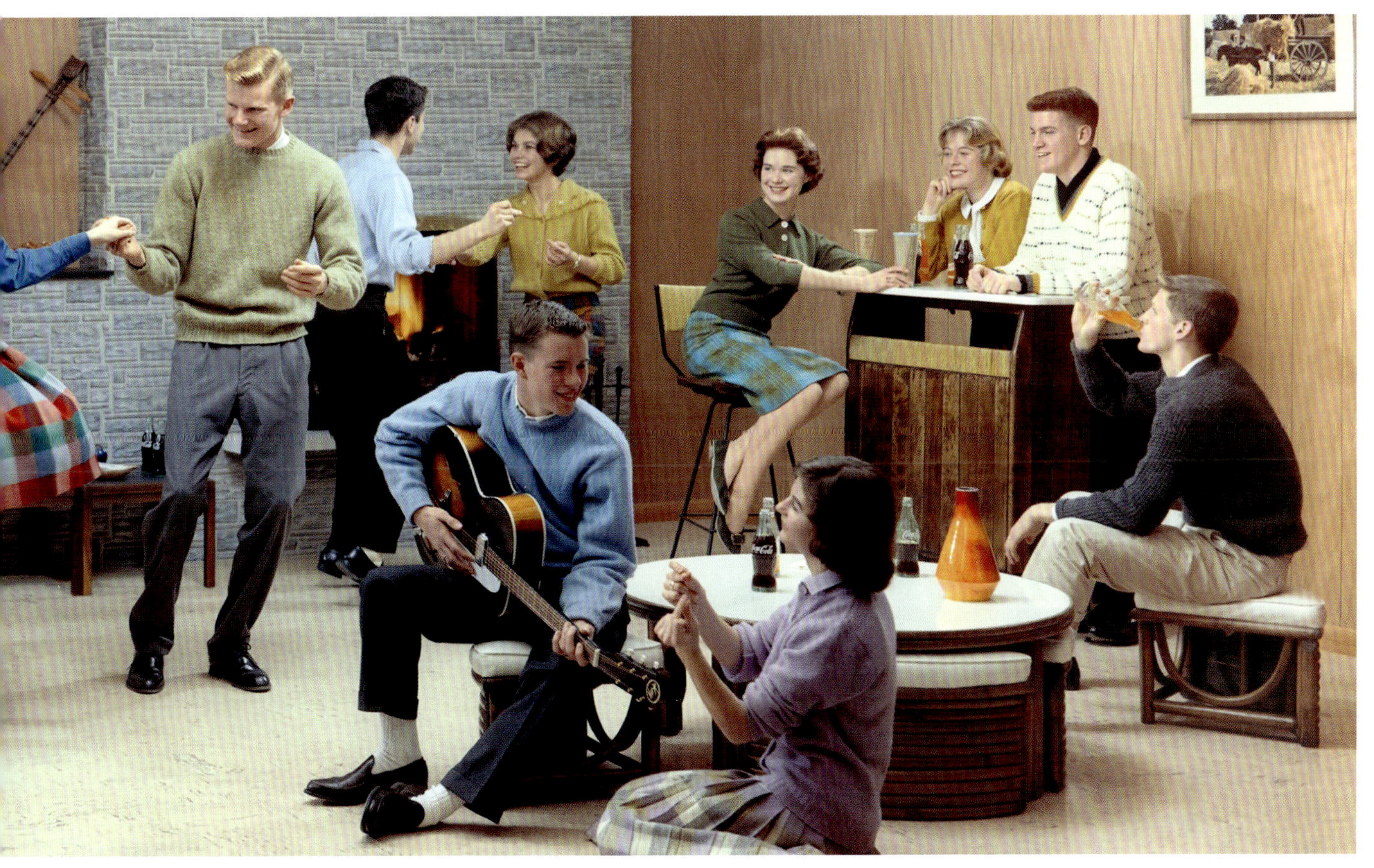

in imitation of the popular Polaroid photograph. It offered filters with names such as '1977', which might bleach the photograph so that it resembled a faded snapshot, or add a vignette. Even the name is a melding of the words 'Instamatic' (Kodak's snapshot camera of the 1960s and 1970s) and 'telegram', romanticising analogue times of the past.

In the 1960s the marketing department of Kodak, through these sanitised scenes of American life, provided an ideology-driven story of a nation. Are the images that we post online also marketing an idealised life – albeit an autobiographical one rather than a corporate, collective one? Could they be read as hundreds of little advertisements for their poster? Next time you take a picture at a party and post it to your social networks, think of this one and compare the story you are trying to tell with Kodak's.

Ralph Eugene Meatyard (1925–1972)
***The Family Album of Lucybelle Crater* (1970–1972)**

An optician by profession, the American Ralph Eugene Meatyard is best known for the last body of work he created, *The Family Album of Lucybelle Crater* – a series of portraits of friends and family wearing masks and enacting low-key, enigmatic scenarios in the Kentucky countryside where he lived. Meatyard never finished his original project, but a revised edition was published posthumously featuring the artist's intended sequencing of images, and adding in missing captions, reproduced in Meatyard's handwriting.

The sequence of photographs is made to resemble a family album. Images bear captions describing the people in them (this image, right, for example, is captioned 'Lucybelle Crater and her P.O. brother Lucybelle Crater' – everyone seems to be named 'Lucybelle Crater') and some of the scenarios follow the formulaic tropes of family snapshots. Startlingly, however, the artist's wife, Madelyn, wears a full-head hag's mask in each picture, while a friend or relative wears a transparent mask that half reveals and half transforms his features. The addition of the masks promises larger stories than a traditional, vernacular album might, making each mundane scenario ghoulish and gothic.

An ordinary photographic album needs a narrator to tell the story for it to be fully understood – that is part of its charm. One can look at the photographs but only ever gain a partial understanding of what is shown: to fill in the blanks, a relative is needed to elaborate and describe, to provide and tell the stories that bind the images together. Meatyard offers us no such context; it is up the viewer to join the dots. We must do this with our knowledge of traditional family albums and how they tell a story and what they do not tell. For example, we know most albums do not reveal negatively life-changing scenarios such as death, divorce or mental illness, but instead concentrate on celebration and togetherness. The masks hinder our ability to read the images and the emotions of the participants, and replace our feelings of empathy with a sense of the uncanny.

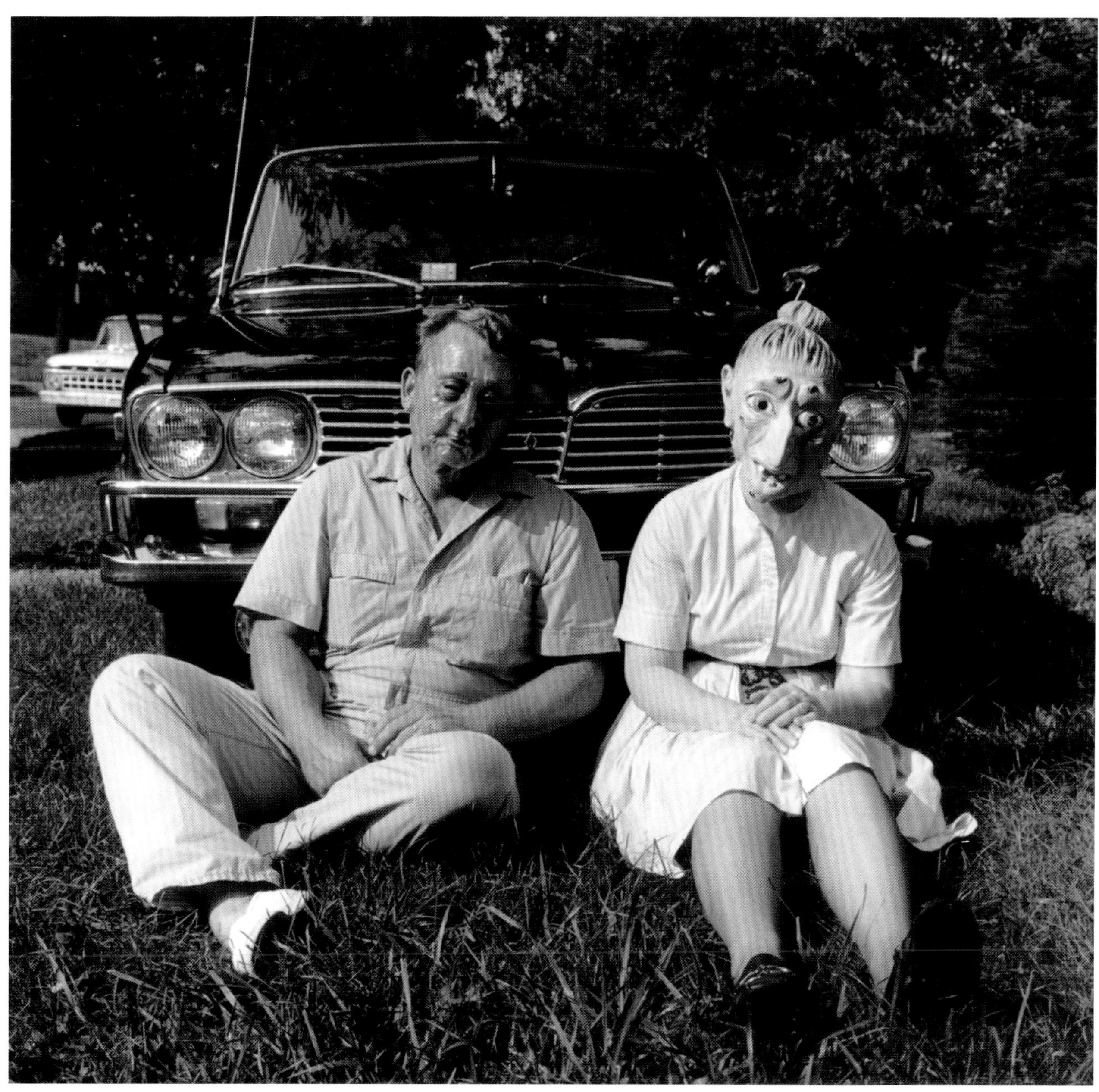

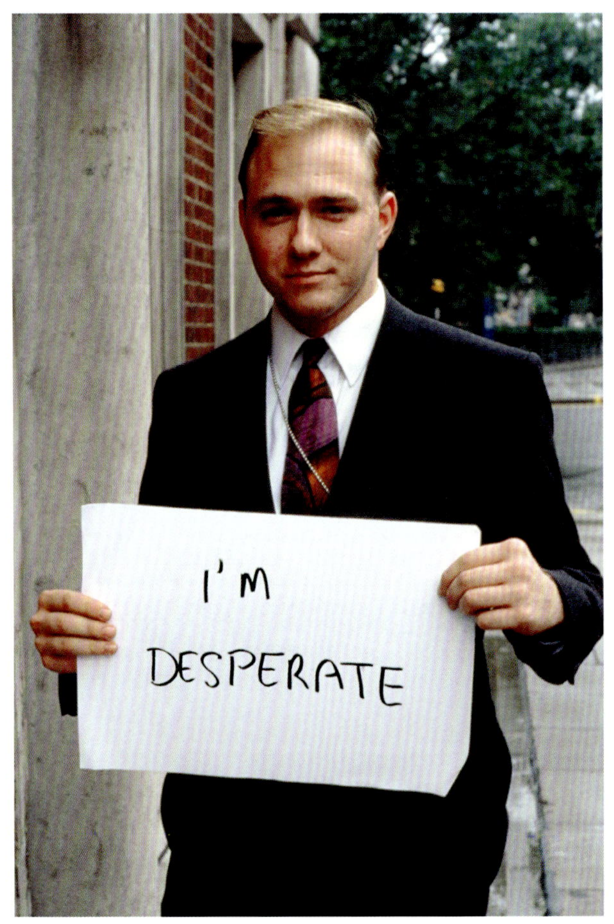

Gillian Wearing (born 1963)
***Confess All On Video. Don't Worry You Will Be in Disguise. Intrigued? Call Gillian Version II* (1994) and *Signs that Say What You Want Them to Say and Not Signs that Say What Someone Else Wants You to Say* (1992–1993)**

The British artist Gillian Wearing is a natural storyteller, using different narrative strategies with each piece of work. For these two works, she respectively used a video and photographs of people holding signs with their thoughts clearly written down – making their stories transparent to the outside world.

For the video (see opposite), Wearing put an advertisement in the weekly London listings magazine *Time Out* with the wording the same as the title of the piece. In a studio, she recreated a modern-day confession box and allowed the participants to confess their sins – typically revolving around sex, theft or revenge – without any interruption or judgement. What is fascinating is how the participants chose to conceal their identity – completely or partially hiding their faces.

In the photographs, Wearing used the reverse strategy so that we see the subject clearly. The contrast between the person's physical persona and their inner thoughts which they wrote on the card is what gives the photographs their charge, as they often seem fictional or hard to believe. So the subject of *I'M DESPERATE* (above) is an affluent-looking man. Another shows a man with a face tattoo proclaimng, 'I have been certified mildly insane!' Are these 'real' confessions and thoughts? Or are the people wanting a moment of fame for the camera? The idea of confession is brought into question. Are they hoping for absolution, as in the Catholic confessional, or for release, as in the 'talking cure' of Freudian psychoanalysis? The result is unclear. In both works, the line between public and private is muddy and the motivations of the artist (and indeed the viewer) slide between the salacious, voyeuristic and bold.

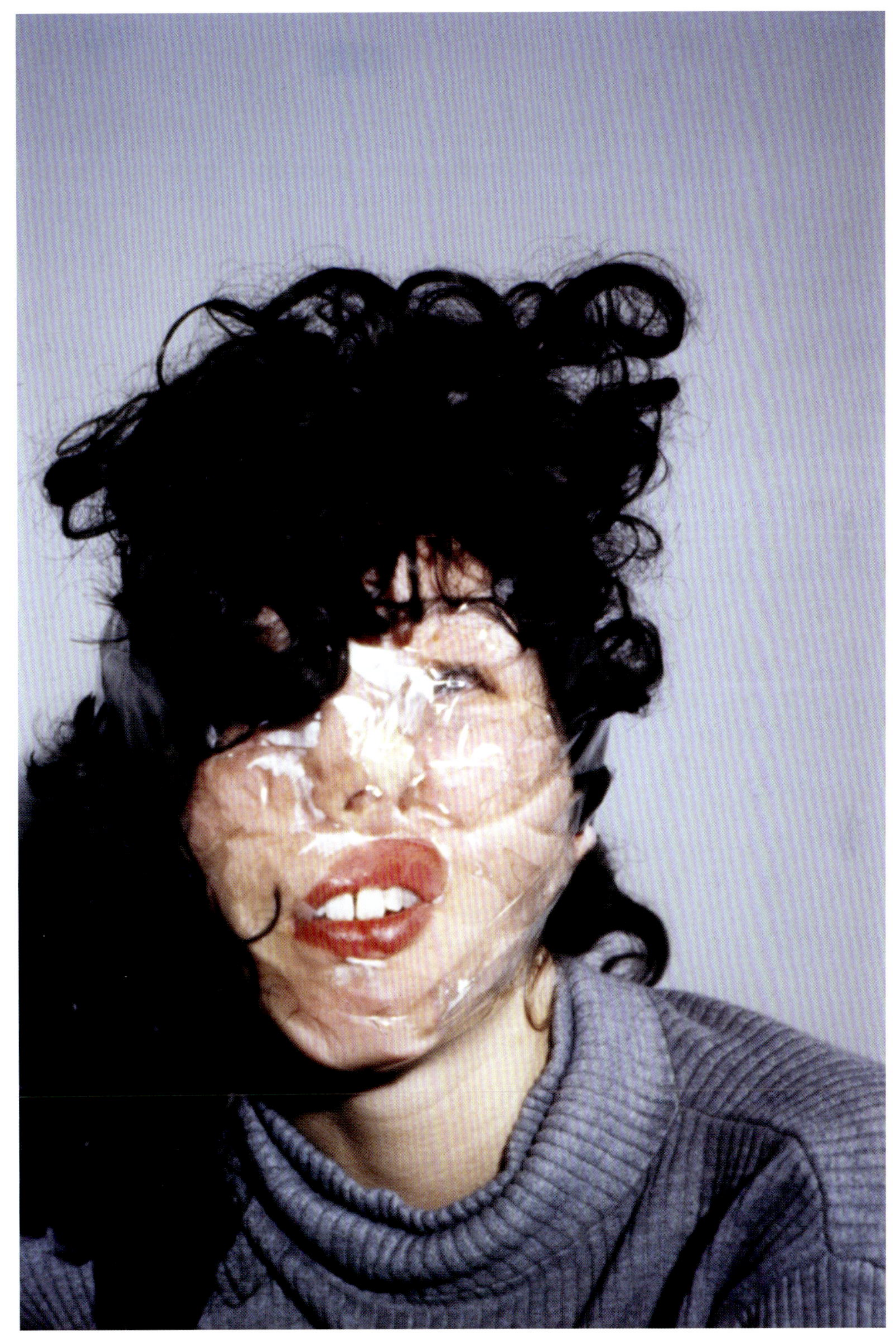

Sarah Lucas (born 1962)
***Sod You Gits* (1991)**

In this work the British artist Sarah Lucas presents a photocopy of a double-page spread from a British tabloid newspaper. However, by removing the object from its everyday context and presenting it as an artwork, she simultaneously revels in and subverts the lurid content of the paper – re-framing its sexist and salacious stories from a feminist perspective. The photographs and text are elevated to the status of an artistic 'readymade'. The role of photography is changed and issues of value and status are brought into question as well as the subject matter of the image.

The presumed reader – the male subject towards whom the erotic, sexist content is directed – is also implicitly ridiculed, as being complicit in the absurdity of the newspaper. The act of taking a 'story' in a newspaper and making it art illustrates the tenuous lines between high and low art which have long fascinated artists and continue to be a constant source of inspiration.

Lucas has often turned to lowly, even base subject matter for inspiration – not only tabloid newspapers but other mundane objects ranging from cigarettes to toilet bowls – while frequently invoking a suggestive, double-edged mode of British humour. A number of her works deploy and satirise the kind of misogynistic language that substitutes female anatomy for food.

What makes the work more complicated than simple critique, however, is that Lucas seems to be slightly seduced by the crassness of working-class British attitudes towards women. Her work, although obviously feminist, is not judgemental. By shining a light on what exists in the world, it puts all value judgement back to the viewer. More than anything, the image highlights that a story can change depending on who tells it, how they tell it and where it is told.

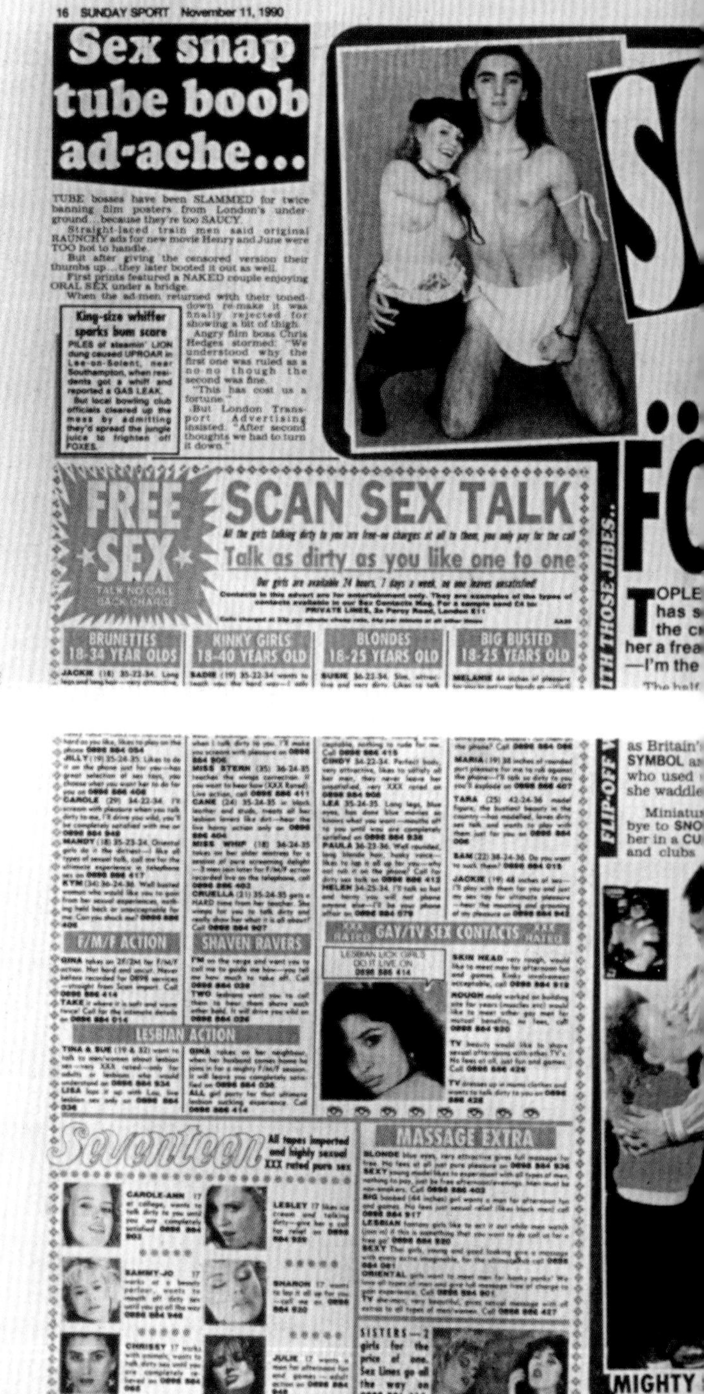

16 SUNDAY SPORT November 11, 1990

Sex snap tube boob ad-ache...

TUBE bosses have been SLAMMED for twice banning film posters from London's underground... because they're too SAUCY.

Straight-laced train men said original RAUNCHY ads for new movie Henry and June were TOO hot to handle.

But after giving the censored version their thumbs up... they later booted it out as well.

First prints featured a NAKED couple enjoying ORAL SEX under a bridge.

When the ad-men returned with their toned-down re-make it was finally rejected for showing a bit of thigh.

Angry film boss Chris Hedges stormed: "We understood why the first one was ruled as a no-no though the second was fine.

"This has cost us a fortune."

But London Transport Advertising insisted: "After second thoughts we had to turn it down."

King-size whiffer sparks bum score

PILES of steamin' LION dung caused UPROAR in Lee-on-Solent, near Southampton, when residents got a whiff and reported a GAS LEAK.

But local bowling club officials cleared up the mess by admitting they'd spread the jungle juice to frighten off FOXES.

FREE SEX TALK NO CALL BACK CHARGE

SCAN SEX TALK

Talk as dirty as you like one to one

BRUNETTES 18-34 YEAR OLDS | KINKY GIRLS 18-40 YEARS OLD | BLONDES 18-25 YEARS OLD | BIG BUSTED 18-25 YEARS OLD

F/M/F ACTION | SHAVEN RAVERS | GAY/TV SEX CONTACTS | LESBIAN ACTION

Seventeen

MASSAGE EXTRA

SUNDAY SPORT November 11, 1990 17

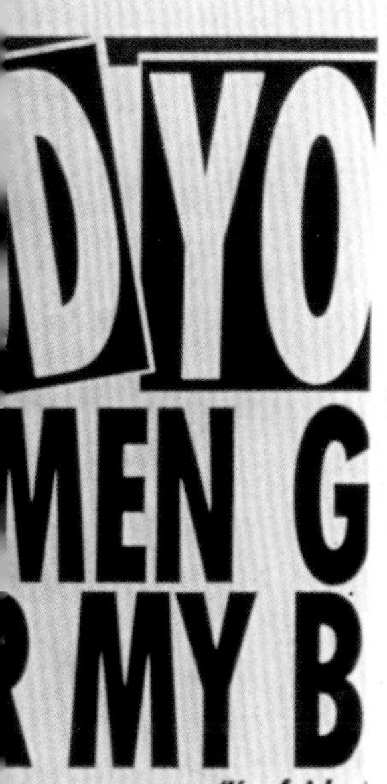

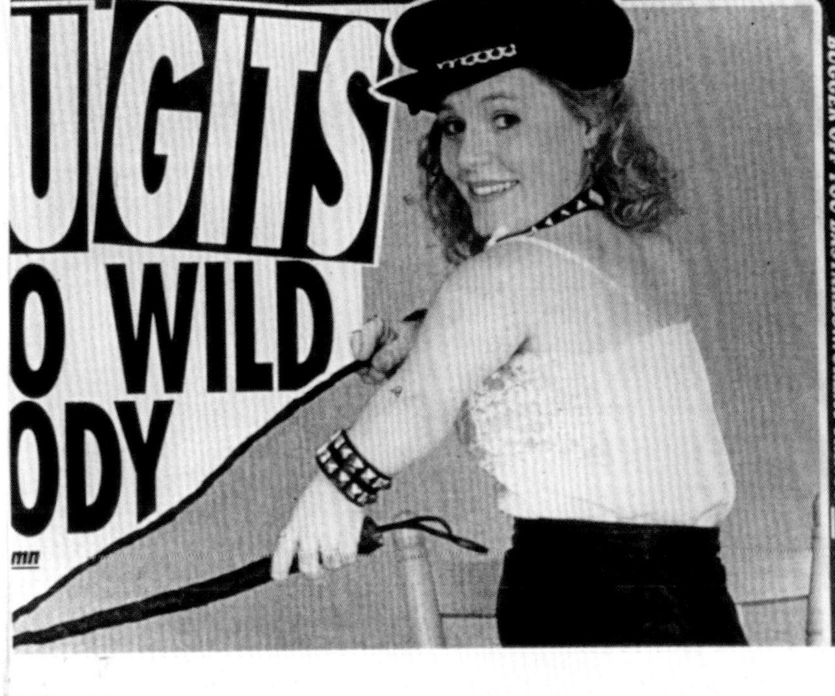

get Sharon Lewis
'O FINGERS UP at
sips who branded
id them: "Sod you
's laughing now."

'I'm fairly d... sexy for m... size... I think'

mn

r matchbox-sized **SEX** k at rotten **BASTARDS** **PENGUIN** at her when ne street.

Sharon has said good- kids who used to lock and is raking it in pubs London as a topless **KISS-O-GRAM.**

The laugh-a-minute **SEX THIMBLE**—who's just 3ft. 2ins. tall—says men go **WILD** for a glimpse of her small but perfectly formed charms.

And when fun-loving Sharon strips off her **ITSY BITSY TEENY WEENY TOP** as part of her saucy act, she tames the **TALLEST** of fellas.

"I'm pretty damn sexy for my size... I think," she squeaked to our newsman at her home in Southwark, South London.

"I have never realised how many men actually wanted to sample me," added the pint-sized sex pot, who strictly **DRAWS THE LINE** at any-sized **HANKY PANKY** with customers.

"I was **VERBALLY ABUSED** for so long and so often I thought men hated me.

"Now I find it a compliement that they go so wild."

Sharon works as a sexy kiss-o-gram with the full support of her hubby Paul—who **TOWERS** above his missus at a **STRAPPING** 4ft. 9ins.

She slips into Mothercare-sized outfits and tours pubs and clubs,

10 whopp... the lon...

1 Tallest living man...
2 Tallest man ever...
3 and woman ... Jini
4 Tallest living woma...
5 Tallest married co... and Anna Bates (7...
6 Shortest person...
7 Shortest man... Ca...
8 Most famous mi... Tom Thumb' Strat...
9 Smallest man livin... measuring 28½in...
10 Shortest twins ... th...

where she does a S... STRIP routine.

Her saucy act i... **WHIPPING** and **STR**... punters before **TOPLESS** herself.

Her delighted Duncan Mundel runs London's Go... grams agency. Sharon is the sought-after kiss... in Britain.

"Calls have flo... since she first wor... me.

"She's got a **CAREER** and is c... different from a... else on our boo... revealed.

"When she arri... the interview, I t... look at her an... "YOU'RE HIRED

But Sharon, 23, ... up with **CRUEL** ... about her height.

Because ... Sharon's only **KNE**... to a **GRASSHOPPE**... child-sized shoe... life's been made h... cruel taunts and n... **BULLYING.**

Although her mum sent her understanding a... school, she was th... of **JOKES** near the

...n' facts giving ...and short of it

...Gabriel Estavao, 8ft 2in
...obert Wadlow, 9ft...
...h, from China, 8ft 1¾in
...Sandy Allen, 7ft 7¼in
...ple... Martin (7ft 7¼in) ...5¼in)
...uline Masters, 21½in
...n Phillips, 26½in...
...et... Charles 'General ...30½in...
...Nelson de la Rosa,
...Matinas, both 76in...

...NKY

...olves ...PING ...oing

...boss ...-who ...eous- ...says ...most ...gram

...ed in ...ed for

...REAT ...ainly ...thing ...," he

...d for ...k one ...said:

...s put ...JIBES

...orty ...-HIGH ...n her ... her ...LL by ...-stop

...oster ... an ...girls' ...BUTT ...amily

home in Banstead, Surrey.

"Some even had THE CHEEK to call me PENGUIN," explained Sharon.

"They said I should have **WORN NAPPIES**, and locked me in a cupboard."

She added: "I cried myself to sleep because of the taunts."

Strip dream comes true

BUT Sharon says the ROTTEN SHITHEADS can stick the ABUSE up their miserable ARSEHOLES.

The **TITCHY 'TEASE** is now making a **MINT** in her amazing career, with her appointments diary **CRAMMED.**

When she first announced she was going to take off her clothes for a living, Paul had a **FIT** and tried to **BAN** her 32-24-36 bouncy figure.

It was only when she agreed to let Paul **MIND** her that her saucy strip dream finally came true.

"I've always wanted to do this. I've had other jobs but they've always been behind a desk.

"They were so boring, I wanted to break out and do something different and exciting."

Punters are AMAZED when the tiny STRIPPER STROLLS into a party to shock an unsuspecting birthday boy.

Wearing a skimpy top, suspenders and carrying a **WHIP** twice the size of her, laugh-a-minute Sharon **STRIPS** her sweating victim of his trousers and boxers and starts **THRASHING** with her leather weapon.

"I don't hit too hard, just enough to make 'em sit up and take notice," she said.

"When I've pulled their pants down, I take my top off to bare my boobs.

"By now they're usually **SPEECHLESS** at what this little thing is doing to them and too shocked to put up a fight. I've never had a failure yet."

And short-house husband Paul, 20, stands by his wife.

"I was very surprised when she first told me that's what she wanted to do," he said from the **LOVE-NEST** they now share in Southwark.

"It's not for me to stop Sharon doing something she really wants to. Now I just **GRIN** and **BEAR IT.**

"I stand quietly a few yards from her and keep an eye on the proceedings.

"My height doesn't mean a thing to me. I can get a bit firm with whoever is causing the trouble. I'm not scared and I've got a few surprises up my sleeve."

With husband Paul keeping his eye out, Sharon runs in and out of their LEGS to stop them getting too near when they get frisky.

"I've got to make the most of my height. Being the smallest stripper in the world is one way of doing it."

10 things shorty Sharon finds a very tall order

1 Playing basketball
2 Changing a light bulb
3 Joining the police
4 Grabbing a saucy mag off the top shelf at the local newsagents
5 Driving a Range Rover
6 Seeing eye to eye with the friendly folk who live next door
7 Reaching the top floor lift button
8 Flushing the chain on an old fashioned toilet without standing on the seat
9 Swapping outfits with her pets
10 Winning an Olympic gold high jump

MIDGET *kiss-o-gram Sharon whips her customers into shape and gives 'em plenty to smile about with her topless routine. Hubby's the minder*

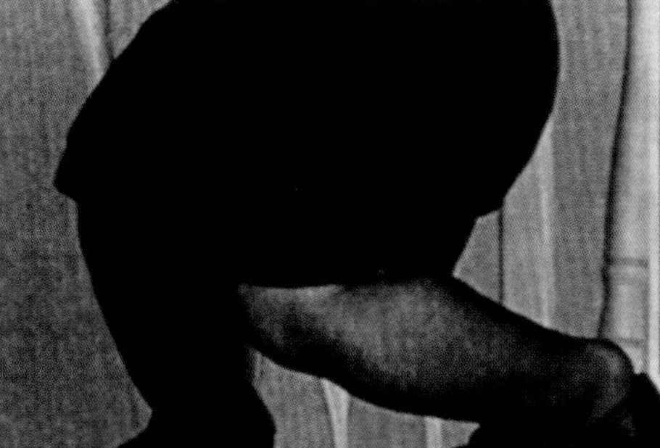

PINT-SIZED HOUSEWIFE B... ...TLES AGAINST CRUEL SHITHEADS WHO CALL HER A PENGUIN...

BUGGER OFF YOU BASTARDS... GREAT THINGS DO COME IN S... ...ALL PACKAGES

SHE'S ONE-IN-A-MILLION...

RAGIN' Russ is angry at comic cons

TV Russ gag for con artists who think it's funny to pinch Abbot howlers

By BEN TRAVERS

TELLY funnyman Russ Abbot has blasted his fellow comedians... for NICKING his JOKES.

The 42-year-old star—whose blockbusting show is the Beeb's Saturday night ratings-topper—said he's FED-UP with rival comics constantly ripping off his best gags.

But Russ, who uses all his own material said HE once pinched a gag off his late idol Tommy Cooper.

He later apologised to the Fez-headed comedian when Tommy complained.

"There's lots of comics who are known for stealing other people's jokes. It's wrong—but there's nothing you can do about it," he stormed.

Promised

"You do all the work developing a routine and the next thing you know somebody's nicked it."

Russ let rip as he prepared to open a new 12-week season of shows at the London Palladium.

Russ, whose Cooperman impersonations are still an audience favourite said: "When I first started with the Black Abbots, I used to do one of Tommy's tricks—taking a handkerchief from a member of the audience and setting fire to it.

"Tommy said he was still using it in his act so I promised not to do it again."

The two comics became friends and Cooper left precious stage props to Russ in his will.

New Russ says widespread cheating in the comedy lark leaves him SEETHING with RAGE.

AIDS CAT-ASTROPHE

CATS are dying from a feline AIDS virus, doctors have revealed. Moggie victims were found on Portsea Island, Hampshire. The bug is harmless to humans.

Can lying
be OK?
Can lying
be OK?
Can lying
be OK?
**Can lying
be OK?**
Can lying
be OK?
Can lying
be OK?
Can lying
be OK?

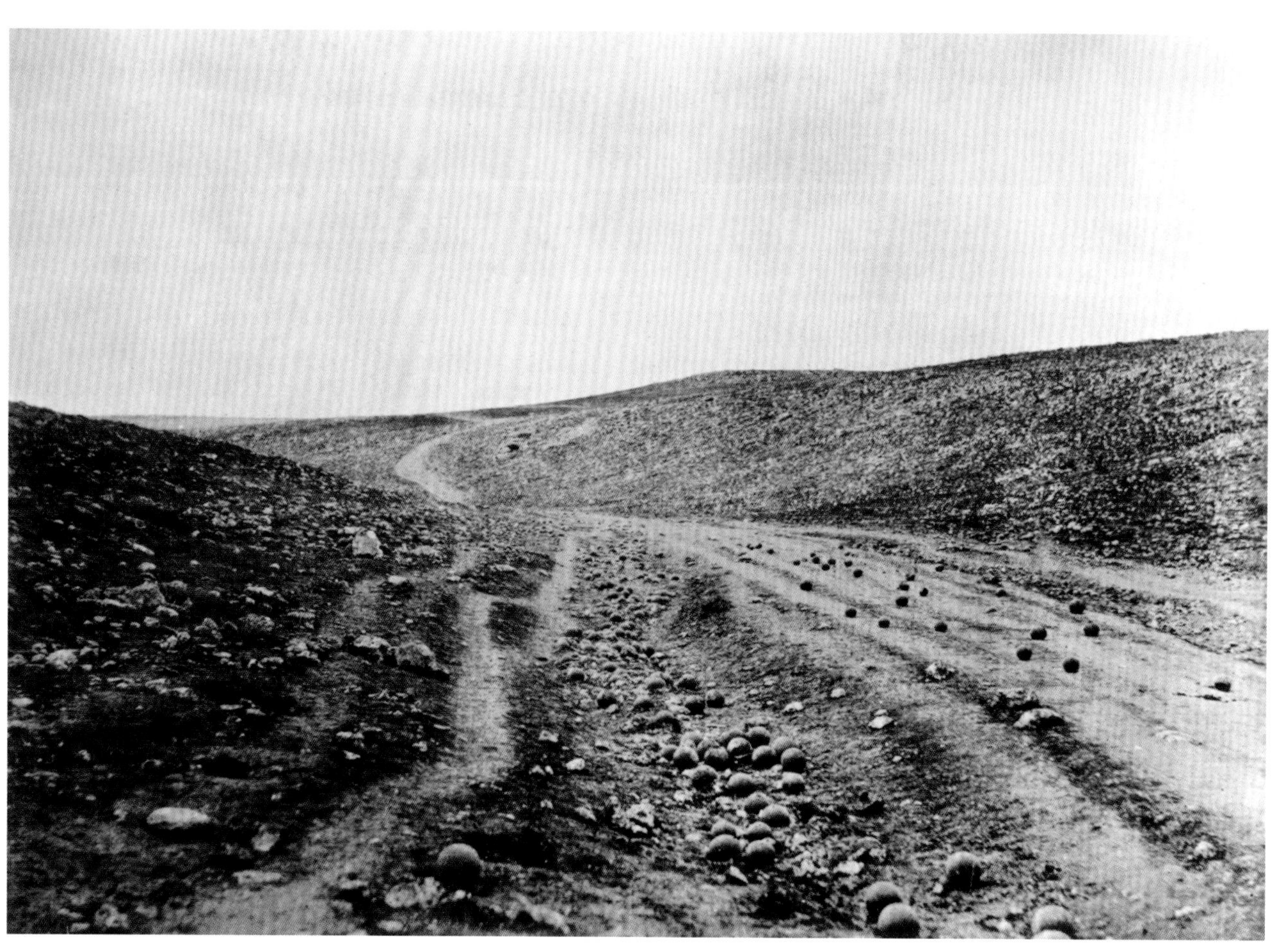

Roger Fenton, *The Valley of the Shadow of Death* (1855)

We want our pictures to show us at our best. If a flash makes us look like a demon, we all probably apply the red-eyes-removal option. We also want the things we photograph to look their finest. If we use a cookbook, we expect the images to make our mouths water – even if we know the vegetables are undercooked to keep their colour, and fruit is sometimes sprayed with hairspray to make it shiny.

As we explored in the first chapter, even if a photograph is untouched, it will still never be a faithful copy of reality. As most of us who have ever tried to capture a stunning landscape know, no matter how brilliant the reality, the photograph will often end up looking flat and dull if we don't apply a filter. In short, we all know that photographs are manipulated. The question is: does it matter that an image has been altered in order to make it as powerful as possible? You could argue that applying a filter to make reality seem more appealing can be considered a kind of lie. So what about shooting an image in black and white – would that be lying, too?

It seems that the fact that photos deceive us on so many levels is something people have come to accept. When it is acceptable to manipulate a photograph and when it is not is a question that has occupied organisations such as World Press Photo, which has spent years trying to formulate a code of ethics – a code that seems to be far from definitive. In press photography, for example, World Press Photo stipulates that a photograph shot in colour and converted to greyscale is an acceptable form of alteration; however, removing a cigarette stub from the ground using Photoshop is impermissible.

It is true that manipulation of images goes back to the earliest days of photography. Roger Fenton (1819–69) worked in photography for just over a decade, but during this short time he undertook a range of important commercial commissions that have reverberated throughout the medium's history. Documenting the Crimean War of 1853–6, he is widely seen as the first official war photographer. It is from the series of work created during the war that his most famous work comes. *The Valley of the Shadow of Death* (left) has been under constant scrutiny since a second picture was discovered in 1981 with fewer cannonballs in the shot. It even spurred the film-maker Errol Morris to visit the site and investigate why this doctoring (or lie) was carried out. Today, it is believed that the second image was the original, and that Fenton added extra cannonballs to make the scene appear more dramatic.

The boundaries of accepted manipulation in multiple domains of photography remain unsettled and are precarious, or even disturbing. Generally, when it comes to photojournalists, we want their work to be as untouched as possible, as only then can we trust them as reliable suppliers of 'real' images. Today, eyewitnesses using smartphones for photographs and live video, and the superfast distribution of images through the internet, in addition to or superseding traditional, professional press photographers, have contributed to a new understanding of documentary photography. Apart from the fact that, optically, mechanically or through software, an image is retouched before it is even shown on our screens, and despite existing protocols restricting the use of Photoshop by news photographers, it has never been easier to falsify images, as can be seen in the example of Eduardo Martins. This 'war photographer' downloaded pictures from other photo journalists' websites, made small changes to them, gave them a different location in the credit line and published 'his' work in media such as the *Wall Street Journal*, *Le Monde* and the *Daily Telegraph*, while also inventing his own heroic biography. He even borrowed photographs from another man's Instagram account to complete his fraudulent identity. What might feasibly have been a clever piece of conceptual art criticising the status of the hero journalist was in fact simply an outright hoax that illustrates the fallibility of the news media's verification procedures. The good news is that increased connectedness might make it easier for stolen or faked images to be distributed, but it also makes the falsehood easier to detect. It took years for Martins's deception to be discovered, but he was eventually found out.

Verification procedures are, however, facing a serious challenge known as 'deep fake news'. Deep-learning network software technology now allows people to create realistic simulations of politicians or celebrities and make them say anything, in real time: the next level in image manipulation. This could potentially cause a great deal of damage, if populations no longer know who to trust, and authentic messages that do not match their prejudices can be dismissed as fake news.

A further obfuscation of reality comes from celebrities themselves, through their self-presentation. One of the best-known examples is Kim Kardashian (right, bottom), whose lifestyle, like that of many other celebrities, especially as distributed through her popular social media channels, is highly tuned and managed. Careful use of lighting, apps and makeup, and the practice of taking hundreds of images out of which just one will be selected, all contribute to achieving the perfect selfie. The Australian actor and comedian Celeste Barber parodies Instagram accounts of the famous and aspirational by 'keeping it real'. She starkly illustrates the extreme poses and situations that people put themselves in, as well as the patently unrealistic versions of their lives they present in order to get more followers and likes. In her 'Celeste Challenge' series, she takes celebrity images from Instagram and, by re-enacting them, highlights the clichés, using the mechanics of vernacular culture to turn them from the aspirational into the absurd. However, they are not ill-natured: she ridicules herself at the same time, and the 'challenge' is really to established ideas of femininity and maternity that are largely regressive, conservative and dictated by ideals. She may use comedy to make her point, but like all images in popular culture, they can be read seriously.

Building a personality cult with the help of photography is something that goes back a long time in politics, too. Propaganda portraits of leaders and dictators, doctored to present their subjects in the most attractive light, have been made and distributed in many countries throughout the 20th century. In our time, the appearance of Italian ex-president Silvio Berlusconi may be seen as an example of life imitating art: rather than altering the photographs, the politician went under the knife to become the 'idealised' image he wanted to present. As can be seen from the photograph of this man (right, top), who has stood trial for many cases of corruption and bribery, however, the result is hardly an instance of propaganda – one could claim that quite the opposite is the case.

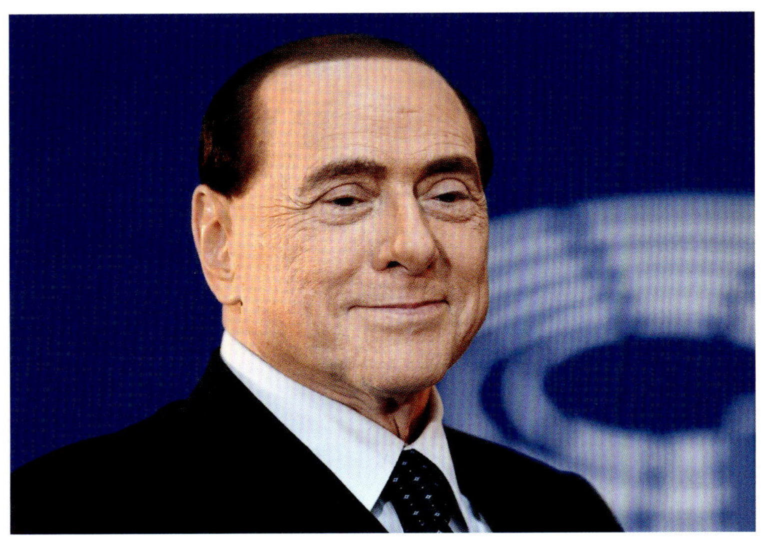

Silvio Berlusconi, Strasbourg, November 2017

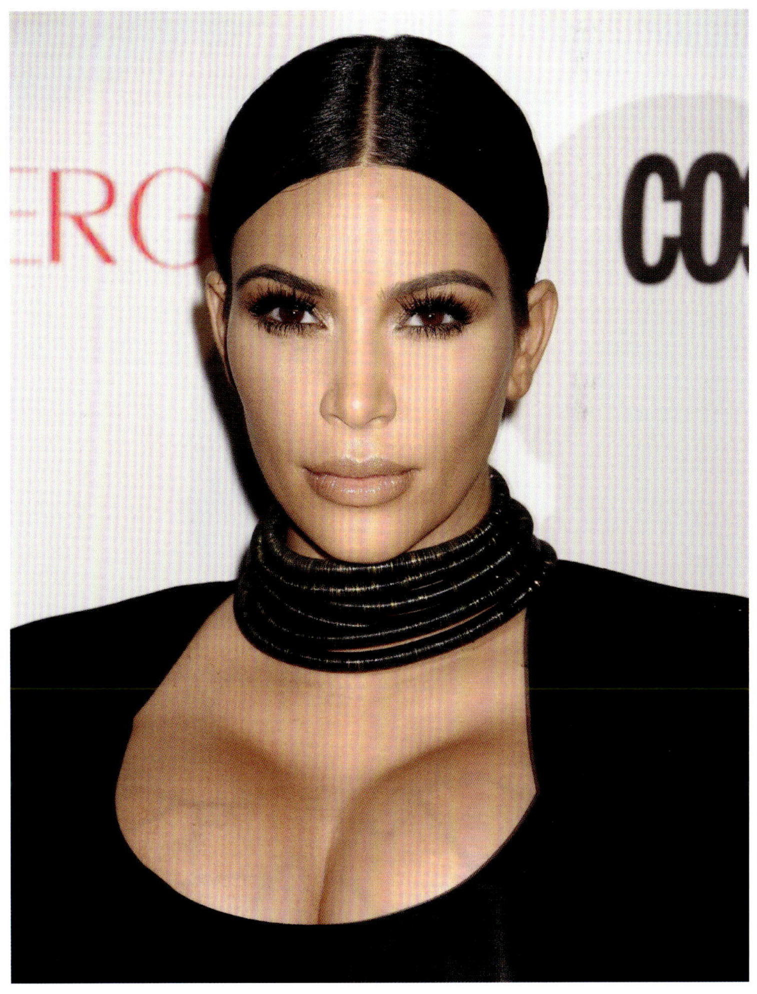

Kim Kardashian, California, October 2015

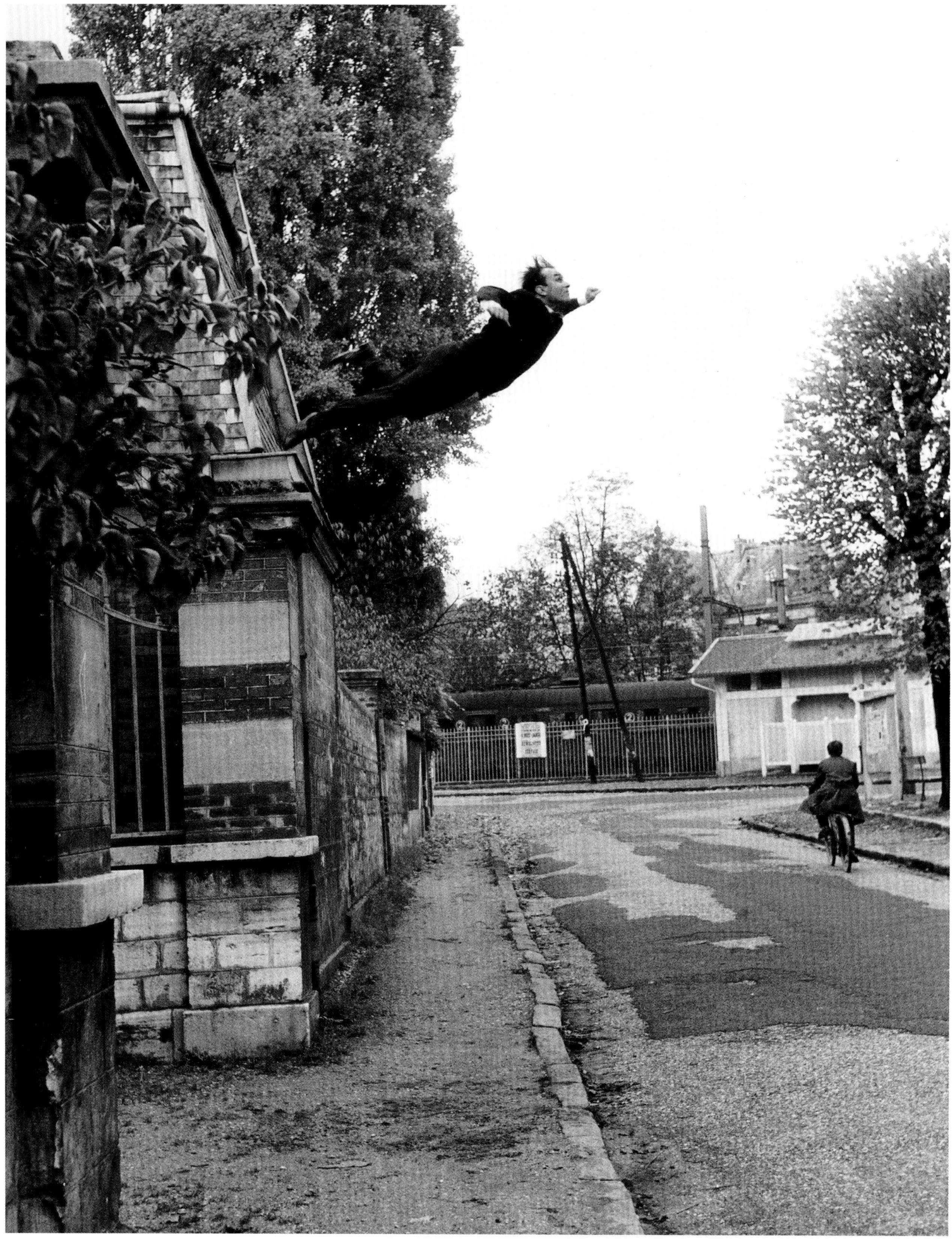

Yves Klein (1928–1962) with Harry Shunk (1924–2006) and Janos Kender (1937–2009)
***Saut dans le vide (Leap into the Void)* (1960)**

Long before 'to Photoshop' became a verb, image manipulation was used within every imaginable context, from advertising to politics and from news photography to art. This particular instance of manipulation started on a French Mediterranean beach, where Yves Klein and his friends decided to divide up the cosmos between them, much as the Greek gods had, with one friend choosing the land, another the sea, and Klein the sky or space. To demonstrate his new affinity with space, in October 1960 Klein undertook a piece of performance art involving a Superman-style leap from the roof of a house in Fontenay-aux-Roses, in the suburbs of Paris. Klein hired two photographers who operated as a duo photographing art performances, especially nouveau réalisme: János Kender and Harry Shunk.

Shunk-Kender created a 'documentary photograph' by combining two negatives: the first showing Klein leaping, face up to the sky, with all the confidence of an Olympic diver knowing he will score high points, while in the street below some of Klein's friends are holding a tarpaulin, waiting to catch him; and the second showing just the street. Part of Klein's performance was a fake four-page newspaper titled *Dimanche* (27 November 1960) distributed among Parisian kiosks, headlined: 'Leap into the Void: Man in Space! The Painter of Space Throws Himself into the Void!' In a rather earthly way, Klein threatened his collaborators with legal action should they ever disclose how the photograph was made.

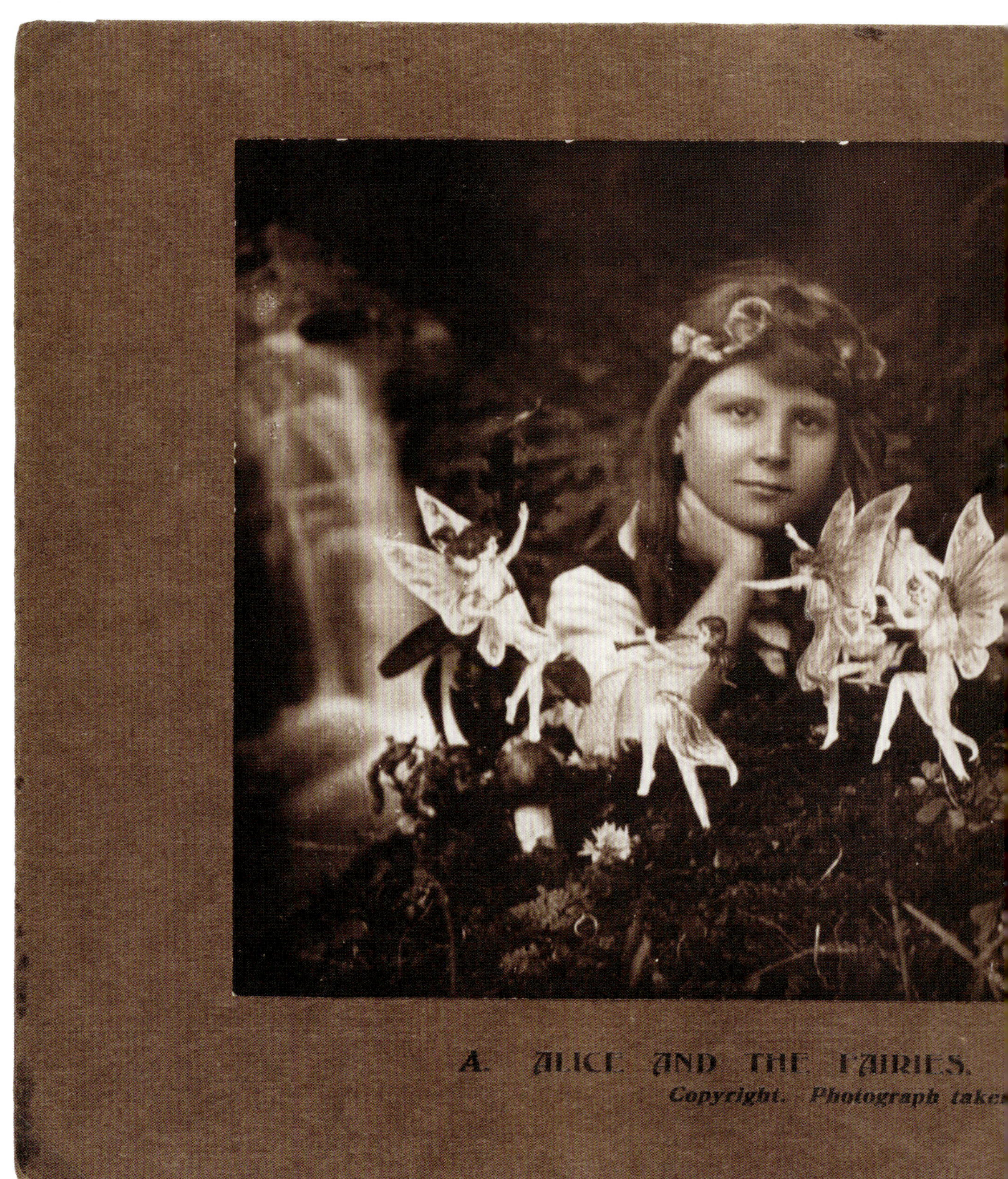
A. ALICE AND THE FAIRIES.
Copyright. Photograph take

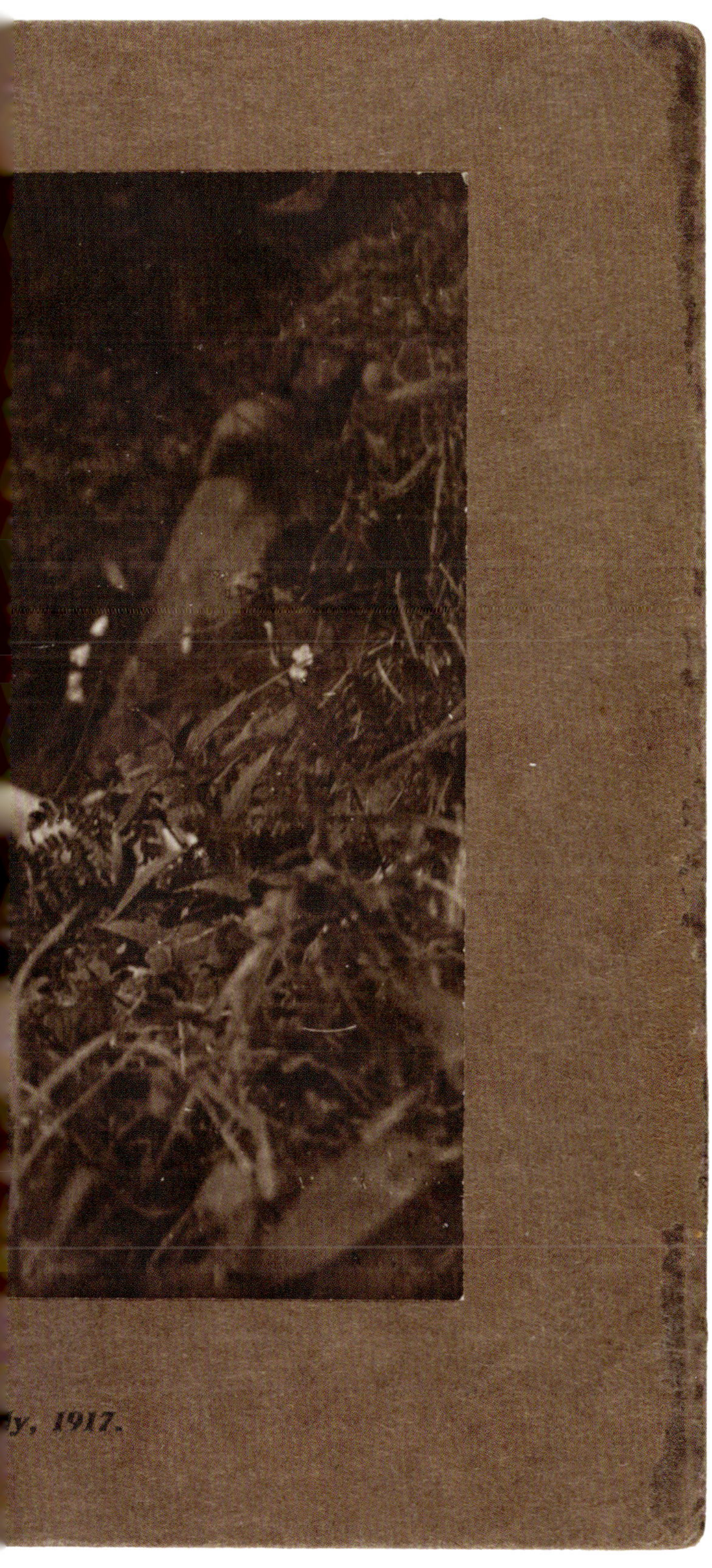

Elsie Wright (1901–1988)
and Frances Griffiths (1907–1986)
***Alice and the Fairies* (1917)**

To understand the strange fascination with this photograph, one must really see photography as primarily a truth-telling mechanism. It is hard to believe now, but at various points during the 20th century many people were prepared to swear that these fairies were real – firstly, and most famously, the author Sir Arthur Conan Doyle, who used them to illustrate an article about fairies in the *Strand Magazine* for its Christmas issue in 1920. Conan Doyle was a committed Spiritualist, and the leap from a belief in an ability to commune with the dead to a belief in the existence of fairies is not so huge. Also contributing to the widespread acceptance of the authenticity of the photographs known as the *Cottingley Fairies* was the fact they were made by children – two young, middle-class girls – and children could not possibly lie in the face of adult authority. Or perhaps it was simply that people wanted to believe in these supernatural miniature beings.

The two children made a series of five photographs, of which this has become the most famous. To create the photographs, the children copied popular illustrations of the day, cut them out and stood them up using hatpins. Given the difficulty of making a photograph at this time, the fact that they were made, let alone circulated, was quite an achievement in itself.

Photography has always been used to 'prove' the existence of mythic and magical beasts. Who doesn't want to believe that a blurry photograph shows the Loss Ness Monster, or a shaky video of a Yeti waving as it heads into the woods? Update this to the esoteric 'aura' photographs in circulation today, and we can see that the desire to see beyond the frame is still intact in photography.

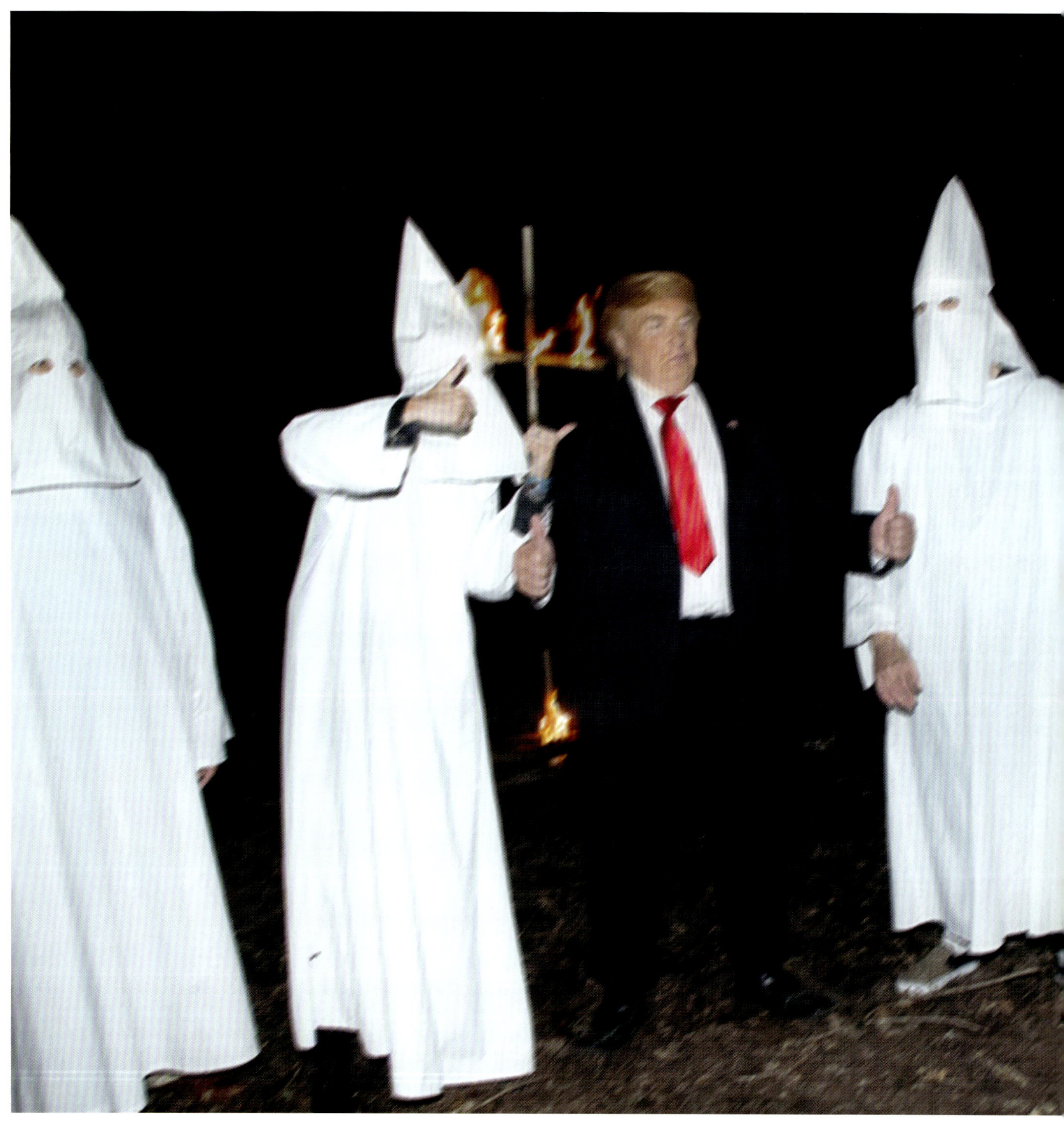

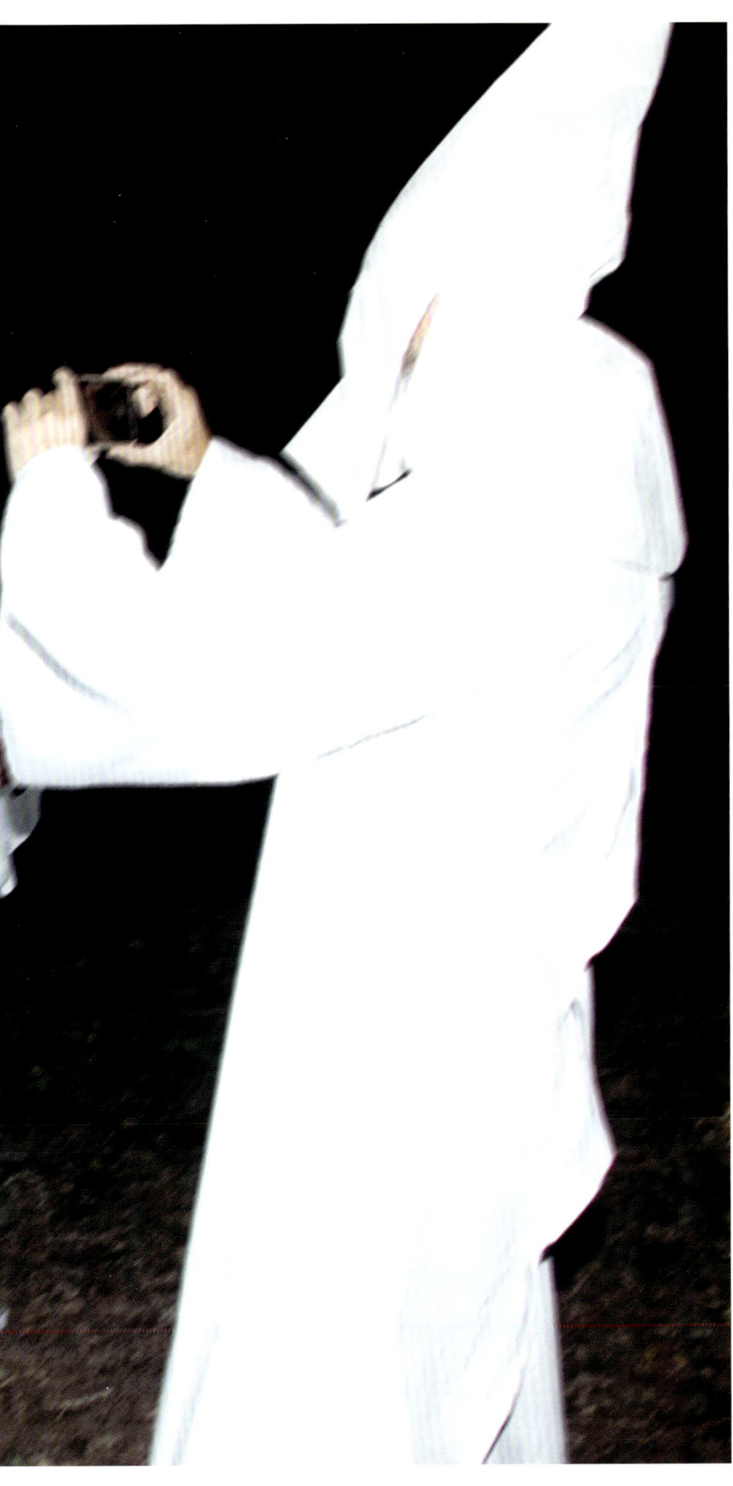

Alison Jackson (born 1970)
***Private* (2016)**

The US landscape photographer Ansel Adams spent more time in his darkroom dodging and burning a print than he spent time taking the actual photograph. Manipulating images in Photoshop is just a way of extending this practice. When the onus is on truth-telling, media may use protocols which require photographers to indicate or limit the degree of digital manipulation in their images. But a lot of the time images are published with no such restrictions, and looking critically is not always easy.

An artist whose oeuvre is dedicated to showing how difficult it is to tell the difference between what is real and what is not in media imagery is the British photographer Alison Jackson. She has used celebrity lookalikes of the British Royal Family, former British Prime Minister Tony Blair, the Clintons and, more recently, Donald Trump, to create spoof images of controversial situations – including this one, in which a fake 'Donald Trump' is shown at a supposed Ku Klux Klan rally. Despite the threat of legal action being taken against her for images like this, Jackson feels the liberties she takes, in terms of truth and manipulation, are an essential part of her freedom as an artist.

Jackson decided to self-publish the book her Trump images appear in, when commercial publishers shied away from taking the risk. Finding the position she was in genuinely alarming, the main battle for Jackson was one against self-censorship. One could ask whether artists should self-censor their work when it could offend people, give rise to protests or endanger their career. While it is usually contentious when documentary photographers manipulate their images, we also demand a certain type of truthfulness from photographers working outside of this genre. The success of this work is dependent on the tension between its unreality and its potential believability, as well as the artist's authenticity of intention. By achieving this balance, Jackson makes a powerful comment on the nature of celebrity culture, media representation, and that phrase that was born simultaneously with Trump's presidential ambitions, 'fake news'.

David King (1943–2016)
***The Commissar Vanishes* (1997)**

Josef Stalin's regime in the Soviet Union lasted from 1929 to 1953, during which time photography played a crucial role in the falsification of history and the elaboration of Stalin's cult as leader. Under him, photographs were doctored, manipulated and censored as he sought to consolidate his rule and 'vanish' those who dared to disagree with him – both in terms of their physical bodies and their presence in the historical record. The mass purges, show trials and executions that occurred during Stalin's dictatorship became even clearer after his death, and ultimately the photographs would serve as evidence of the thousands of people who opposed him politically while he was in power.

The pairing of the doctored photos with their originals was the painstaking work of the British writer and photographer David King, whose vast collection of Stalin-era photographs highlighted the airbrushing, cutting, defacing, cropping and other more or less crude methods adopted by the regime. A fraction of them were published in King's book *The Commissar Vanishes* in 1997. Looking through the many examples, it is fascinating to note how badly or clumsily done some of these obliterations were. One hopes that this was done as a deliberate act of resistance.

This pairing shows the 'disappearance' of Nikolai Yezhov, successively People's Commissar for State Security, Internal Affairs and Water Transport, who was obliterated from the original 1937 photograph after his execution on 4 April 1940. Yezhov was himself the architect of the Great Purge, so it is somewhat ironic that he should have met the same fate as those he was responsible for blotting out of history. This is just one of thousands of examples of similar scenarios involving other Commissars. These photographs have a renewed significance today as they remind us that photography can never be taken at face value – not now, and not at the birth of photography in 1846, when William Henry Fox Talbot's apprentice Calvert Richard Jones removed one of the figures from a calotype of Capuchin friars in Valetta, Malta, using nothing more than a blot of India ink.

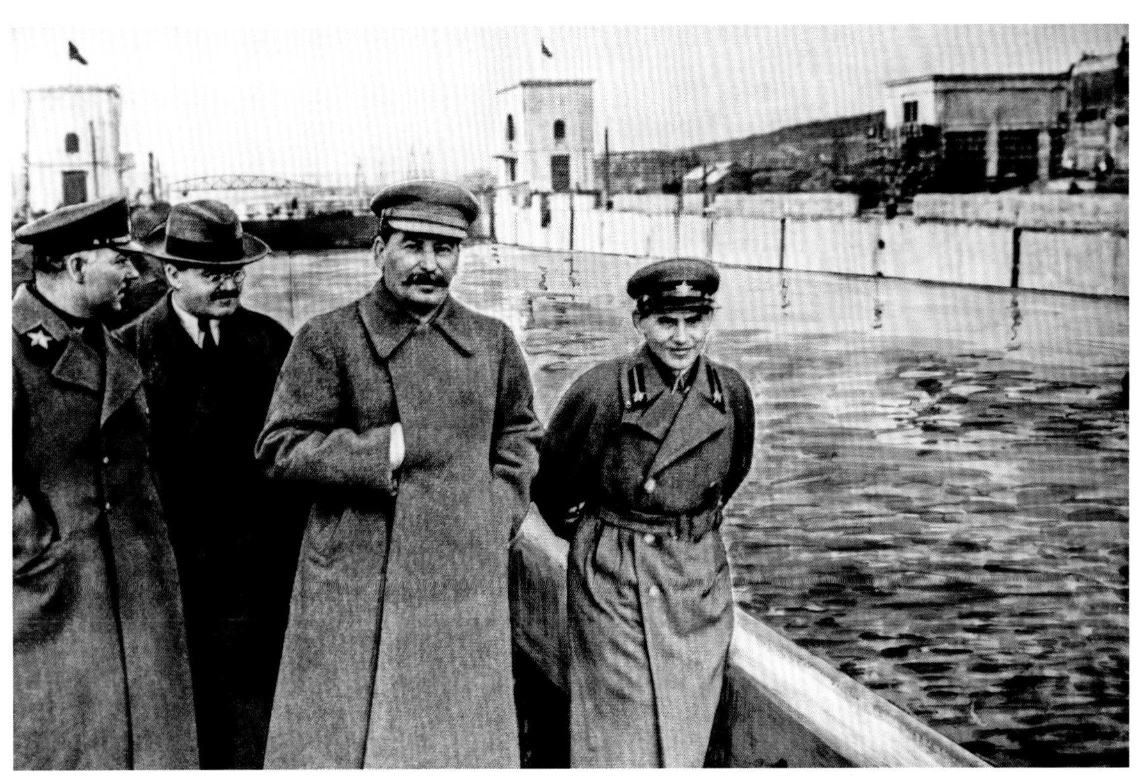

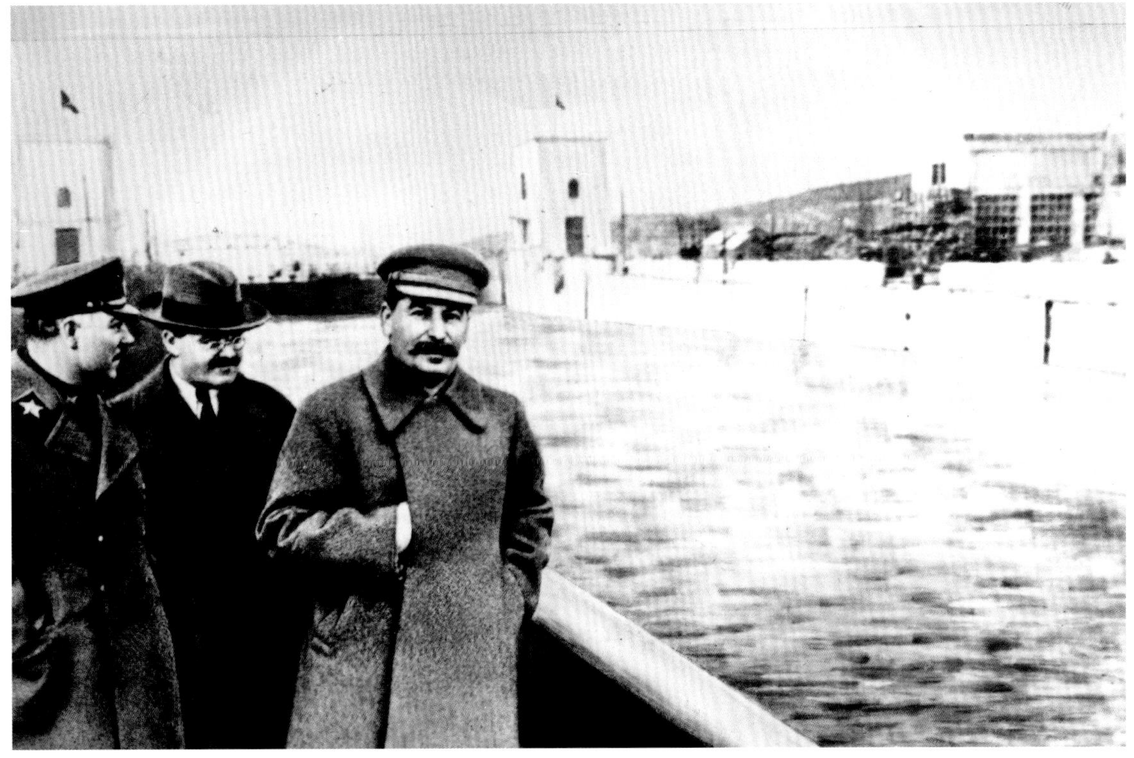

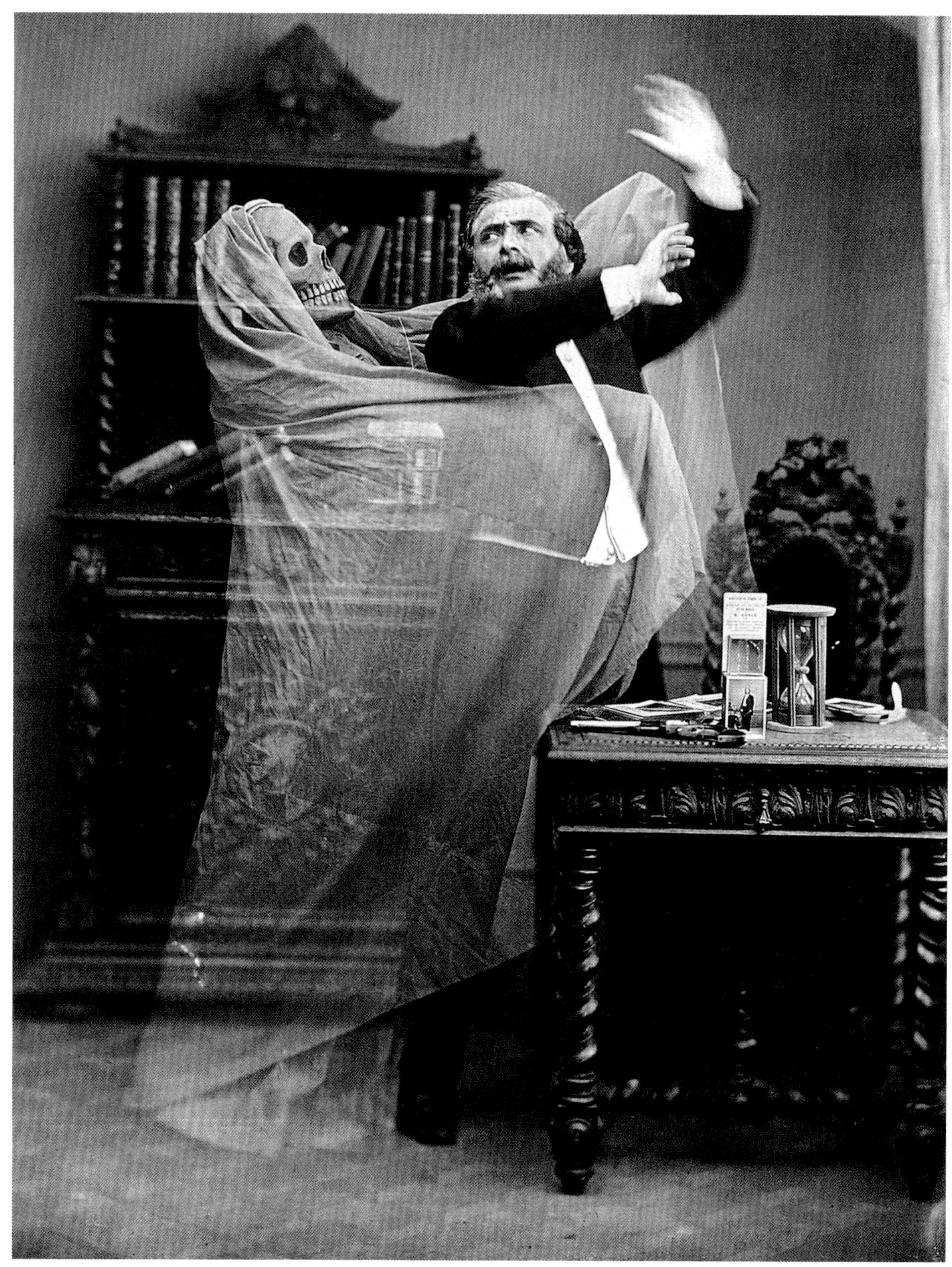

Eugene Thiebault (1825–unknown)
***Henri Robin: Conjurer and Ghost* (c.1860)**

The spirit photographs that were made in relatively large numbers in the 19th and early 20th century should not be regarded simply as jokes or amusing theatrical tableaux. Not only were many of these images taken seriously as proof of the existence of ghosts and the reality of the afterlife, but they also reveal attitudes toward death and grieving and the enduring fascination with the supernatural that has long infused science, art and religion. While, to contemporary eyes, the images seem hammy, ridiculous and obviously fake, they closely follow a powerful tradition in the visual arts – found especially in paintings and engravings – depicting spirits, angels and ghosts that were cultural projections of human emotions, especially the fear of death.

What must also be remembered is that people experienced death far more regularly in the 19th century. Many mothers died giving birth, and child mortality was high. Disease was rife and many sicknesses incurable. People died at home, so death was not abstract and sanitised as it is today in many Western cultures. The bereaved mourned openly, and the new art of photography played an important part in this, with, for example, images of the deceased placed in lockets and other items of jewellery. Spirit photography was only another manifestation of this preoccupation with death, remembrance and the afterlife.

Thus, while a picture like this may seem almost laughable today, a clear example of 'trick' photography, it is important not to underestimate its original seriousness, with deception ironically practised not so much to deceive but to offer consolation and evidence for the life eternal. It is important, too, not to lose our sense of wonder regarding photography. The alchemic blending of chemicals and the appearance 'out of nowhere' of a picture in a darkroom using analogue processes, and the ability of an image to digitally reproduce itself infinitely, may lie in the realms of science, but it certainly holds a touch of magic, too. Even today, the union of science and magic seems not to have quite disappeared, even if it manifests itself in different ways to this image of a magician 'conjuring' up a ghost.

Christoph Bangert (born 1969)
***War Porn* (2014)**

News websites, TV channels and newspapers subtly yet dominantly set conclusive limitations on what we see. Keeping a shocking photograph away from the audience may generally not be considered a form of lying, but not being shown certain images is a form of censorship we usually don't think about.

Everybody knows that fake news can be dangerous when it is used to spread propaganda, more so as it deflects attention from real news. Hard enough as it is to separate real from fake news, it can be just as difficult for readers and viewers to form a personal opinion if they are not given full access to press photography, which may also influence the public opinion.

In his book *War Porn*, German photographer Christoph Bangert published the images which the international news media he worked for considered too disturbing. The book functions as a perturbing reminder that helps us to understand how press censorship in democratic states distorts our understanding of suffering in places of war. The photographer witnessed the most harrowing scenes and shot the most soul-racking images of conflicts that took place in seemingly faraway places like Iraq, Gaza and Afghanistan, images that would have been brought to your home if not censored by the news media.

Some of the pages in the book are not cut apart, initially hiding the images from immediate consumption. The viewer is expected to make a conscious decision as to whether they want to peek between the perforated pages, or rip them open to see the full horror. Bangert poses the fundamental question about how we can refuse to watch and acknowledge a photograph depicting gruesome incidents, knowing that other people are forced to actually live in those atrocities. This small yet grand book not only encourages people to think about how the media uses censorship, but, ultimately, how the reader actually applies censorship themselves by consciously avoiding images and looking away.

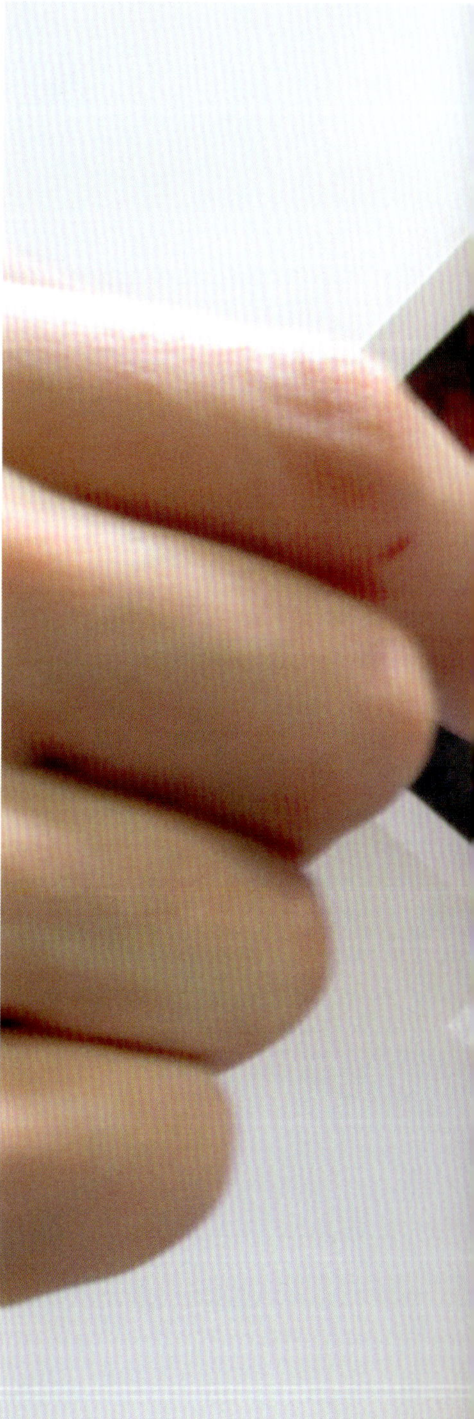

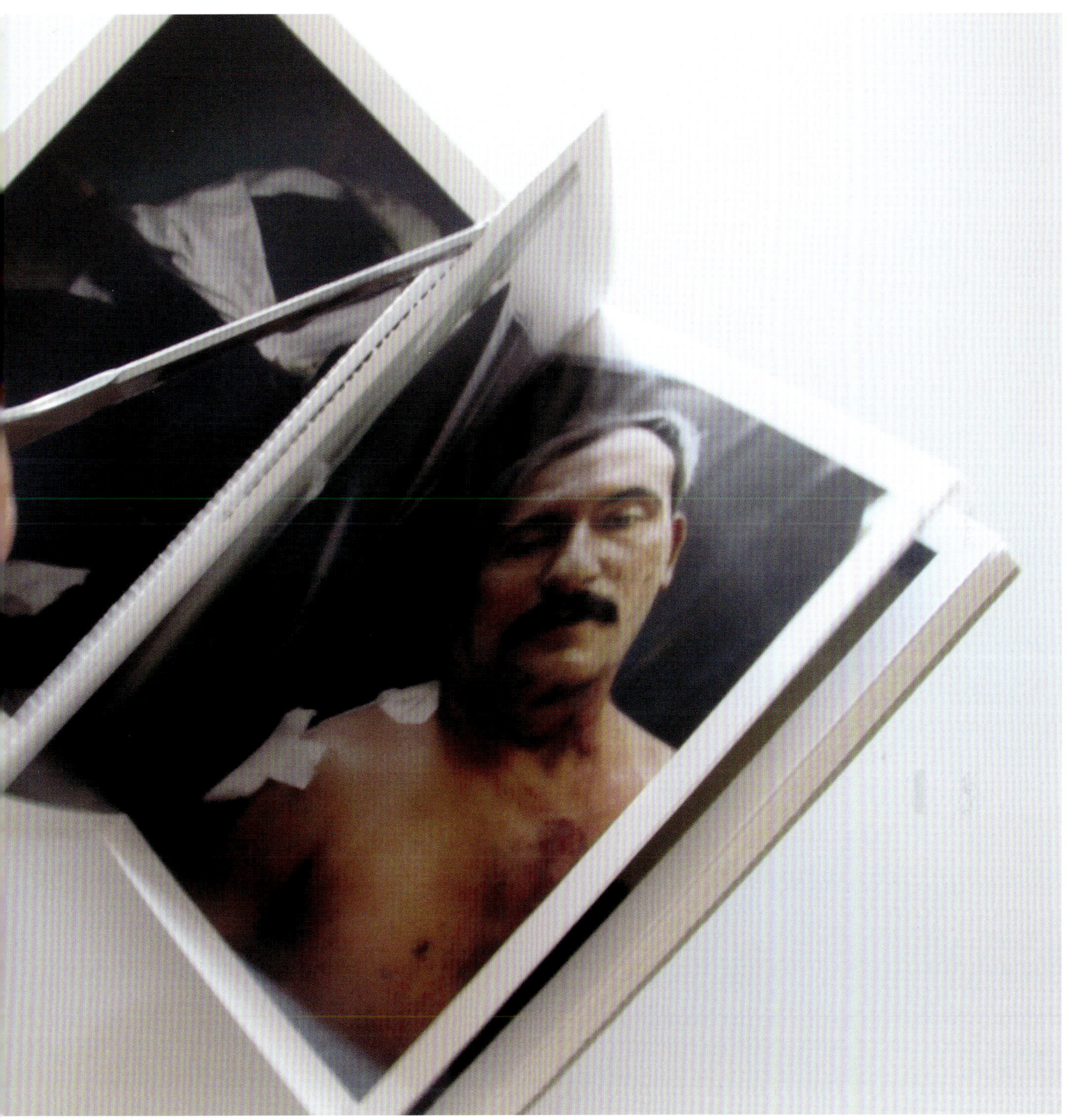

What goes
where?
What goes
where?
What goes
where?
What goes
where?
What goes
where?
**What goes
where?**
What goes
where?

and your love's like an overdose
with your hands wrapped around my throat
using sex like an antidote to the pain

brett anderson

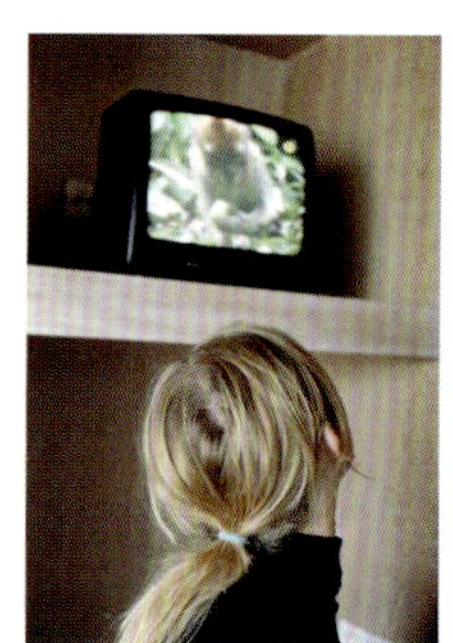

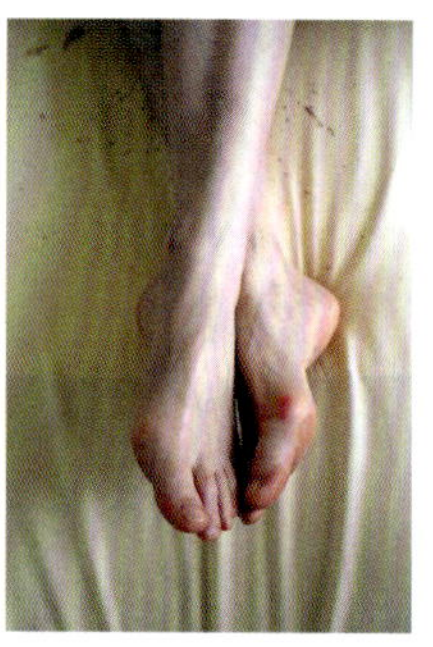

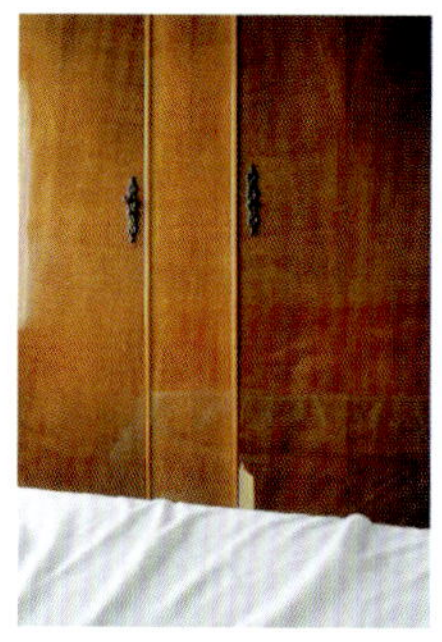

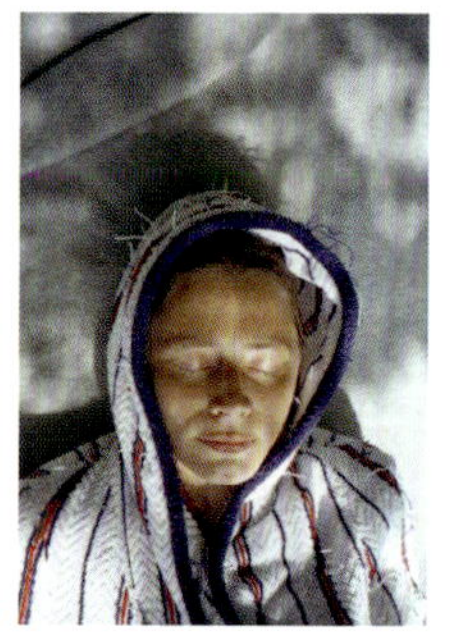

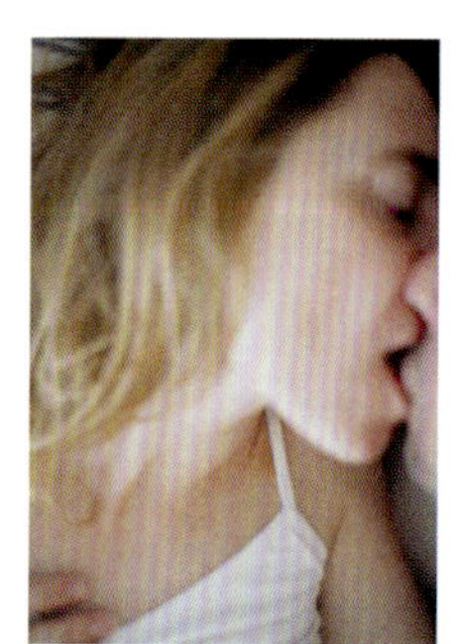

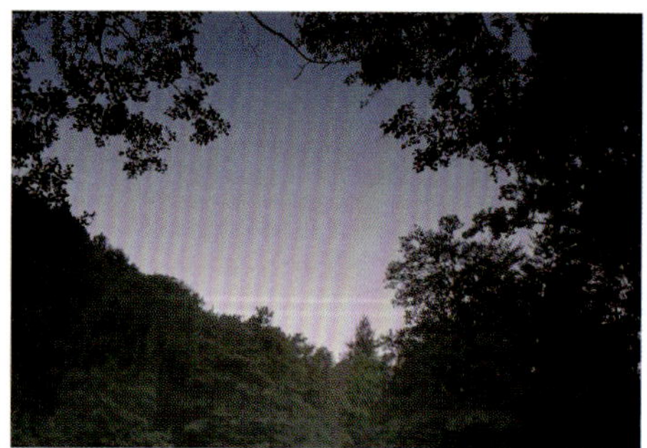

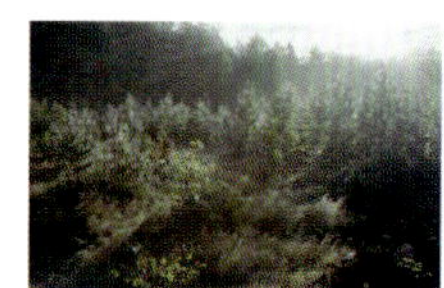

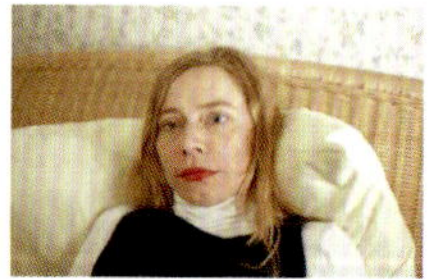

Fred Hüning, pages from *einer* (2010)

The American artist Nan Goldin once said that everybody can be a photographer, as anyone who takes a hundred pictures will have made two good ones. Whether you agree with her or not, wandering about your local town or city taking pictures from the hip does not necessarily make you a street photographer – much as a three-year-old is not an Abstract Expressionist merely by virtue of the quality of her drawing. Incidentally, Robert Frank set the bar much higher than Goldin: he shot 27,000 photos (760 rolls of film) from which he chose the 83 pictures that make up his classic book *The Americans* (1958); only one in 325 was good enough in his eyes.

Photography is, of course, a trickier business than just pointing a camera and pressing a button. The selection of an image – editing – is at the very heart of photography. Think of how many pictures you take before you choose the one that you think is best. What are the criteria for choosing the 'right' one? What makes a good photograph? What makes a bad one? With the advent of digital photography, the editing process has become all the more important as we don't have to worry about wasting film to get a picture, which means we tend to end up with more than ever before to choose from.

There are many ways to edit. Much of it depends on context. A newspaper or magazine will be edited very differently from an art book, which in turn is very different to a wedding album. In each instance, a story has to be told. A single photograph can do this on the front page of a paper, but different instances need a different flow, logic and pace that suits the context. Think, for example, how a cookbook uses only a few pictures, but a food blog may have many more. Blogs are not restrained by the commercial limits of book making and can afford to show the process unfold in a way a book cannot.

Art photography often works as a sequence rather than as a one-off photograph. The best way to illustrate this is in a photobook. Photobooks are now becoming as collectable and as important as photographic prints, and their success or failure rests on the edit. A careful consideration of what goes where gives the book life and its identity and character.

An autobiographical work might take the form of a diary, mixing text and images. An example of this is the trilogy *einer* (2010), *zwei* (2011) and *drei* (2011) by the German artist Fred Hüning (born 1966; see left). These photobooks do not present a linear story, but instead weave photographs, poems and prose in a fluid, non-chronological form. The jump-cut style, the fragmentation and the entwining of past and present together create a work of great immediacy that is part memoir, part lyric and deeply self-conscious about the act of making and editing.

This form of editing is storytelling, and as such, it can be manipulative – the pictures and the sequence in which they are presented can work to pull the audience in a certain direction.

Migrant Mother by the American documentary photographer Dorothea Lange (1895–1965; see opposite) is a perfect example of a brilliant single image within the context of a wider story (the US Farm Security Administration employed several photographers including Lange to document the effects of the Great Depression). Lange's choice of image is the 'best' picture in that it responds to the conventional theme of the Madonna and Child in the way it is structured. The subject's face is worn out and worried and the turned-away heads of the children provoke an emotional response of sadness. The photograph operates on both an emotional and a universal level.

Because this one picture has been so frequently reproduced, it is only when we see other photographs from the contact sheet that we realise that Lange actually took five different exposures of the woman in the tent (three of which we see here). Seeing the pictures together allows the viewer to explore the way in which the photographer edited her pictures, and consider its iconic status in comparison to the others. This kind of storytelling is very different from a news story that needs an image that says everything with one very quick glance. There is no need for universal meanings to resonate. Graphic qualities and obviousness are key to how news pictures work.

Editing is the most difficult stage in photography, because it requires the photographer/editor to grasp the importance of narrative and understand how to convey it, sometimes using only a single image. Similarly, in a sequence of images, as Hüning shows, editing is about much more than simply selecting one extraordinary single image after another. There is a certain analogy with film to be made: Robert Frank's use of a contact sheet was as important to him in the editing process as a storyboard to a film director. This process ideally takes place over a longer period of time and a number of different phases, each phase being more and more meticulous in its attention to context and narrative progression.

If anything, the art of editing is even more important today, when our cameras have the capacity to store thousands of images, and the ability to choose and keep only the best images is increasingly crucial. This is as true of our personal photography as it is of commercial and journalistic photography, where whole departments are given over to picture editing, and where stories and aesthetics are very carefully mediated and controlled.

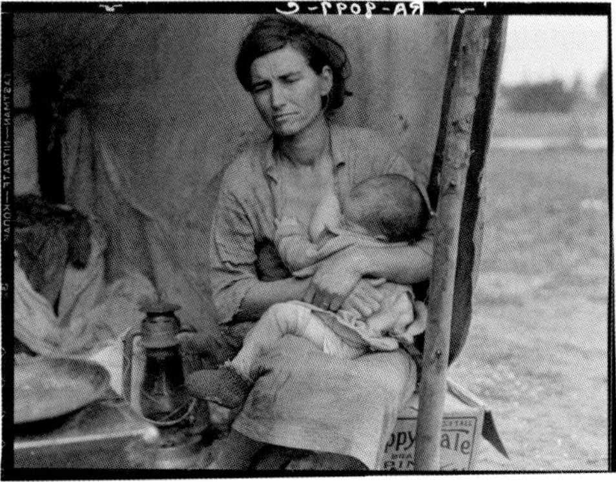

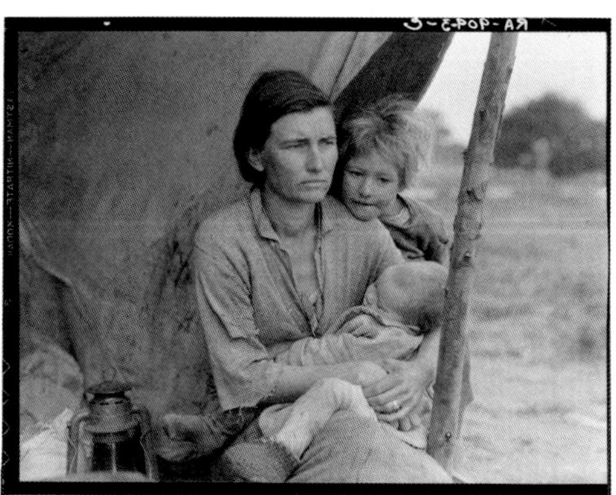

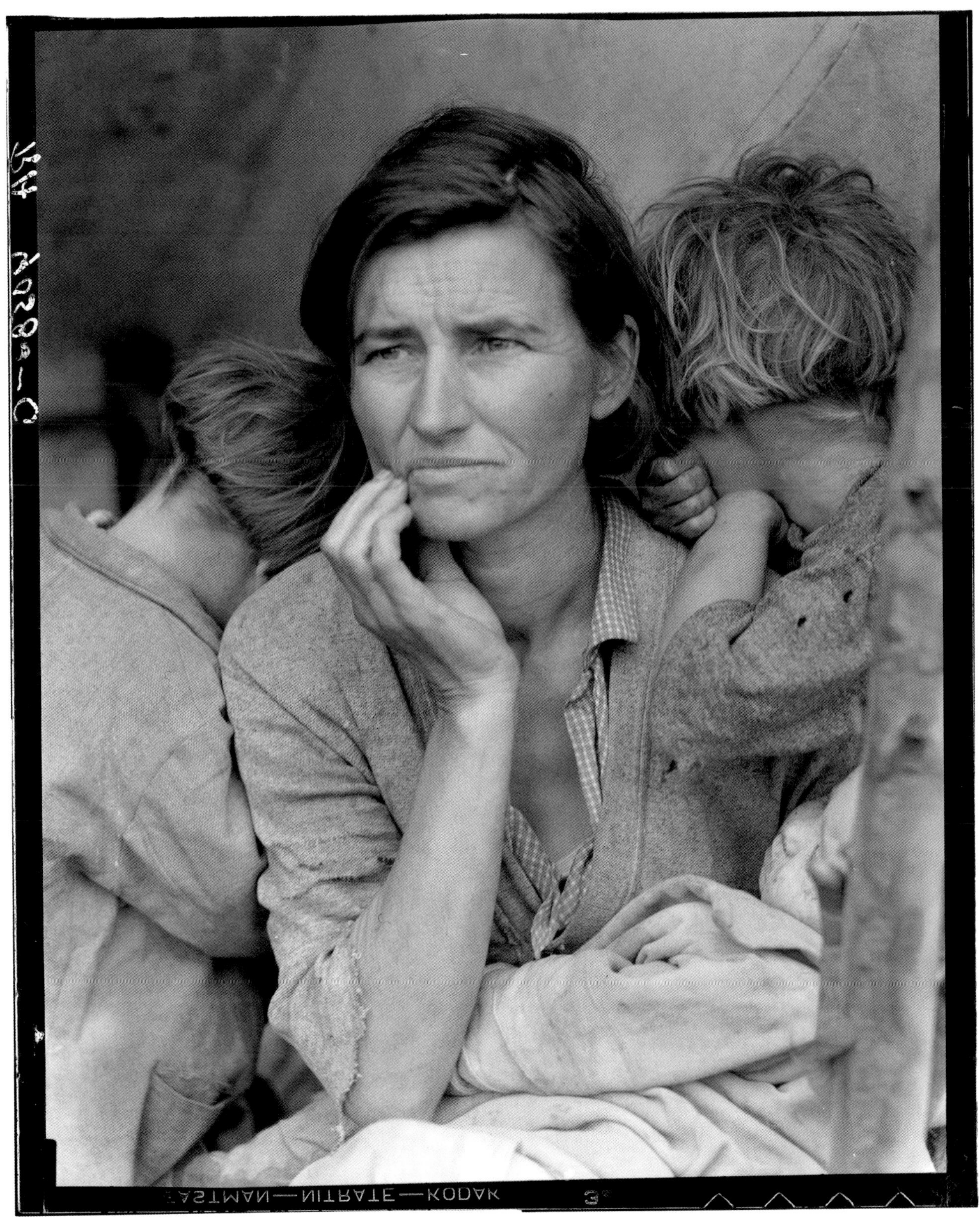

Dorothea Lange, *Migrant Mother* (1936)

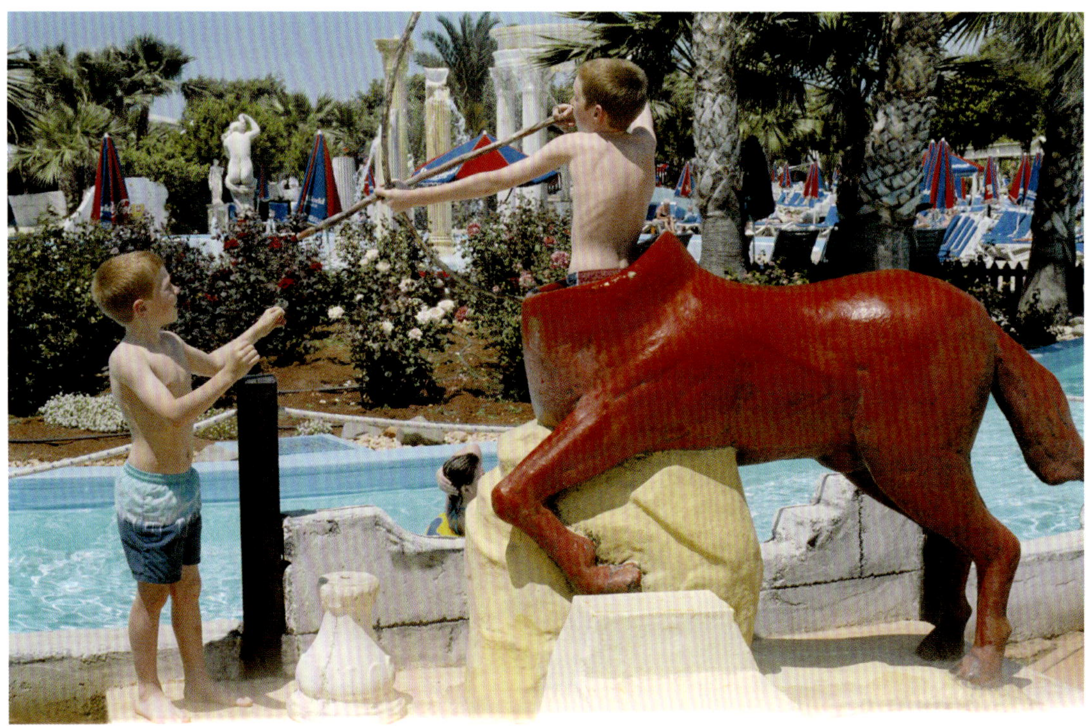

Phil Collins (born 1970)
***free fotolab* (2009)**

Philip-Lorca diCorcia (born 1951)
***Heads* (2004)**

What the two images shown here, as well as the bodies of work to which they belong, have in common is an erasure of the artist by the use of found photos or an automated process. Nonetheless, the artist's hand can be seen in the editing process – controlling what is seen, and how this is displayed to the viewer.

The British artist Phil Collins's *free fotolab* (see above) is created from a series of 35mm slides – of a sufficient number to fill the carousel of an old-fashioned projector. The artist sourced the images by issuing a public call for undeveloped film, then edited what was submitted, choosing to leave many images out as he sought to evoke a particular mood of melancholy, surrealism and pathos. Displayed over a nine-minute period, they show a range of everyday activities and scenes – from holidays to quiet moments in the garden – and their power lies not only in the eerie familiarity of what they depict, but equally in the sequencing and the hypnotic sound of the slides dropping into the light for projection.

The American artist Philip-Lorca diCorcia created *Heads* by remotely triggering a long-lens camera and strobe, so that people walking through New York City's Times Square had their portraits taken while being completely unaware that the act was happening. The shots were taken in broad daylight, so the flash would be unnoticeable, but it isolates the subject from the crowd as though they are caught in a dramatic spotlight. Thousands of photographs were taken, so the skill of the artist really was in the editing and production of the series, for which only 17 shots were chosen – including *Head #13* (2001), shown here.

The production of both of these works relies on a mix of spontaneity and method. On one level, the formalism and simplicity of diCorcia's headshots seems far removed from the more haphazard snapshots presented by Collins, but both have a resonance with daily life and are at their most effective when viewed in sequence, as the artists intended.

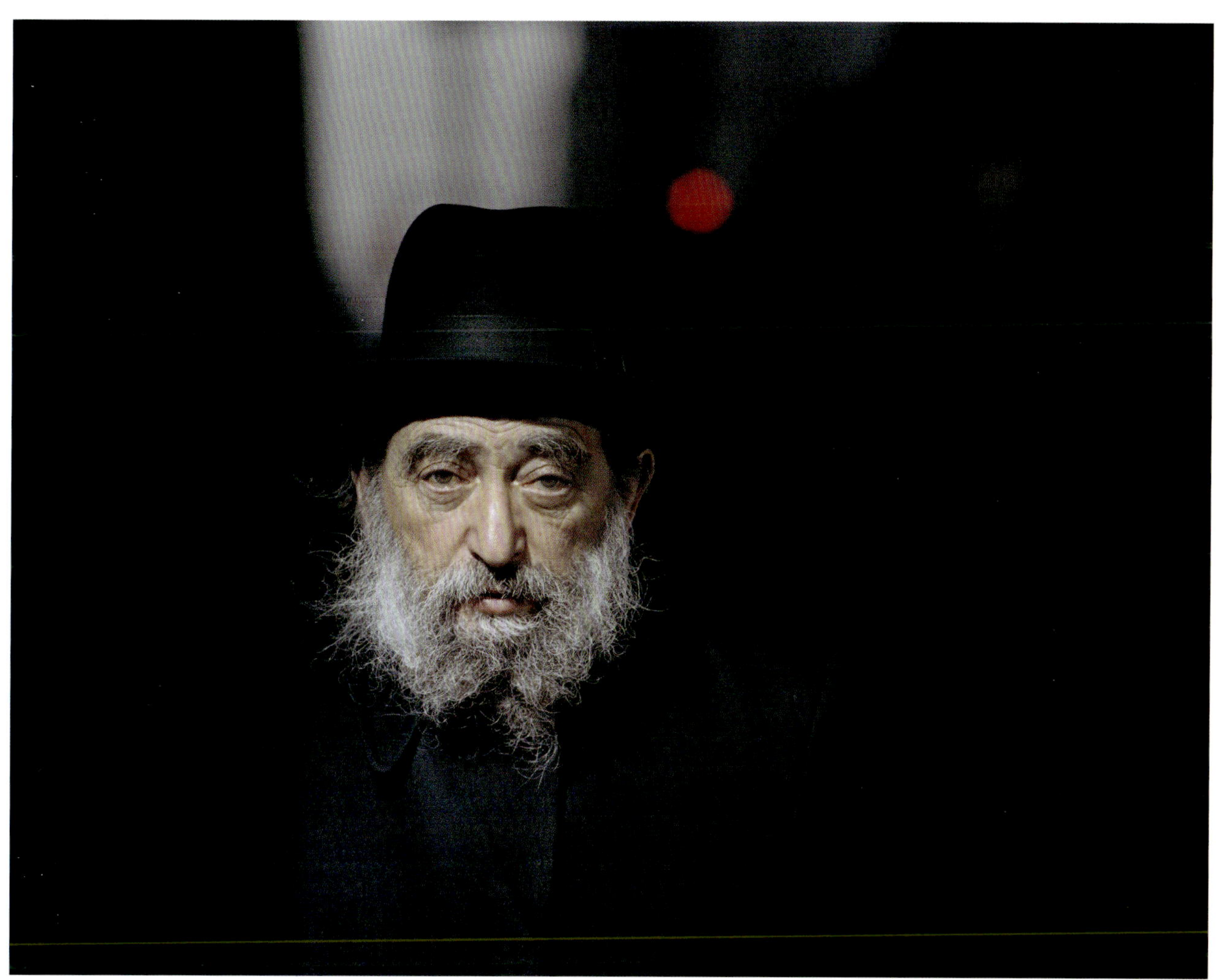

Oliver Chanarin (born 1971)
and Adam Broomberg (born 1970)
***Holy Bible* (2013)**

'Right from the start, almost every appearance he made was catastrophic ... Catastrophe is his means of operation, and his central instrument of governance.' This quotation from the Israeli philosopher Adi Ophir was the starting point for the *Holy Bible* project by the South African artists Adam Broomberg and Oliver Chanarin. The 'he' of the quotation is Yahweh, the God of the Old Testament, and the quote refers to the idea that when God reveals himself, it is often to catastrophic effect for the world and humankind.

With Ophir's words in mind, the artists investigated the Archive of Modern Conflict in London to find images that would illustrate, contradict or subvert the text of the Bible, in the King James Version. For example, where the phrase 'And it shall come to pass' appears in the Bible (as it does 120 times) they show a photograph of a circus or a magician. The archive is an eclectic one, so while there are sometimes pictures of magicians, there are also photographs of atrocities. By placing photographs of the latter against text that refers to equally violent ideas, a correlation between ideologies is created. Why might this be considered blasphemous? It is certainly provocative, because many of the images are distressing. Indeed, for the Bible to be tampered with at all might seem transgressive – even without the graphic photographs. Through their intervention, the artists comment on power, both on its abuse and those who abuse it.

The project amounts to an extraordinary feat of editing, with every included photograph considered in terms of how it works with or against the text and how it changes the overall meaning of the words. The disasters of the Old Testament are made to seem very real by their similarity to real-world disasters. The end product was a limited-edition photobook with tipped in reproductions of the photographs from the Archive, something that also comments on the desire of humans to photograph and look at images of crisis and human suffering.

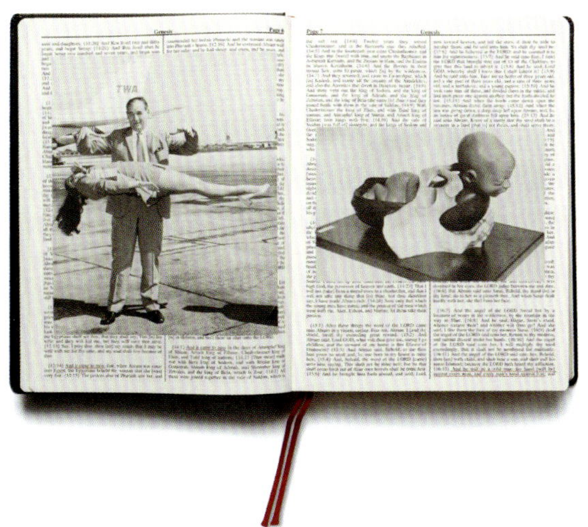

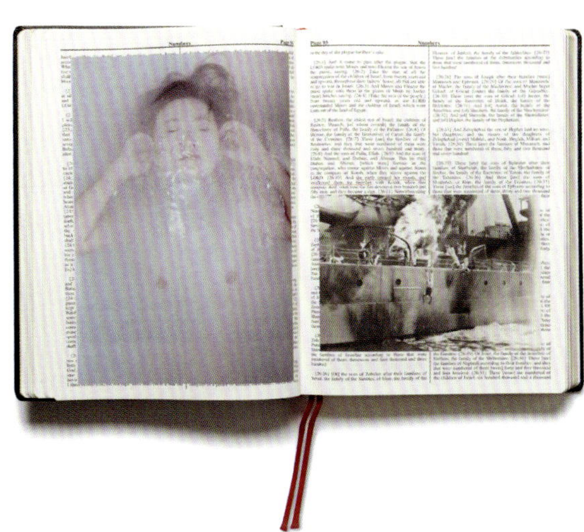

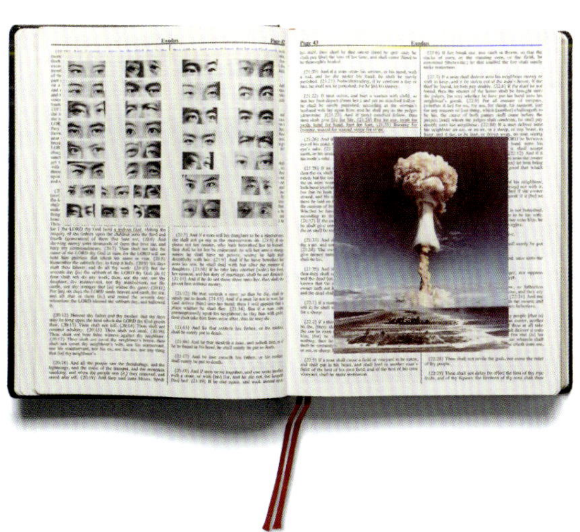

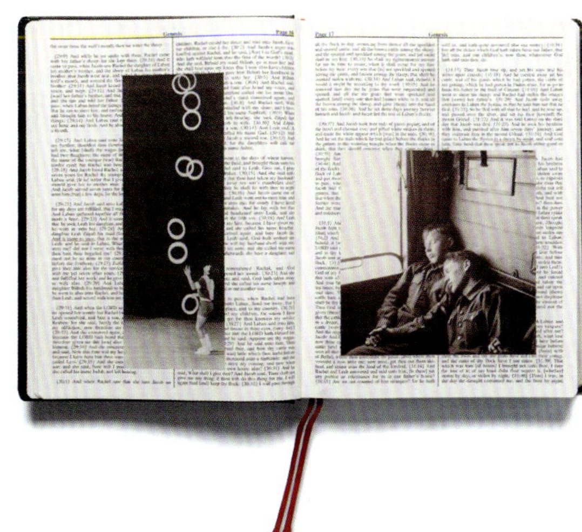

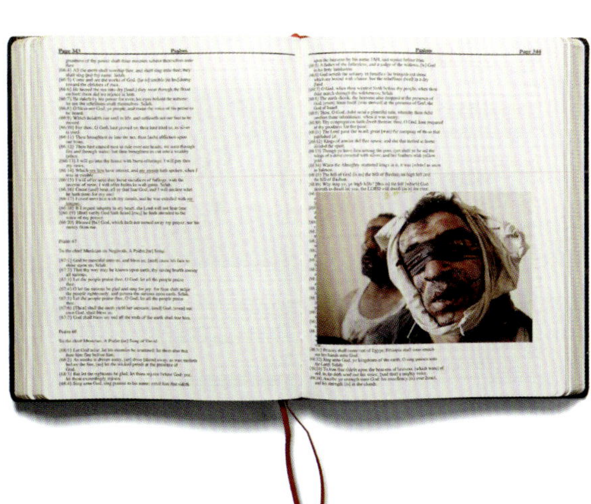

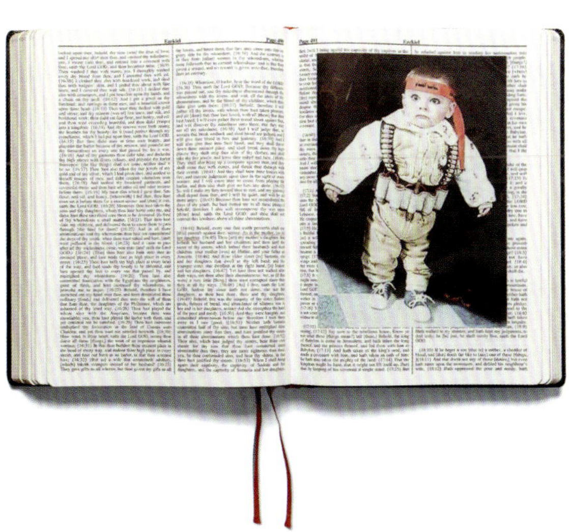

Larry Sultan (1946–2009)
and Mike Mandel (born 1950)
***Evidence* (1977)**

Another example of found photographs being used to strange and disconcerting effect is *Evidence*, a book of 59 photographs that the artists selected after poring through 2 million images housed in the archives of a variety of US federal agencies, corporations and industrial bodies over a two-year period. Removed from their original context, the images appear funny and absurd, devoid of any meaning beyond what they show. We can try to guess, but the images are often so specific to the situation they were originally tethered to that it is impossible to know what is going on. The selection of the images is vital to the book's success. The images play off one another and encourage the viewer to invest them with their own interpretations.

Now almost half a century old, *Evidence* continues to be highly influential, especially to a generation of artists working today who grapple with photographs that constantly appear out of context on the web. The book also highlights issues of authorship and ownership: should the photographers who took the images be credited? Ambiguity is often key to conceptual photographic practices. *Evidence* adroitly engages in this. Firstly, the title – evidence of what? Secondly, many of these photographs appear experimental, which seems antithetical to the fact and clarity the word 'evidence' implies. The structure of the book makes the United States of the 1970s look like a mysterious and strange place, and although the images were clearly taken with objectivity in mind, they seem imbued with a Cold War aesthetic.

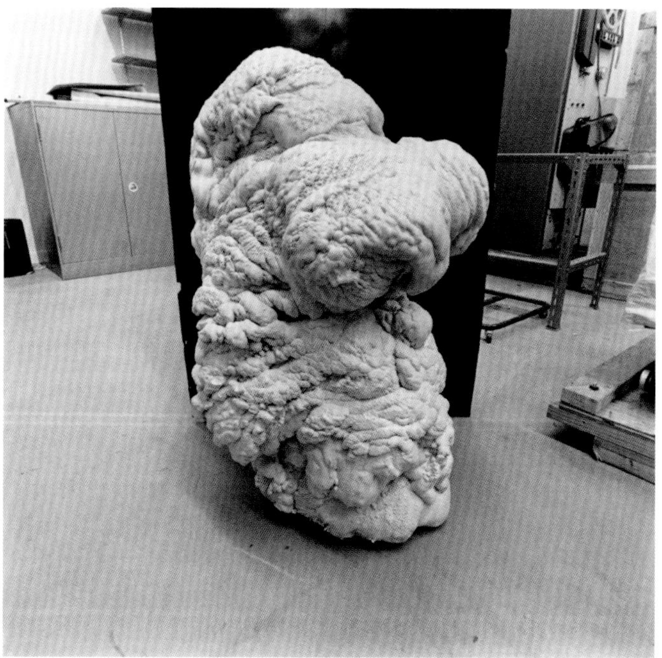

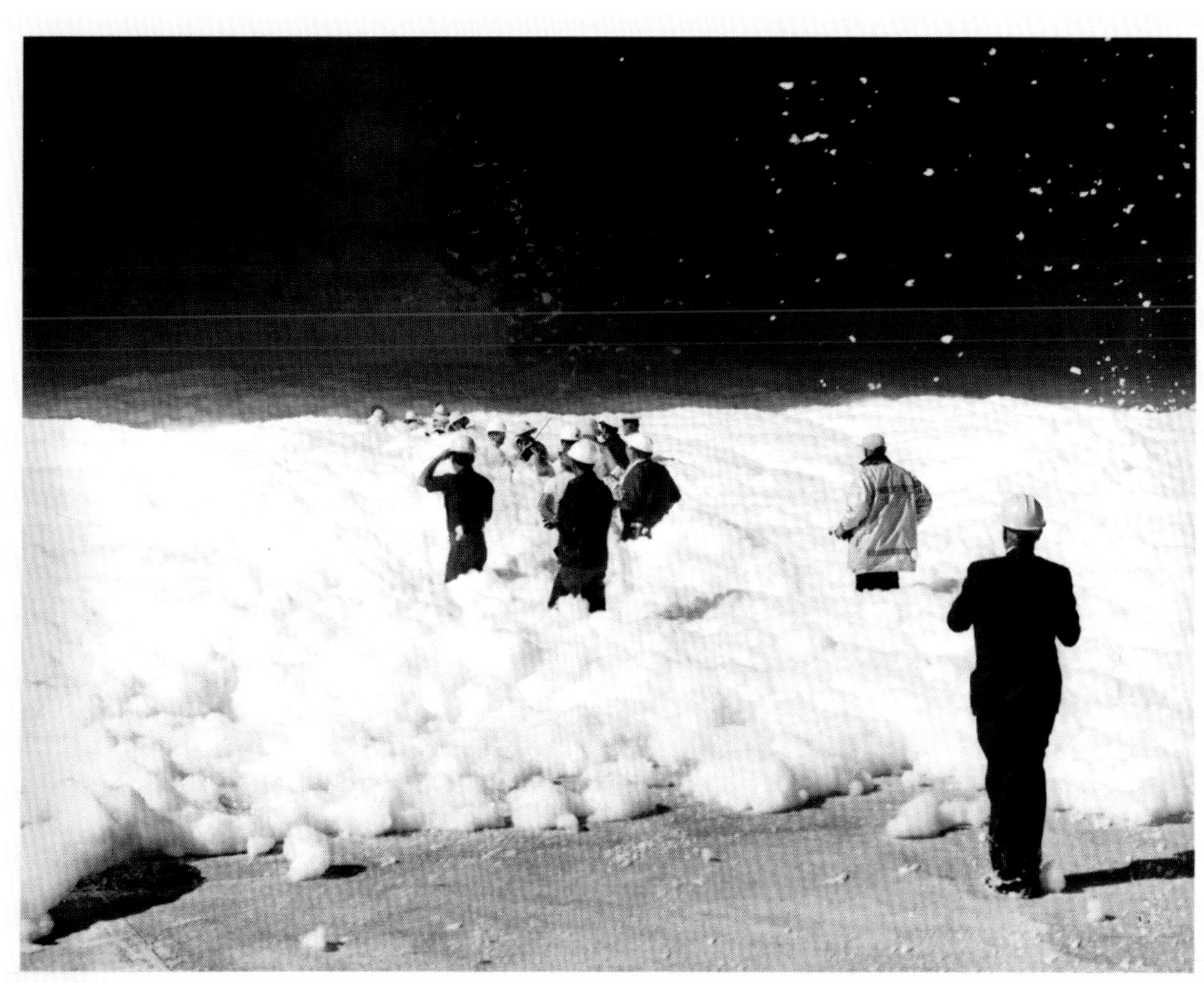

Eadweard Muybridge (1830–1904)
***Animal Locomotion*, Plate 535 (1887)**

In 1879 the British photographer and inventor Eadweard Muybridge introduced to the world the zoopraxiscope, an early device for projecting moving images. Indeed, while he first won renown for his majestic images of the Yosemite Valley in 1868, his best-known images, from later on in his career, are reminiscent of frames from a film. It was motion, above all, that obsessed him.

This example here shows a partially hidden, masked man, sitting at a table against a dark backdrop, beating time with his hand. Muybridge made many similar studies with other human and animal movements, some of which reveal aspects of motion that are otherwise imperceptible to the human eye. Famously, he was the first to prove through photography that there is a moment in a horse's gallop when all four hooves leave the ground at the same time.

Muybridge produced many thousands of serial images analysing movement, often using several cameras simultaneously so as to capture the same action from different angles – as here. With his sequences, Muybridge made his contemporaries believe the illusion of movement even when there was none. His working proofs, however, reveal that he edited his images carefully and that he altered the order to get the result he desired. Although it makes his work less scientific, his manipulation does not diminish the value and artistic quality of his work, nor the lasting effect that his oeuvre has had on our lives.

Muybridge's ground-breaking technological achievements have been immensely influential: from Thomas Edison's motion picture camera to special effects in computer games and Hollywood films. One way to generate a frame sequence is to set up a series of still cameras and have them take a series of shots that can later be played back in sequence. The same principle that Muybridge invented has been exploited in films such as *The Matrix* (1999), where it was used to create the sequence with the bullet, the trajectory of which should not be visible to the human eye, yielding the eponymous name for the technique known as 'bullet time'.

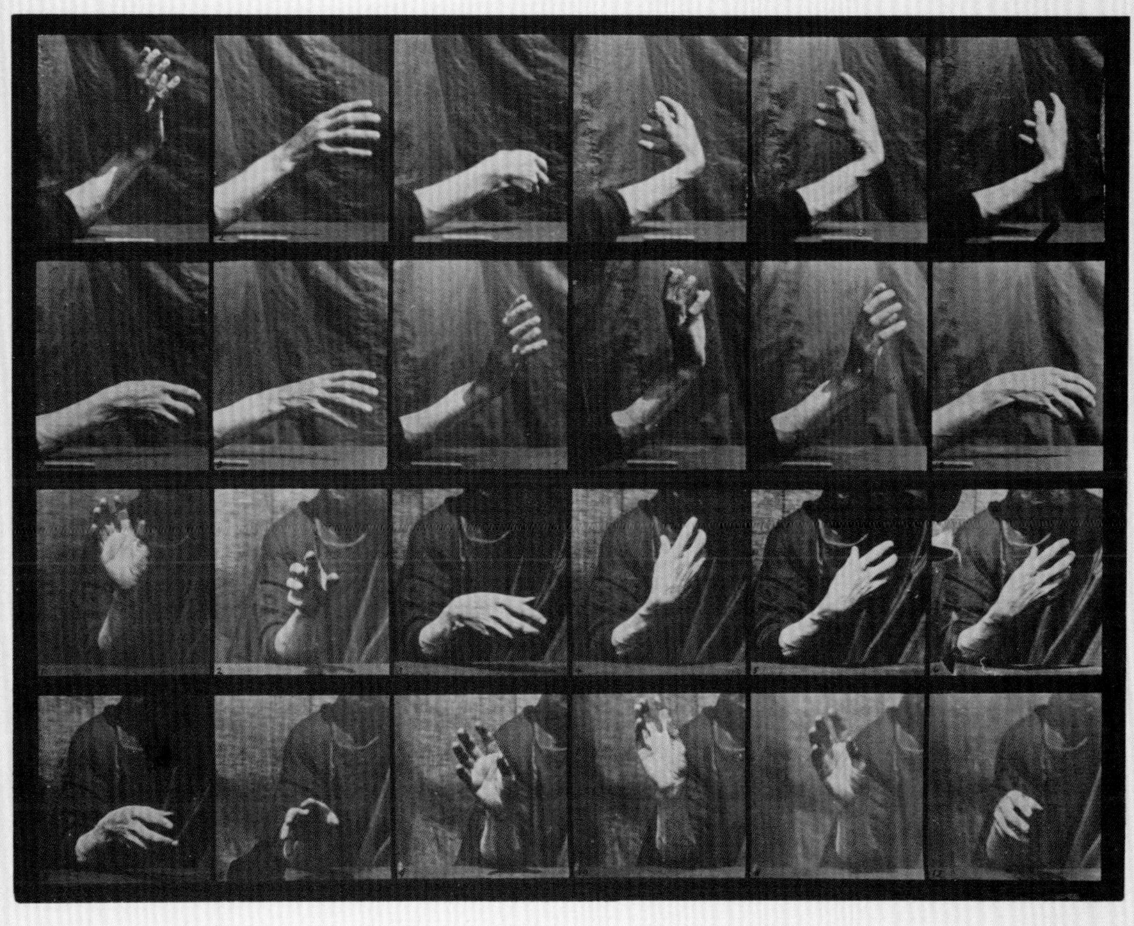

Animal Locomotion. Plate 535

Copyright, 1887, by Eadweard Muybridge. *All rights reserved.*

Jan Hoek (born 1984)
***Maria* (2014)**

The Dutch artist Jan Hoek consciously works on the edge of controversy. He has photographed Ethiopian homeless people with mental health problems, addicts, a girl without limbs, and members of a Lonely People's Club that he himself founded. His portraits rarely meet the expectations of those portrayed, because, as a maker, he often looks for something very different from the way his subjects want to show themselves or expect to see themselves reflected in their photographs. In Hoek's portraits, he tests the boundaries of what is ethically sound, all the while wondering how far he can go. Hoek wants to explicitly show this in his work because he thinks that crossing the line in terms of the ethics of representation is something that is too often concealed by his fellow photographers.

When he shot the subjects of his book *New Ways of Photographing the New Masai* (2014), he asked them to decide how they wanted to be photographed, in an attempt to offer an alternative to the caricature of the Masai that we know from earlier photographers such as Leni Riefenstahl, who showed them as athletic men and women who stand close to nature, either naked or dressed in traditional garb. After taking the portraits, Hoek asked his subjects to indicate their preferences, which Hoek included as notes in the final piece, prominently showing the sitter's first choice. By incorporating the choice of the Masai in the final work – the person who is portrayed decides what goes where – the question of whether he has exploited people by photographing them seems to become less urgent. Still, Hoek challenges viewers and fellow photographers to take a position.

Maria (33 years) animal keeper

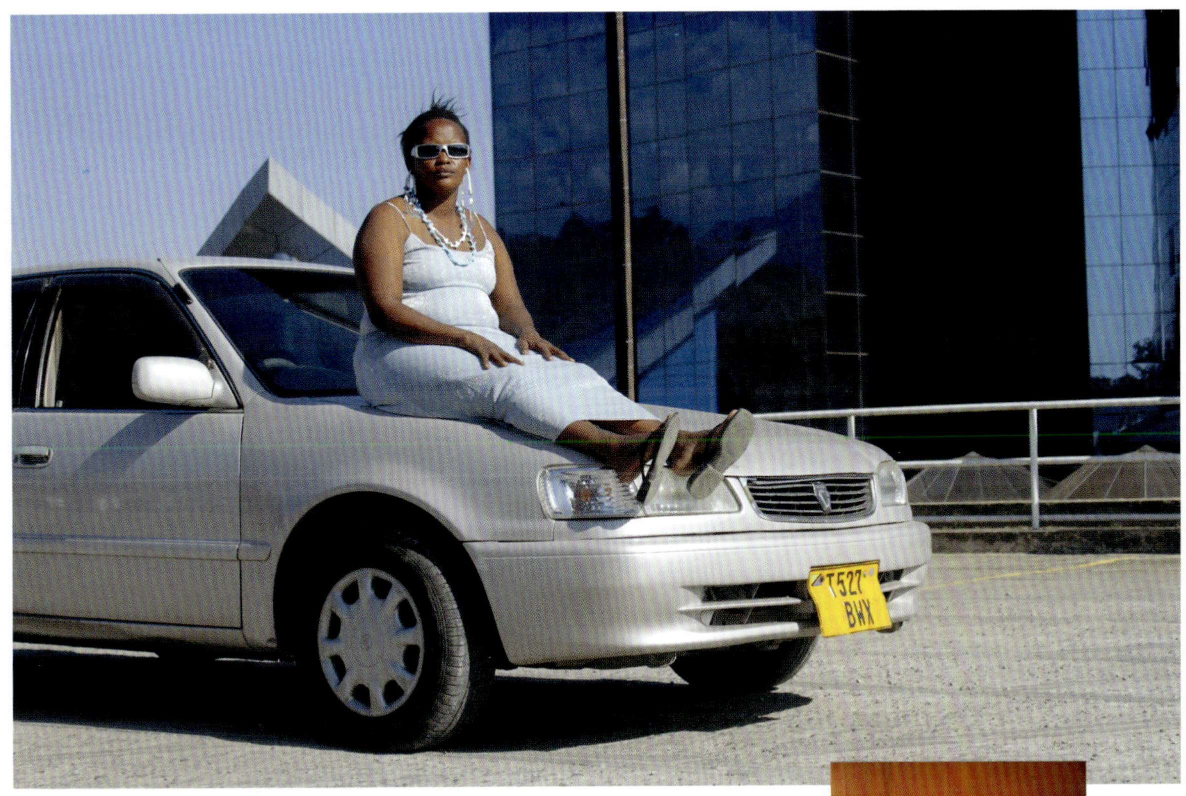

↑
1st choice

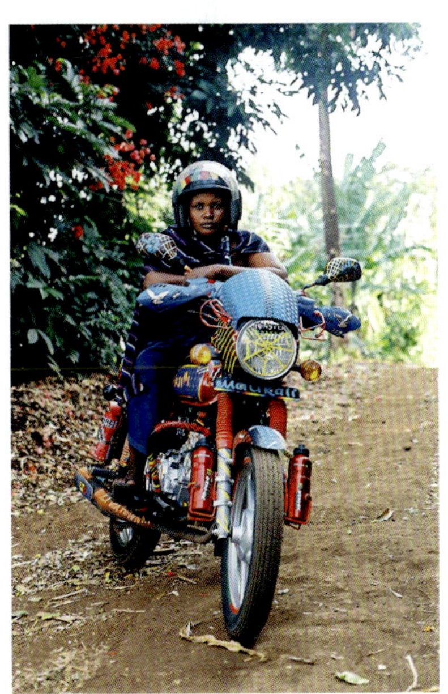

Likes:
silver and to be photographed happy and smiling

Doesn't like:
sad photos

← 2nd choice

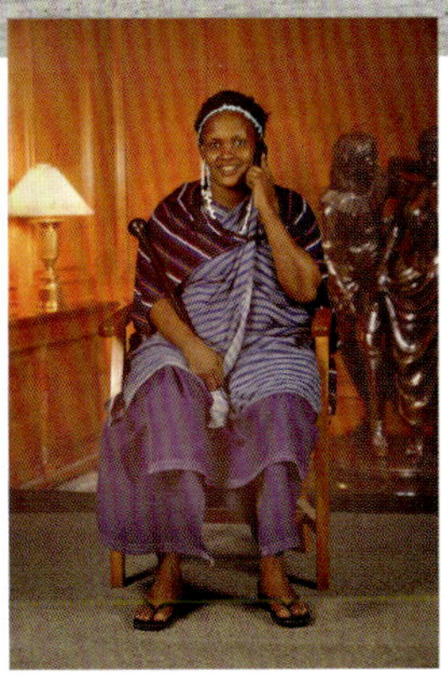

↑
3rd choice

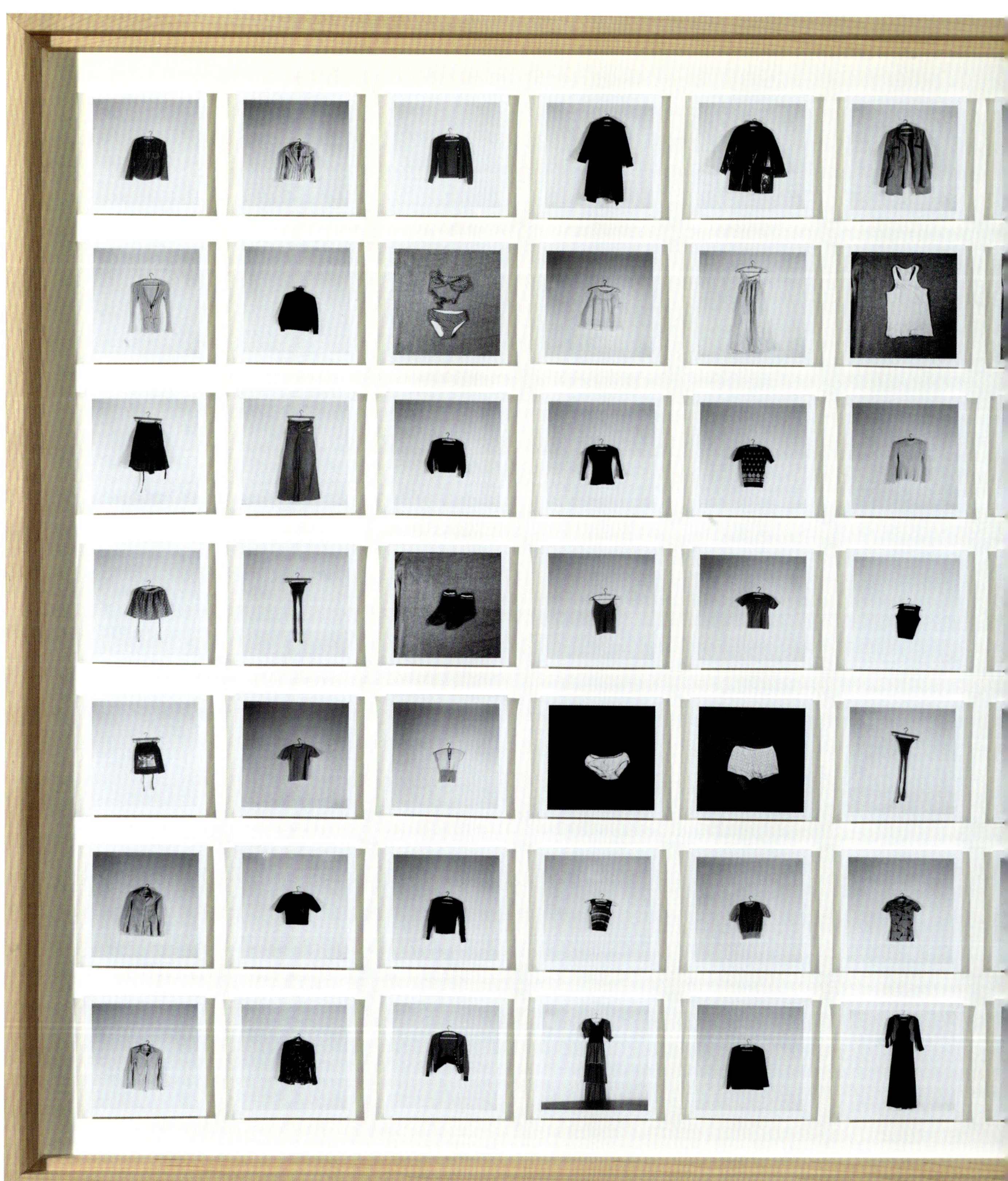

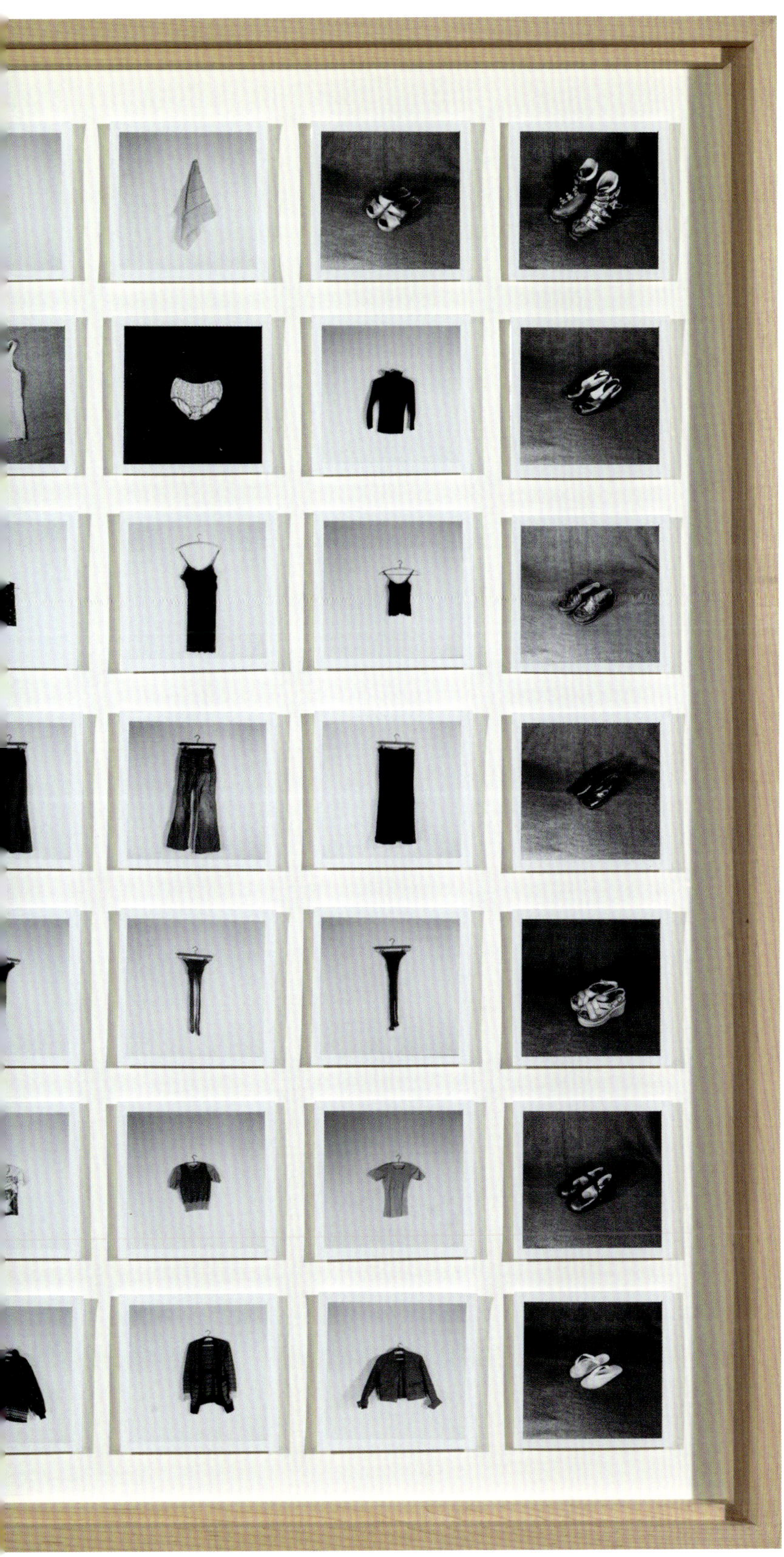

Hans-Peter Feldmann (born 1941)
***All the Clothes of a Woman* (undated)**

The work of the German artist Hans-Peter Feldmann includes painting, collage, archives and collections of images. However, he is best known for his booklets of black-and-white photographs, each one dedicated to a banal subject such as unmade beds and women's knees. On the other side of the Atlantic, the American Ed Ruscha has worked on similar photographic catalogues. Intricate theories about both artists' work have been unleashed – Feldmann's work has been called conceptual, politically motivated and full of moral issues. He, however, has more than once rejected such theoretical interpretations.

The title of this work is indeed an indication that he is averse to such language. What you read is what you get. The collection of photographs shows one woman's entire wardrobe. It can be seen in terms of presence in absence, and associations have been made to piles of clothes in Auschwitz. A young viewer, however, might be just as easily reminded of online shopping options, or a common contemporary desire to catalogue objects. Asked by the Danish artist Mikkel Carl about the logic or selection of works in this piece, Feldmann replied: 'If I had come on to her [the woman] in the streets, or somewhere else, she would probably have slapped me in the face, whereas with this approach it was all a bit more sophisticated ... *All the Clothes of a Woman* was all about the woman, not the clothes. Anyway, I take things, I arrange them in a certain way, and that's it.' This seems like an elementary and wonderfully unpretentious view of the process of making art, to be topped only by the British conceptual artist and Turner Prize-winner Jeremy Deller. Asked in 2017 what, in his opinion, is the question facing artists today, he replied: '"WTF?" That's the question facing artists today.'

Why is it famous?
Why is it famous?
Why is it famous?
Why is it famous?
Why is it famous?
Why is it famous?
Why is it famous?

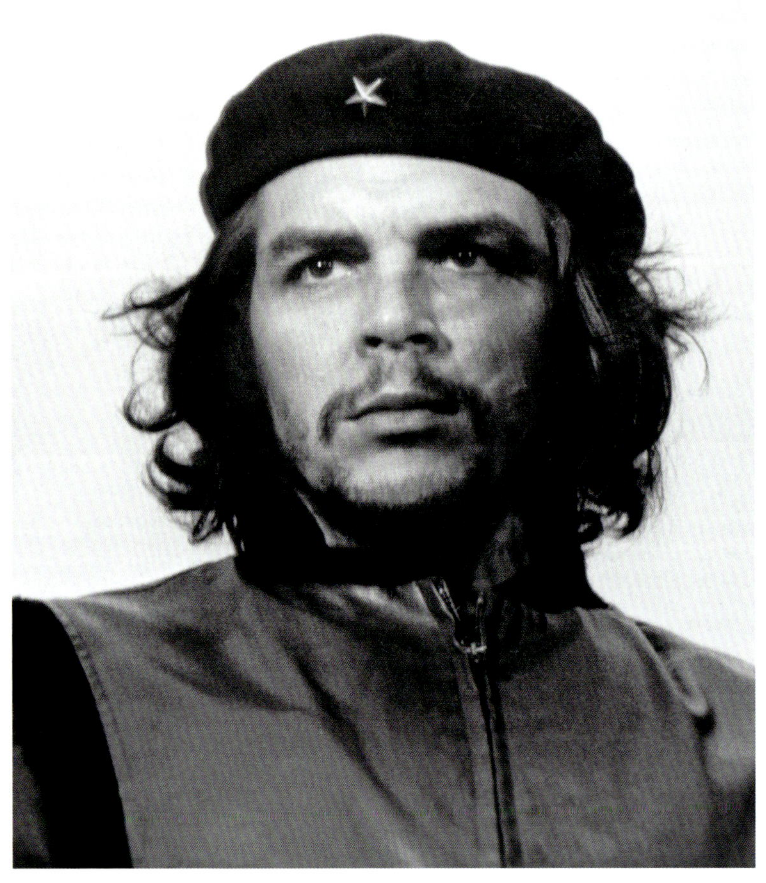

Alberto Korda, *Guerrillero Heroico* (1960)

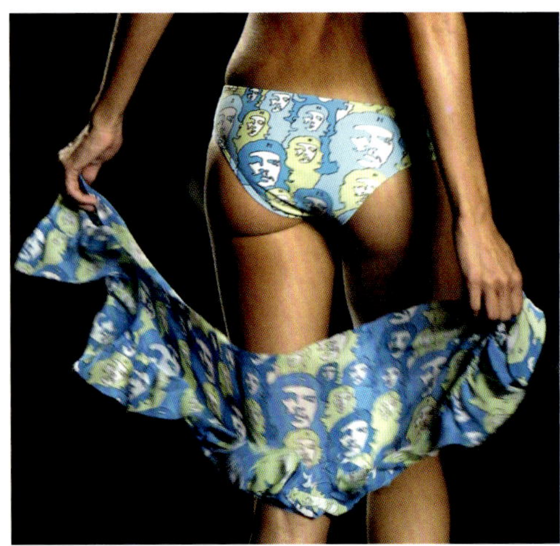

Che Guevara bikini, worn by Gisele Bündchen for Cia Maritima (2003)

In a world where billions of photographs are taken every day, it's hard to imagine one (just one!) making it through the visual noise to the point where it becomes iconic. However, the 20th century is marked with such photographic moments. Now imagine that all the pictures in the world have disappeared apart from two. One is *Guerrillero Heroico* – a portrait of the revolutionary leader Ernesto 'Che' Guevara – by the Cuban photographer Alberto Korda (1928–2001; left, top), and the other is *The Ultimate Confrontation: The Flower and the Bayonet* (1967; overleaf) by the French photographer Marc Riboud (1923–2016). Only one of these images can survive. Which will it be? This thought experiment can help us to understand the factors that go into making an image so readily recognisable that it reaches what we might refer to as iconic status. By what criteria can we decide which photograph has more value, and therefore survives? First, we might ask, what is the social value of the image? And, second, does it reinforce or undermine dominant ideologies? To address these questions, we need initially to look at the context: what were the circumstances of the photograph? Where does it sit in the history of photography and in social history? Does it have any metaphorical messages beyond the frame? Why is it so popular?

Both Korda's and Riboud's photographs are of historical importance and are considered 'iconic' in the history of photography. This means they are instantly recognisable, even when their political context has been stripped away. Of Korda's image we can safely say that it has been overused. Does that make it more worthwhile saving, or less? The Riboud image may strike us as a bit 'hippy', emblematic of the 1960s counter-culture and the slogan 'Make love, not war', but clearly there is something about both images that resonates. They both register on emotional levels around the issue of protest, and their original handmade prints have capital value at auction. More importantly, however, they convey a particular meaning to nearly everyone who sees these images.

Both images were made for popular consumption from the outset. The Korda photograph was made as part of a journalistic assignment but not immediately used. It later became a poster. The Riboud image was for *Look* magazine. This popular consumption has increased in their enduring lifecycles and now both images are equally popular on the Internet or a museum wall. From here on, it is only a small step to postcards and mugs. This may seem a shallow way of understanding what may or may not become iconic, but popularity and familiarity certainly play an important role in how we value images and their importance to culture at large.

Korda's portrait of guerrilla leader Che Guevara, taken when he was 32 years old, has been reproduced on posters, T-shirts, mugs, baby bodysuits and bikinis (see opposite, bottom). You can even buy a coolbox featuring this portrait to make your picnic look revolutionary. But not everyone is aware of the causes he fought for. In the same way, other photographs by Alberto Korda and other portraits of Che Guevara are not so familiar. There are well-known photographs taken after his death, and several where he is smoking a cigar. However, none are as famous as this image that has transformed from a would-be news photograph to a global symbol of rebellion and subsequently the epitome of commercial exploitation of a portrait. It's all somewhat ironic considering the politics of Che himself and the communist Korda, who resisted the commercialisation of the image.

When a photograph like *Guerrillero Heroico* becomes one of the most reproduced images in the history of photography, it perfectly illustrates the discursiveness and multiplicity of traits so intrinsic to the medium. A 'classic' postmodernist approach to photography suggests that photography cannot be understood as having a static identity or singular cultural status. John Tagg states, 'photography as such has no identity … its nature as a practice depends on the institutions which define it and set it to work … its history has no unity'. Contexts and meanings shift and change. Divorced from its original context, the initial meaning and substance become more diluted and the image today works almost purely as graphic icon. What was a symbol of militant Marxism has ironically become a device of capitalist appropriation.

Of course, part of the image's iconic strength lies in its effective use of certain photographic strategies. Shot from below, the subject appears big and heroic. It was cropped for dramatic effect and all extraneous photographic information has been removed to make it more graphic. The starkness of the blacks and whites were further emphasised when the image was first printed. The upturned gaze into the distance, too, suggests vision and strength. In 2006, a poster showing presidential candidate Barack Obama under the 'Yes we can' slogan would adopt similar strategies.

What contributes greatly to how Korda's picture nestles in our collective consciousness is that it was unprotected by copyright for more than 40 years. Reportedly, Fidel Castro wanted the image to represent the Cuban Revolution worldwide. The journey of this photograph and how it was endlessly reproduced is a case study of iconisation, commercialisation and mythic fantasy. It perfectly illustrates the discursive and slippery nature of photographs where ownership and authorship are more complex than in many other types of art. It also demonstrates the clash of the opposing ideologies of communism and capitalism. And on a different level it raises the question: would Che's portrait have iconic status today if he were twice as old and half as handsome?

Apart from its representational function (a crucial characteristic of any icon), issues of communication and transcendence must also be acknowledged when considering why a certain image is more famous than another. An image must be evocative and transcend what it depicts into some larger context, recognisable not only to a small group of people in the know, but to many. Marc Riboud's photograph shows an American student protesting against US involvement in the Vietnam War in Washington in 1967, but to numerous people, it represents a broader protest against war, hate and violence. The picture is one of two halves. On one side a young woman, 17-year-old Jan Rose Kasmir, holds a chrysanthemum up to her face. This strongly contrasts with the phallic weapons that are held up to her by the men in helmets facing her on the other side of the photograph. She does not look afraid. 'All of a sudden, I realised "them" was that soldier in front of me – a human being I could just as easily have been going out on a date with,' Kasmir said later of the men. 'It wasn't a war machine, it was just a bunch of guys with orders. Right then, it went from being a fun, hip trip to a painful reality.' The contrasts between their clothes, their gestures and their 'weapons' demands a difference between them, but really they are just all young people doing what they believe is right. The photograph transcends the actualities of the event by representing the Flower Power movement, gender politics and perhaps simplistic symbolism of guns equal war and flowers represent peace.

The photograph is imprinted in the minds of many and it can be seen to be embedded in a more recent photograph, *Taking a Stand in Baton Rouge* by Jonathan Bachman for Reuters, showing Leshia Evans taking part in a Black Lives Matter protest in 2016. Consciously or unconsciously, the image directly references the earlier photograph's graphic and symbolic strategies of gender stereotypes of aggression and resistance.

Whether a photograph becomes iconic relies on many factors beyond the actual image. Graphic strength and aesthetics count, but often photographs have become famous or iconic because they relate to a specific event. This, of course, is changing as we increasingly rely more on moving images to cement memories or visualise famous events. Combined with all other forms of media attention surrounding the events, the photographs are reproduced repeatedly over time and become fixed in the minds of the public consciousness. The number of times we see it, where we see it and why are all crucial to a photograph being considered an iconic image.

Riboud's photograph seems to resonate more today than ever as protests increase around the world and political tensions are high. It is an easy image to read, playing on ancient symbols of innocence and experience, good and evil, supposed feminine virtues of peace and male aggression. One wonders if the image would resonate so effectively if the person holding the flower were a young man instead of a young woman?

So, to return to the question that opened this chapter – what image holds more value and should therefore survive if only one could? Can we even consider photographs like this without issues of taste and preference coming into the equation? So perhaps the question should change from which one into why. Why are these images iconic and why is that?

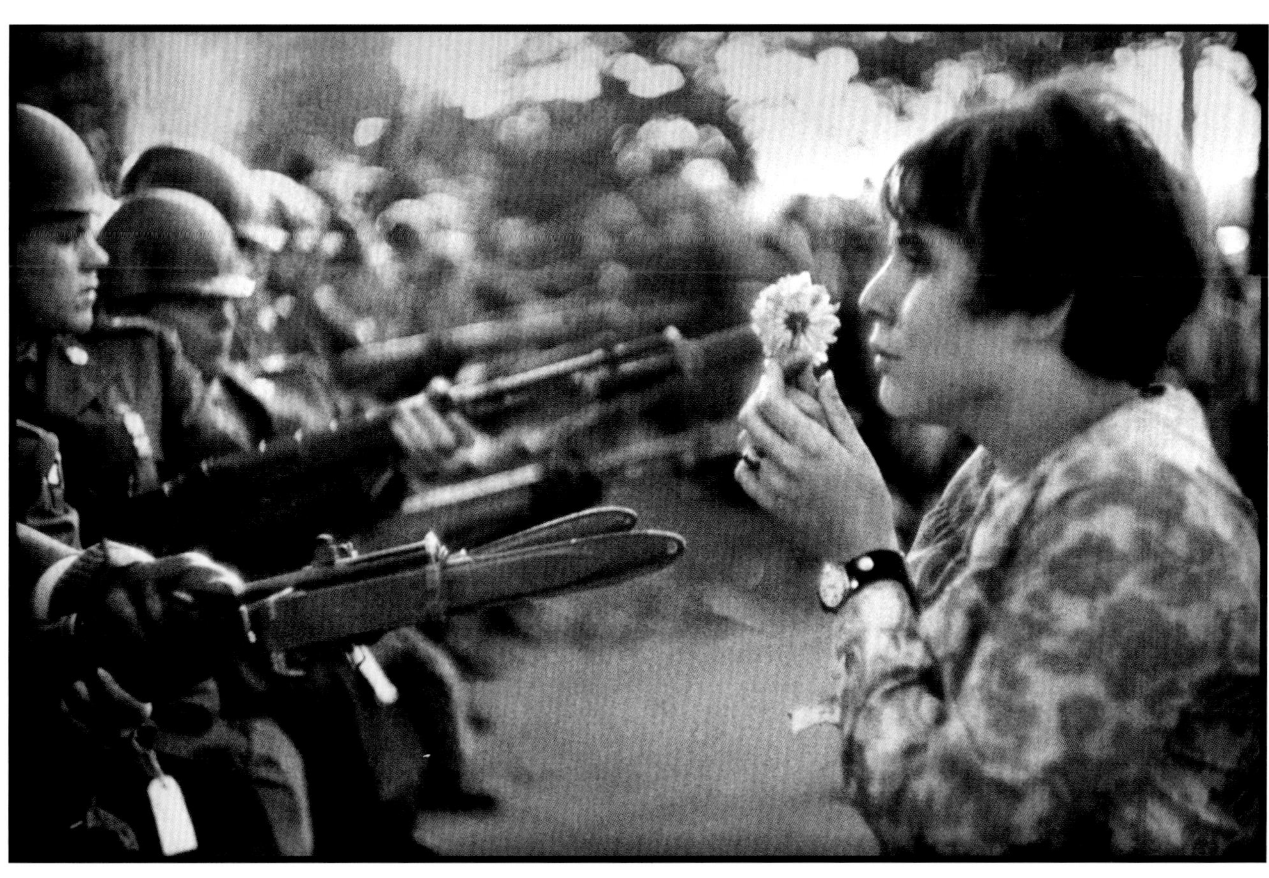

Marc Riboud, *The Ultimate Confrontation: The Flower and the Bayonet* (1967)

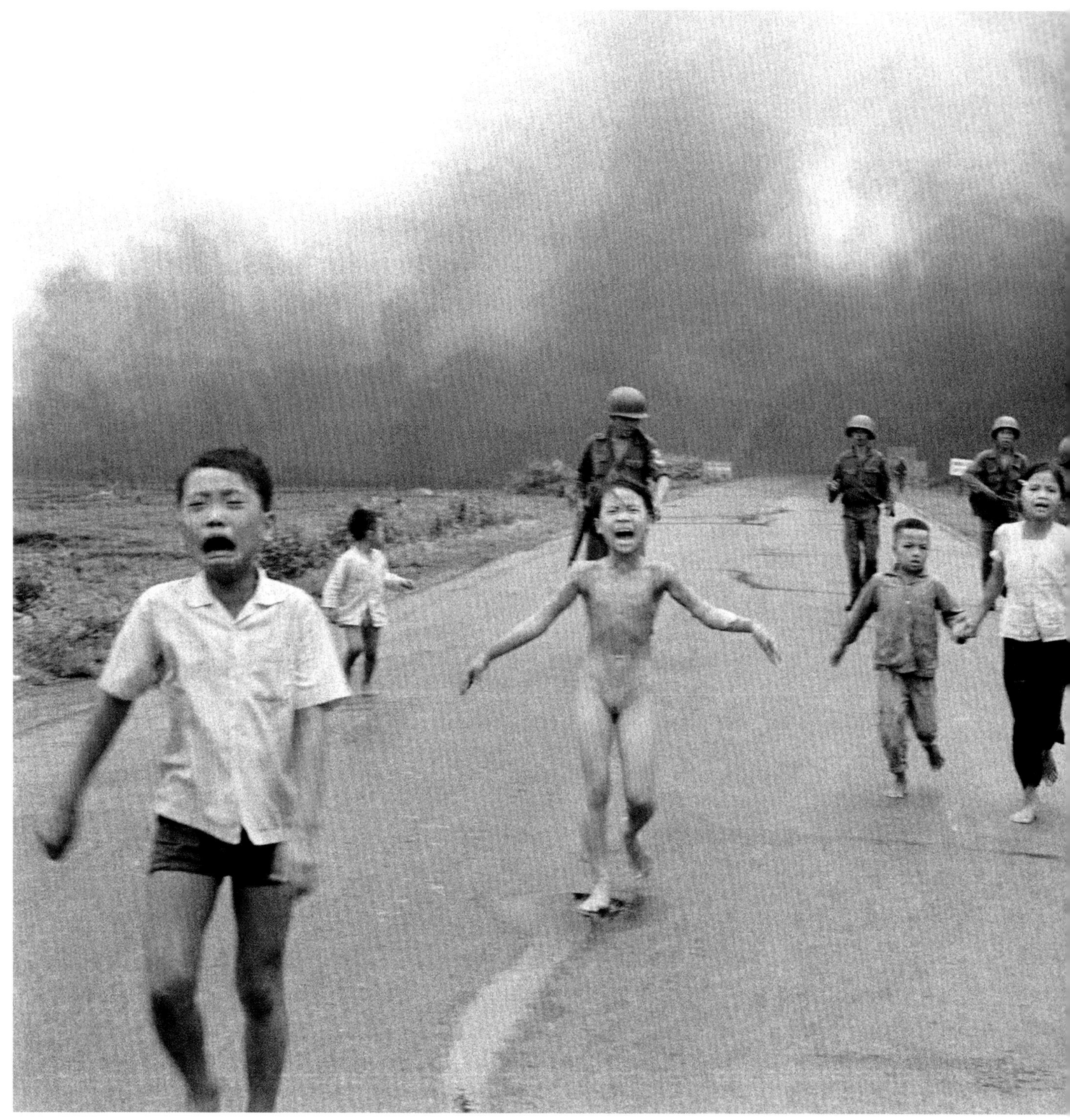

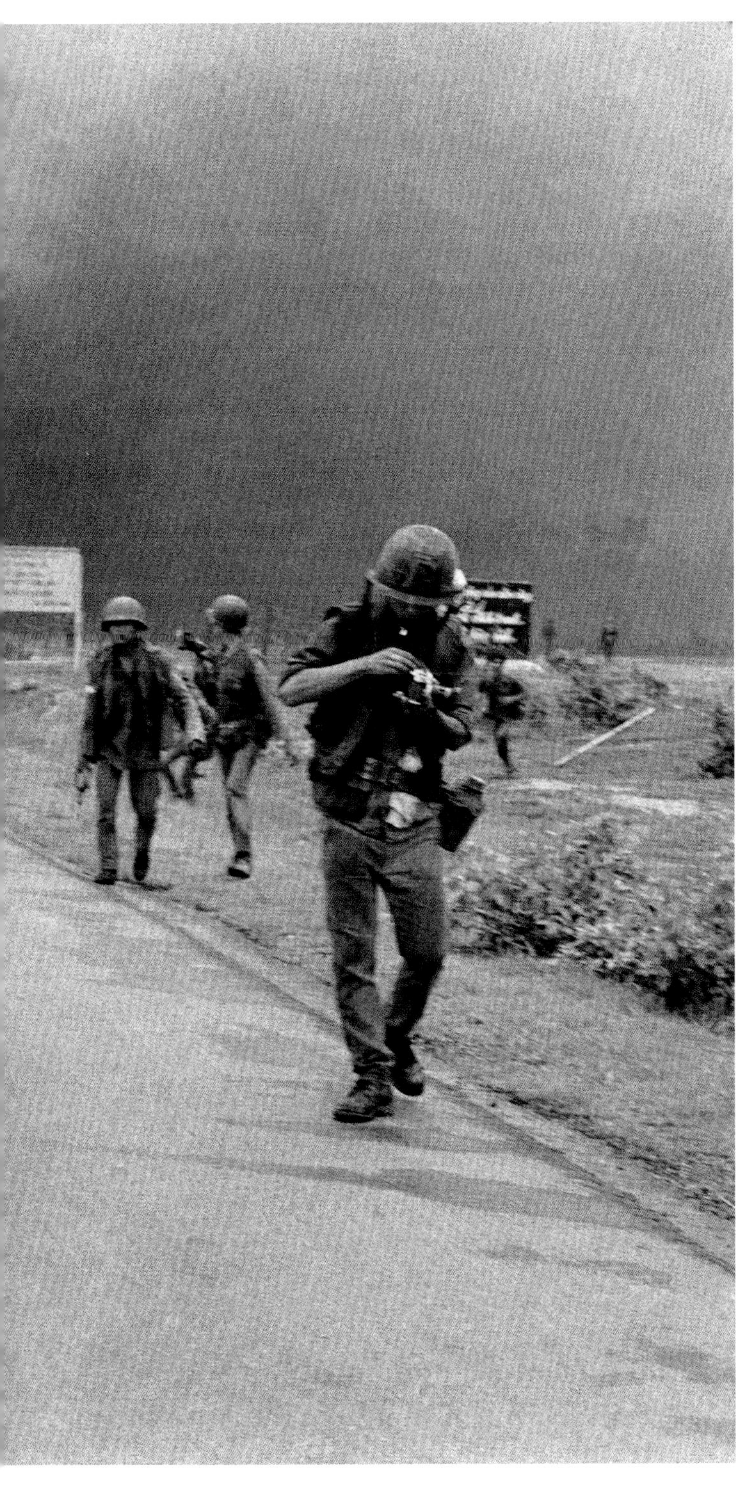

Nick Ut (born 1951)
***Napalm Girl* (1972)**

This harrowing photograph is probably one of the most famous in this book, and certainly among the most memorable images of the 20th century. Nonetheless the circumstances surrounding it are largely unknown, often forgotten or wrongly described. The picture shows children running from a napalm attack outside Trảng Bàng, a village about 19 miles (30 kilometres) outside the South Vietnamese capital, Saigon (now Ho Chi Minh City). The napalm was dropped by a South Vietnamese plane mistakenly, so this photograph depicts a result of what is known as 'friendly fire'. The open-mouthed horror on the face of the boy in the foreground, and the nakedness and outstretched arms of the screaming nine-year-old girl at the centre of the image, Phan Thị Kim Phúc (the 'Napalm Girl'), who had torn off her burning clothes as she fled, are shocking and disturbing to look at. Superficially, it is unclear from the photograph alone whether the soldiers are friend or foe, whether the soldiers are haranguing the children or helping them escape. Indeed, the difficulty of determining which was the 'right' side and which was the 'wrong' was something that many of the photographers who documented the war attempted to show in their work.

Photography played an important role in the Vietnam War, bringing home its horrors to a wide public. It has been argued that this photograph along with Malcolm Browne's *Burning Monk* (1963) and Eddie Adams's *Saigon Execution* (1968) raised awareness and did much to sway a strong resistance movement in America. One can ask whether photography alone has that kind of power. Can it really change the course of world events? Expectations of news photographs have always been high, but it is vital to remember to keep them in context.

The fact that the young girl was naked was one of discussion at the time, as many newspapers had policies excluding full frontal nudity. However, it was decided by the editors that this picture was too important not to show and it was widely disseminated worldwide. Unlike some of the photographs in this book, this photograph has not dated and is as upsetting today as it was when it was first published, even if the full circumstances are not as widely known as the image itself.

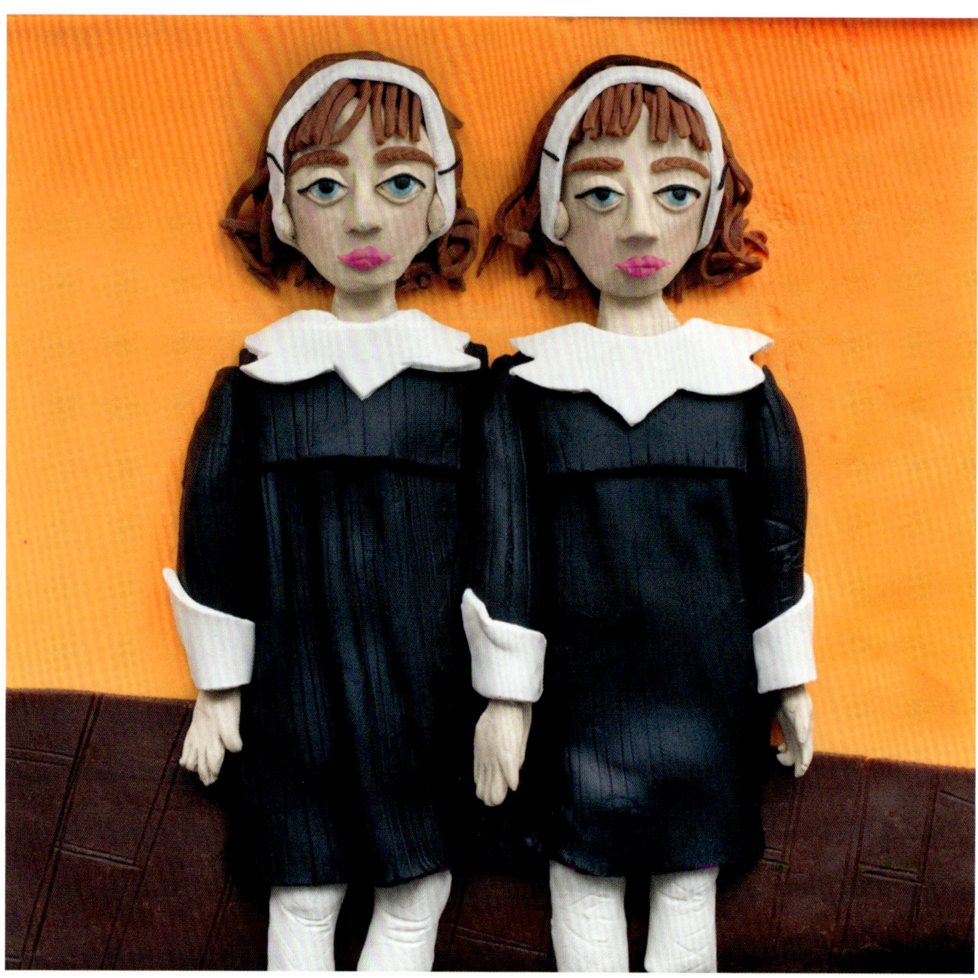

Eleanor Macnair (born 1976)
***Original photograph: Identical Twins, Roselle, N.J., 1967 by Diane Arbus rendered in Play-Doh* (2015)**

At the heart of this fun and funny project is a continuation of conceptual investigations by many artists to disrupt and question the hierarchies of art and photography. By dismantling the nature of high and low art the viewer is left asking why a particular photograph – here Diane Arbus's unnerving photograph of identical twin sisters in matching dresses – has become so famous and iconic in the first place. There are many ways in which artists have done this: dot-to-dot drawings (MacDonaldStrand), colouring book-style outlines (Martin Parr), or remodelling scenes out of food (Vik Muniz). The British artist Eleanor Macnair uses Play-Doh, creating a whole series of tableaux that take on the work of some of the 20th century's most celebrated photographers including William Eggleston, Claude Cahun and André Kertész.

It is this that makes Macnair's project so joyous: Play-Doh is fun, it's for kids, and there is a sense that, in making these tableaux, the artist does not take herself too seriously. The effect of Macnair's reworking is that it defuses the menace and restores a certain childhood innocence to the picture.

The pieces are also really skilful. Another reason these photographs are popular is that Macnair's website and the image-sharing site Instagram were initially the two main outlets for her work (even if subsequently they have also been shown in galleries and museums around the world). Both these ways of encountering her work are far removed from the art gallery or the newspaper in which many of the original photographs were, and continue, to be found.

By dismantling a photograph and reducing it to shapes and primary colours, the artist encourages the viewer to look more closely at an image rather than just scanning it, as we are so accustomed to doing with photographs now.

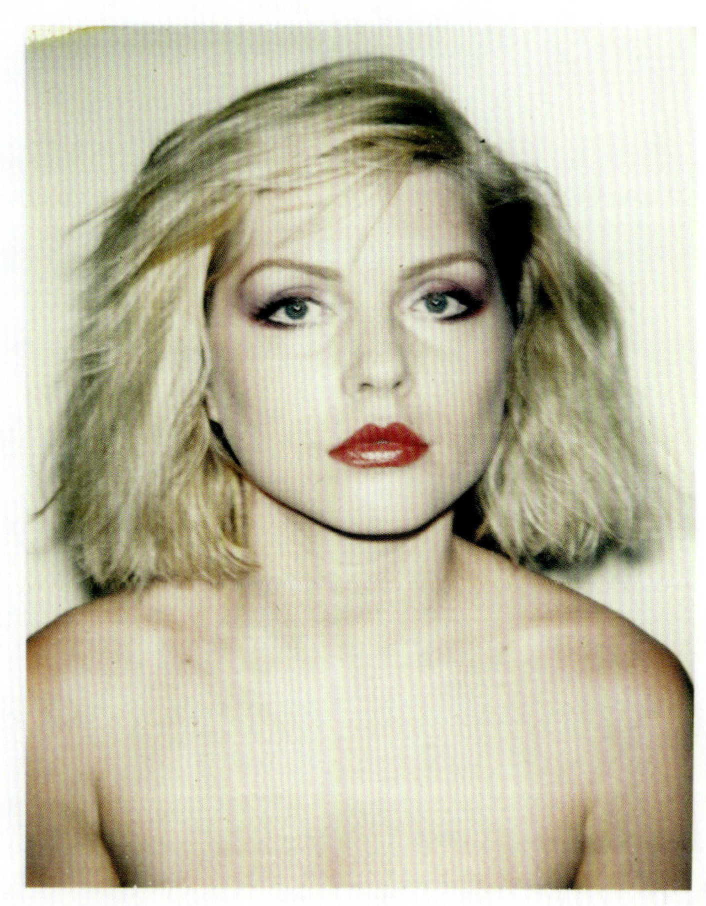

Andy Warhol (1928–1987)
***Debbie Harry* (1980)**

Which celebrity picture is iconic to you? This probably depends on your age and gender. What often is meant by 'iconic' is just 'famous and recognisable'. Is this image iconic purely because it is instantly recognisable as a Polaroid photograph by Andy Warhol of a famous singer? To truly deserve the appellation, an image should also carry with it a connection to a larger, preferably universal meaning. Thus, Warhol's *Campbell's Soup Cans* (1962) is not just a multiple-canvas work depicting tomato soup cans; it has come to symbolise pop art and tells us something about the relevant era, especially the commercialisation of culture, repetitive mass images and a desire for speed and ease in American culture.

By making instant pictures of friends and celebrities, Warhol documented his life in a way Instagram documents our lives today. However, his portrait of new wave band Blondie's singer Debbie Harry also captures an important moment in musical and cultural history – a female singer who was as rebellious as she was glamorous. The fact that she is incredibly photogenic certainly helped her become an icon for both men and women worldwide. The combination of Harry and Warhol works to cement the credibility and status of both artists. He lends her art-world exposure, and she admits him into a world of cool celebrity. Their individual fame helps bolster the other.

The Polaroid was then used as a template for his famous silk screens of Harry in 1980. The washed-out blondes and beiges that made the Polaroid technique so particular are gone, replaced by vivid pinks. With the transformation of Harry from photograph to silk screen the hierarchies of painting and photography are brought back into play. By giving her his signature treatment, her iconic status is sealed – not just by her musical achievements, but also by the fact she has been 'Warholed'.

Sergeant Ivan Frederick (born 1966)
Ali Shallal al-Qaisi at Abu Ghraib Prison (1994)

The distasteful practice of 'trophy photography' has a long history. The term originally applies to game hunting where hunters pose behind the animals which they have killed, but it has also been used to describe the use of photography when photographing the dead in warfare. Few examples are as shocking as those taken in Iraq in 2003, the first instance in which photographs taken in conflict were captured digitally and shared across different platforms. This photograph is just one of many taken at Abu Ghraib, a prison on the outskirts of Baghdad which the US military were using as a detention centre. It is not by a professional photographer but a sergeant in the military who, along with several of his colleagues, tortured and humiliated Iraqis who were being detained. Photographs of the American soldiers torturing inmates revealed the dubious ethics of the war and, as in the Vietnam War, highlighted the fact that not all US allied soldiers were heroes or indeed saviours.

This photograph became the most reproduced and therefore the most famous, as it was the least graphic in many ways. Several elements of the photograph nonetheless make it disturbing. The outstretched arms of the Iraqi prisoner, Ali Shallal al-Qaisi, make him resemble Jesus on a cross, and the electrical wires tied to his hands add to the macabre theatricality, while the hood strips the prisoner of any remaining dignity.

The term 'war porn' has been attached to the Abu Ghraib photographs and other similar gratuitously violent and explicit images that are often circulated without context. This image is perhaps the first to be understood in this way and as a lasting icon of the war in Iraq it illustrates the changes in how photography is taken, disseminated and understood at the turn of the 21st century. It has not gone through the filters of an editor and shows that 'citizen journalism' is not always taken with noble intentions.

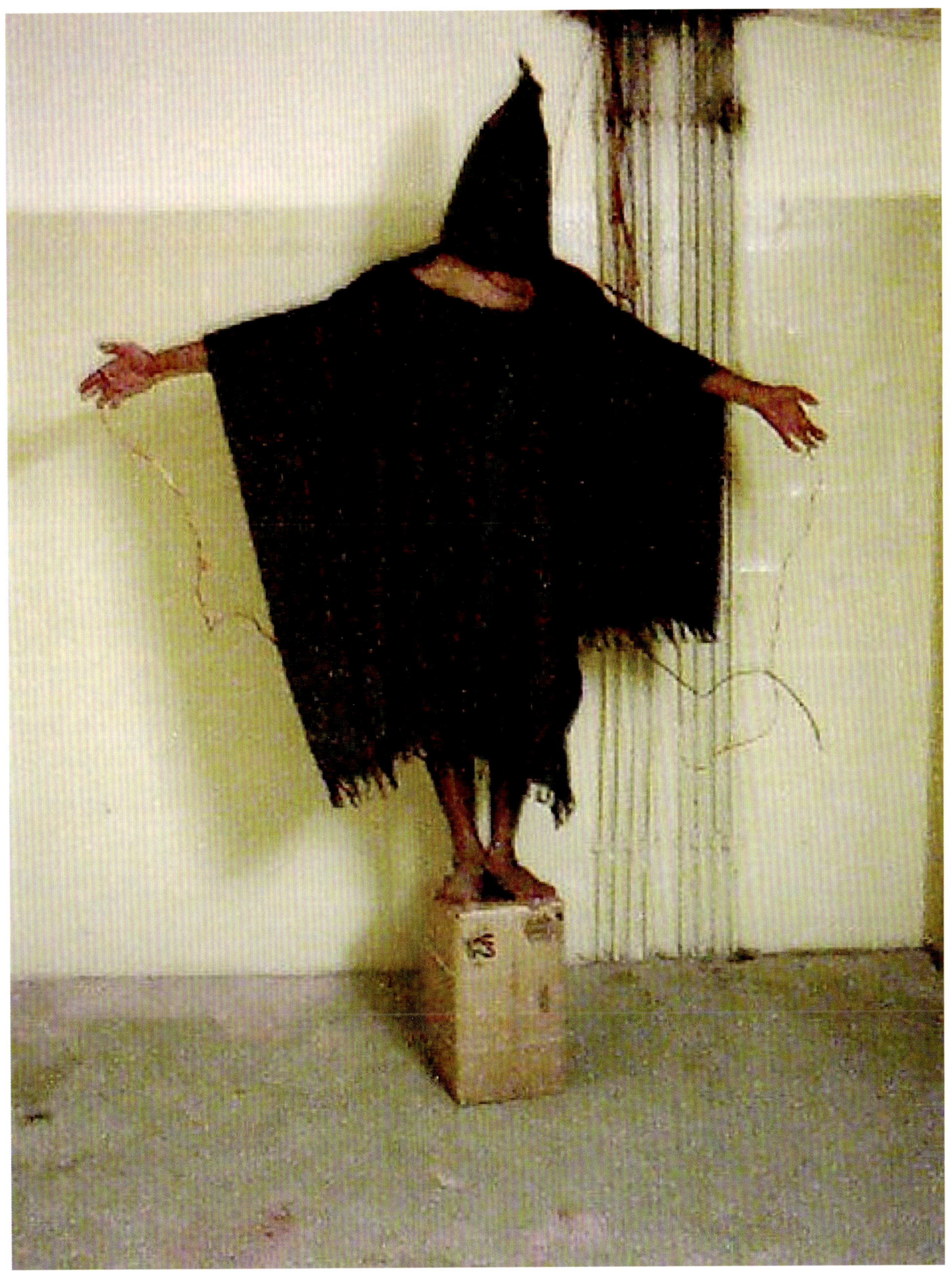

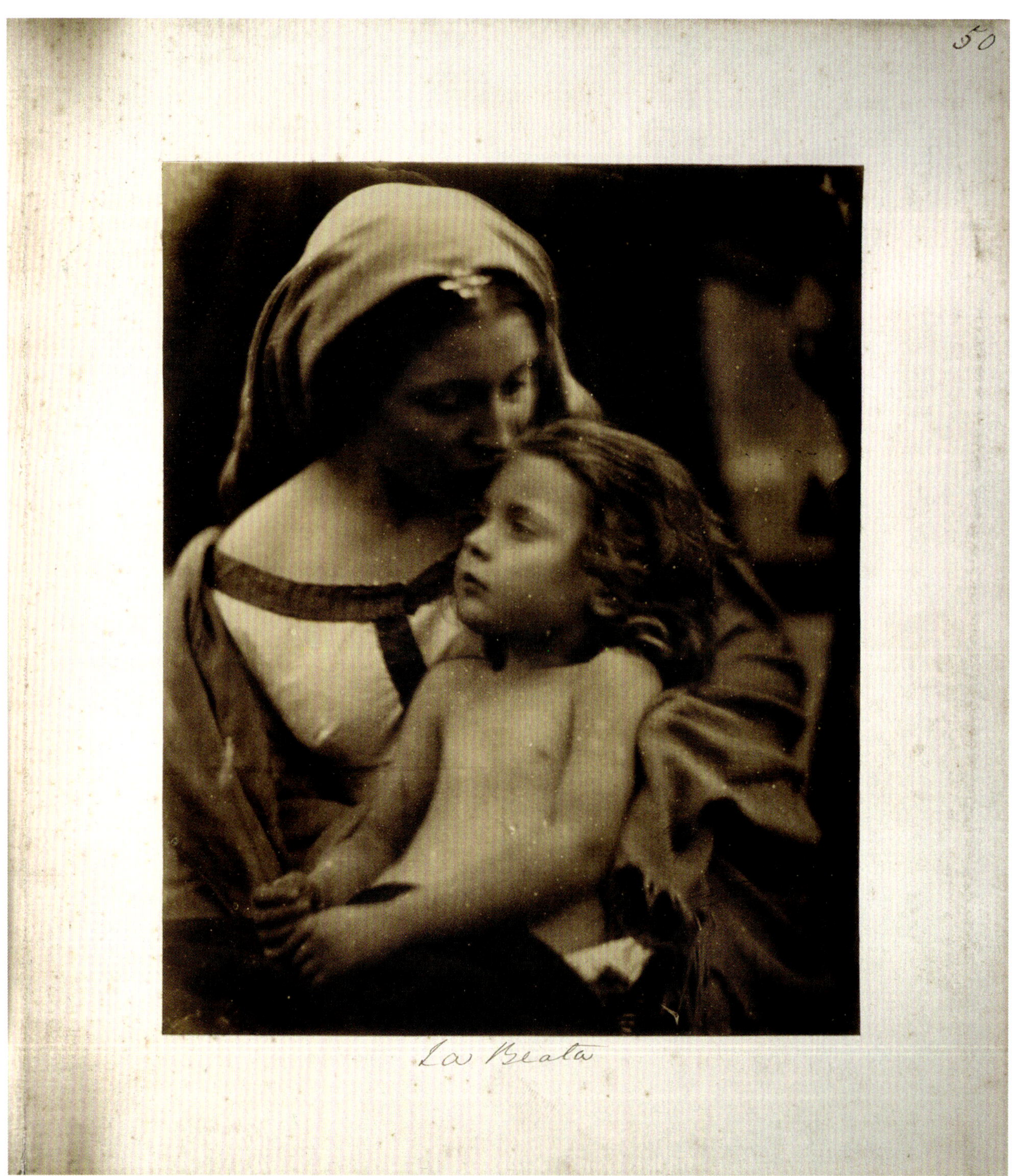
50
La Beata

Julia Margaret Cameron (1815–1879)
***Blessing and Blessed* (1865)**

During the Italian Renaissance, the hitherto prevalent image of the Virgin Mary with the Christ child was replaced by the Madonna of Humility, an icon which humanised both mother and child, and was understood to represent universal human feeling and experience. Here the mother protects, feeds and derives hope from the new life; an ultimate idealisation, partly by identifying the child with Jesus Christ and the mother with characteristics such as tenderness, compassion and love.

Photography followed painting in representing this tradition as one of the noble genres of art. One of the most famous examples of this can be found in the work of Julia Margaret Cameron, an amateur photographer who photographed the image of the Virgin Mary many times over her short working life. She drew inspiration from religious iconography for this portrait: she covers her model's head, and the slight blur of the camera and the folds of clothes give an outward dramatisation of inward emotion – a reference that dates back to very early Byzantine Virgin Eleousas. In addition to the symbiotic and vulnerable relationship between mother and baby, we see an idealised and romantic image; motherhood as a holy calling.

Cameron's Madonna-and-Child images reverberate with universal, religious and personal symbolism and she purposefully calls upon the signs and symbols of religious art, making her work accessible and instantly recognisable. To this day, we see the compositional structure of the triangle of the Madonna painting, even in documentary photography, although in this genre a reality is shown in which the life of mother and child is neither idealised nor romanticised.

Kevin Carter (1960–1994)
***Starving Child and Vulture* (1993)**

Some images do not make it into a newspaper because they violate a journalistic code or because photo editors consider them too shocking for their readership. This image by the South African photojournalist Kevin Carter, taken during the 1993 Sudanese famine, did get published. There is no bloody scene, there are no dismembered limbs, and there is no face with recognisable emotions we can relate to. Instead, the photograph features a young, starving Sudanese child, who (according to the caption in the *New York Times*, where the image was first published) collapsed on the way to a feeding centre. As Carter was photographing the child, a vulture landed close by. After taking this picture, Carter drove the vulture away.

The image was used in charitable campaigns, and so became an iconic depiction of famine that helped forge public opinion. In addition, it quickly became a prominent case study in the debate over whether and when photographers should intervene during their work in crisis situations. Some readers of the *New York Times* criticised Carter for not immediately coming to his young subject's rescue. Carter later said that he hated this photo, even though he won a Pulitzer Prize for Feature Photography for it. A few months after he won the prize, he could no longer live with the depression he'd battled for years, and he took his own life.

Perhaps the fundamental question is: How much should viewers see of the world's miseries? And when confronted by scenes like this, is it the photographer who should take action, or the people who see their images?

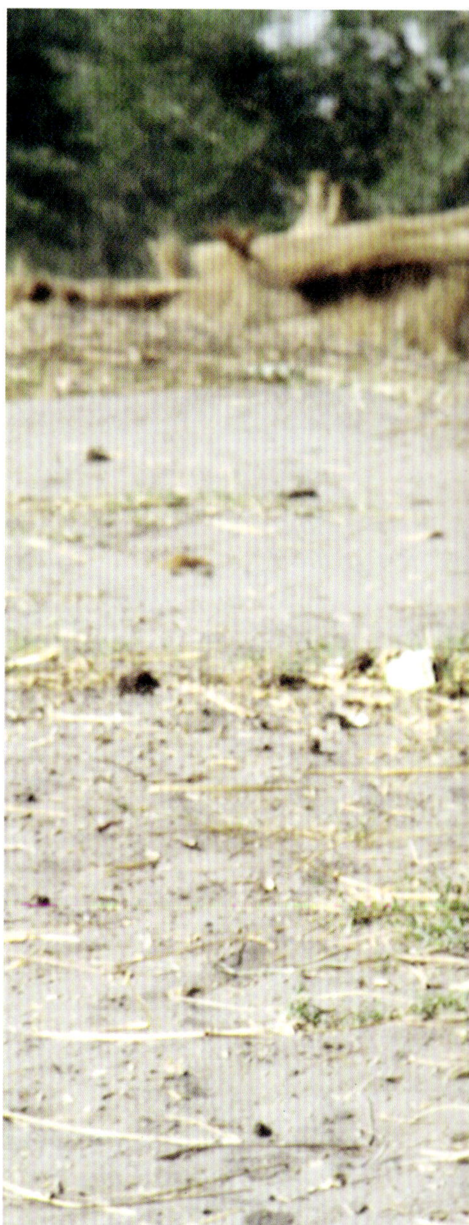

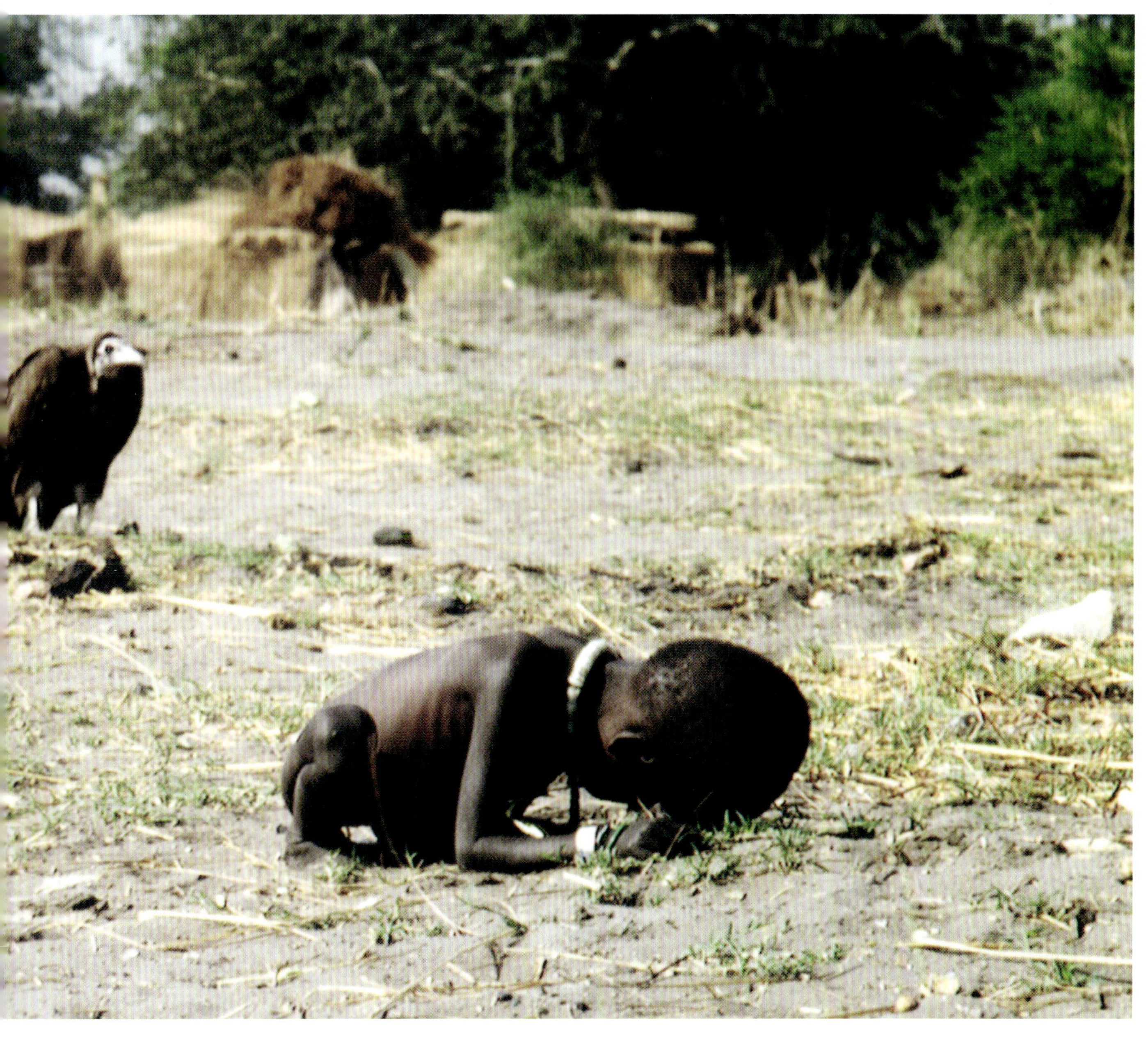

Joel Meyerowitz (born 1938)
***Amy, Cape Cod, Massachusetts* (1981)**

In 1992, the Dutch artist Rineke Dijkstra made a series of 'beach portraits' of girls and boys in their early teens (and sometimes younger) in the USA and in Western and Eastern Europe. Irrespective of where they come from, or however expensive or handed down their swim suits look, her subjects all seem equally self-conscious: on a museum wall, they look like monuments to teenage awkwardness. The fact that we have all been that age, which is glorious and terrifying at the same time, might well explain the iconic status of Dijkstra's photograph of a Polish girl in a green bathing suit, which is often compared to Sandro Botticelli's *Birth of Venus* (1484–6). However, in the Renaissance painting Venus rises from a shell in the sea close to the shore, whereas Dijkstra's muse, standing firmly on dry land, is less bombastic and does not demand our admiration. The Polish girl was not asked to strike a contrapposto pose; she did it unconsciously.

In 1987, Annie Leibovitz took a photograph of Willie Shoemaker and Wilt Chamberlain at the beach in Malibu, California, for an advertising campaign for American Express. Although the two men appear more confident than the young Polish girl, their poses are strangely reminiscent. In 1983, years before Leibovitz and Dijkstra made their beach photos, the American street photographer Joel Meyerowitz photographed this shy young girl on a beach in Cape Cod.

The fact that each image was created entirely separately makes the resemblance between them all the more remarkable. The three photographers and their subjects all seem to be taking inspiration from a collective unconscious, to represent something universal.

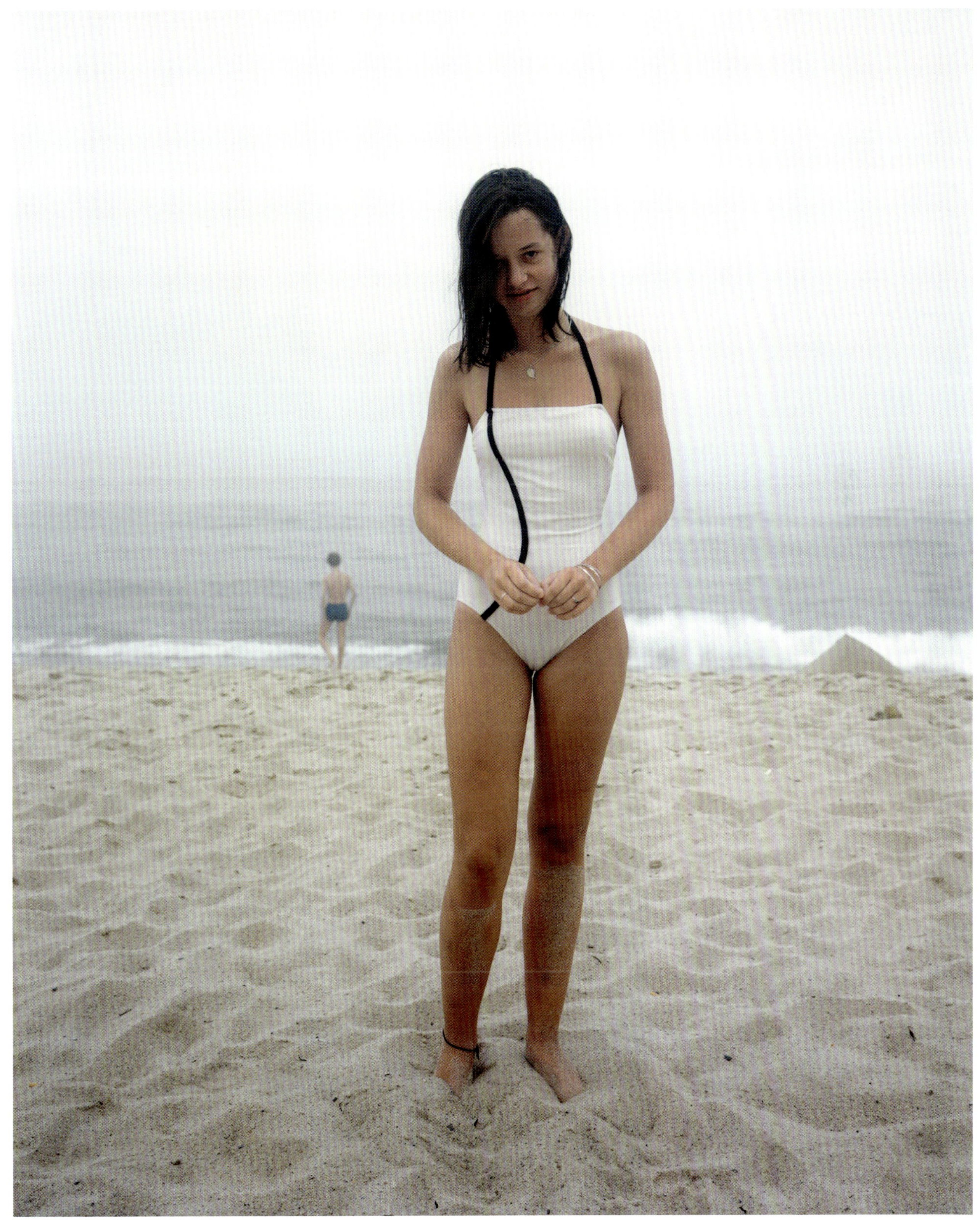

What makes it problematic?
What makes it problematic?
What makes it problematic?
What makes it problematic?

What makes it problematic?

What makes it problematic?
What makes it problematic?

The 19th-century psychiatrist and pioneering photographer Hugh Welch Diamond (1809–86) made portraits of his female patients at the Surrey County Asylum in the UK (see right). He claimed to use these photographs for diagnosis and treatment, as he believed that his patients' mental disorders were manifested in their facial expressions. The efficacy of his photo-therapy is obscure, yet the intentions of the photographer are clear. As a fervent amateur photographer, the photographs are far from being 'medically objective', and his subjective artistic aspirations are indicated by the use of props and different backgrounds. The series of photographed women raises questions not only of medical confidentiality, consent and voyeurism, but also class and power. When Diamond continued his psychiatry practice in a private asylum in Twickenham, he no longer photographed his patients. Apparently taking portraits of poor patients in a public institution was less problematic than photographing his wealthier, private ones.

The questions around consent are complex, and again it is not always a matter of what the photograph shows, but where and when it was taken and the context in which it is received. A contemporary example can illustrate this. Say you're a young street photographer. You are driven and sharp, and you never leave home without your camera, always ready to capture a scene or take a portrait. Your talent is recognised and your series of photographs of drunkards, who merrily posed for your camera, becomes a hit. The numbered and signed photographs are sold for high prices by a gallery and they find their way into museum collections. Ethical questions arise. While consent was given at the time the photograph was taken, were you, the photographer, exploiting someone's condition? Could your subjects in their inebriated state have been fully aware of the ramifications of that consent? Would it have made a difference if one of your photographs was sold to news media only?

The same issues of consent also occur when parents take photographs of their children. The children may have agreed at the time – but were they – could they be – fully aware of what they are agreeing to and the contexts in which their image will appear? This is particularly relevant to the field of blogging, where parents publicly share the quotidian moments of their lives with the children.

One can ask, then, if there are certain kinds of subjects who should not be photographed. Should we photograph the mentally unwell, victims of crime or natural disaster, or the dead? As in comedy, are there certain themes that can never be funny? Genocide or rape, for example? There is a fine line between communicating something important

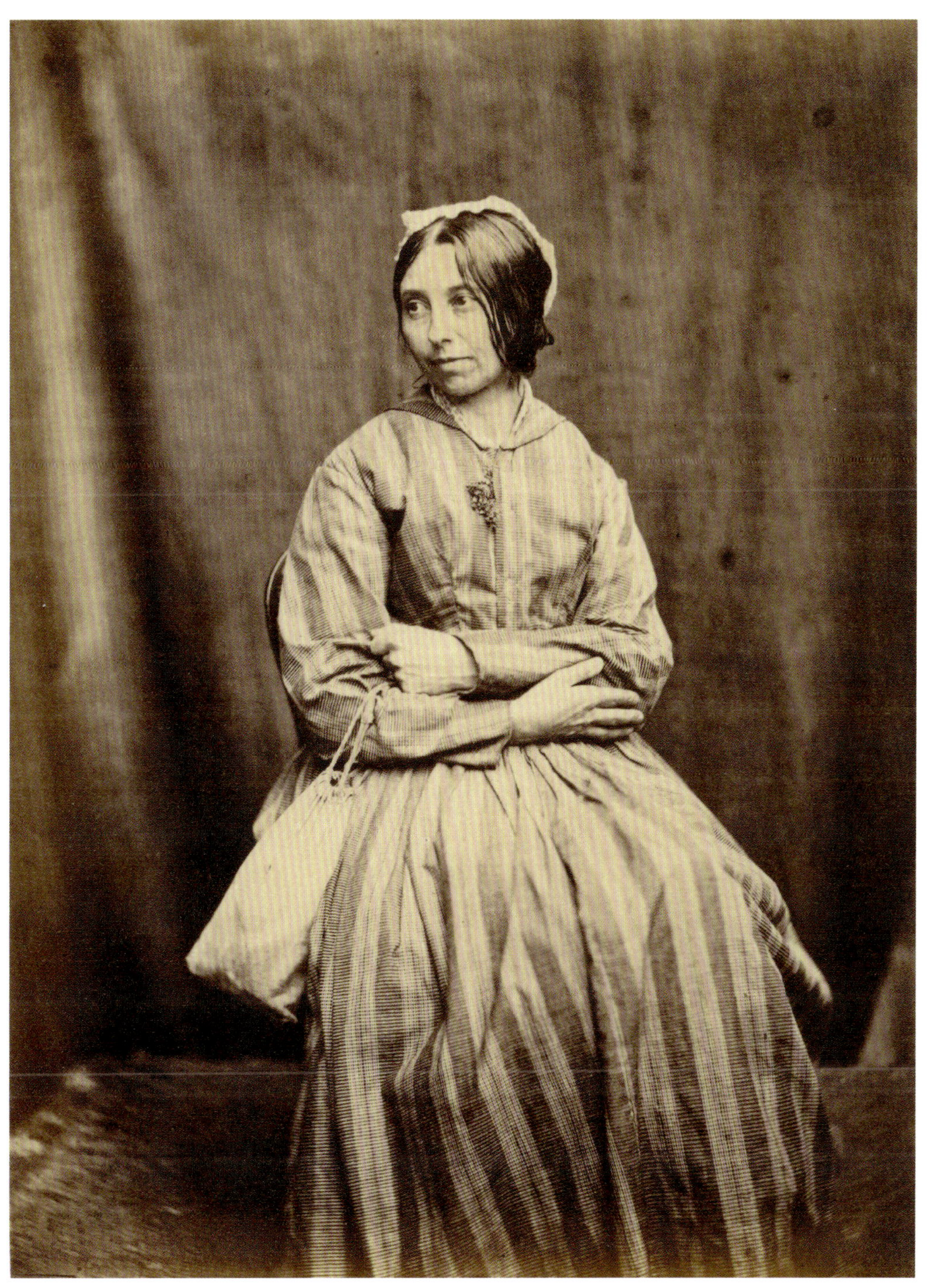

Hugh Welch Diamond, *Seated Woman With a Purse* (c.1855)

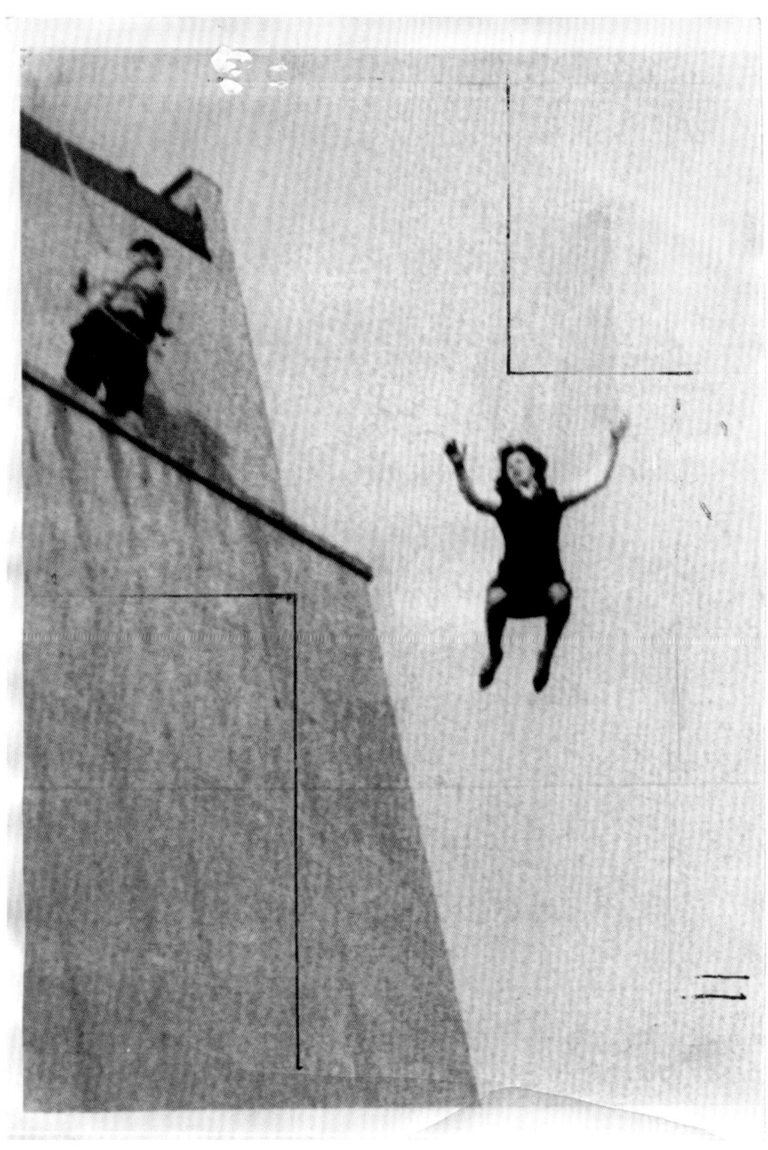

Unknown photographer, *Suicide Attempt by Ona Lee Fuller, Harlem, NY, April 1964* (1964)

and exploitation. Issues around censorship and the necessity of protecting free speech also apply. Rarely is it obvious, and each case really needs to be considered on an individual basis. This news photograph (left), for example, of a girl named Ona Lee Fuller was taken by a United Press International photographer in the 1960s, just as she leapt off the six-storey-high Salvation Army headquarters in New York City. According the caption on the back of the photograph, firefighters and police rescue units had tried to dissuade her. She landed in a net and was hospitalised. It could be argued that the photojournalist was profiting from Ona Lee Fuller's despair. Photographers regularly make a profit out of other people's misery, often risking their own lives in order to get a photograph. The lines that are drawn, the importance of the photograph and the context in which it is seen is something that each photographer must feel comfortable with.

In the traditional media, there have always been ample opportunities to censor images. Even on social media, images can be censored before and after being posted. In live streaming, however, this is complicated because while text can be screened for keywords, image-based content is much harder to screen, so even when the same ethical standards apply, there may not be the opportunity to impose them in real time. For a company like Facebook, which has to determine the rules of conduct for 2 billion users, dealing with the use of controversial imagery and at the same time achieving worldwide consensus has proved to be virtually impossible, despite its army of thousands of moderators.

The same applies for subtleties around humour and satire, and issues such as gender, race and religion, and sex and nudity. Take the iconic picture of a group of Vietnamese children fleeing after a napalm attack (see pages 116–7): it was banned by Facebook due to the nudity, which was detected by algorithms. Facebook initially defended its decision stating, 'While we recognise that this photo is iconic, it's difficult to create a distinction between allowing a photograph of a nude child in one instance and not others.' It later reversed its decision due to widespread criticism from news organisations and media outlets around the globe accusing it of censorship.

Similarly, people from different backgrounds have very different, culture-bound ideas about the definition of an unethical picture. Photographs of people mistreating animals may cause indignation in Western Europe, but this may not be the case in parts of the world where animals are not accorded the same status and rights. According to Facebook, using this kind of imagery is permitted as it can contribute to awareness of animal welfare. Distinctions become even less clear when such images are displayed as works of art – as can be seen when a video piece titled *Dogs That Cannot Touch Each Other*, included in the exhibition *Art and China after 1989: Theater of the World* at the Guggenheim Museum in New York in 2017, provoked protest and was eventually removed.

More than half a century after the photograph of Ona Lee Fuller was published, it is highly unlikely that any newspaper would release an image of someone trying to commit suicide (although online the ethics codes are more hazy). Most media work in the West has to conform with a code for responsible journalism, as the way in which a suicide is represented could evoke copycat behaviour. Professional societies such as the American National Press Photographers Association (NPPA) ask their members to adhere to a code of ethics. The NPAA code says, for example, that photographers should not intentionally stage a scene, should give consideration to vulnerable subjects, should provide context, and should avoid altering images in a way that is misrepresenting of subjects and misleading to viewers. This clearly leaves ample room for grey areas. For example, Facebook will allow users to livestream attempts to self-harm because they want to be sure that friends and family members can provide support and help, and the company 'doesn't want to censor or punish people in distress who are attempting suicide'.

The large quantities of distressing images found on all social media platforms resonate with a 'blink' mentality. In digital communication, nuances become increasingly rare, which seems to encourage competitive pursuit of an ever-escalating shock factor. You notice these kinds of images quickly, which is the point. With Facebook struggling to censor imagery adequately and appropriately, one would think the answer to the question of how to avoid making and spreading unethical pictures might be found in legislation, local customs and the users' good taste. However, as noted, each of these will differ according to where you are from and your cultural values. Simple answers to questions of taste and respectability in an increasingly global culture become ever more tangled, as legal answers and guidelines fail to keep up with technology.

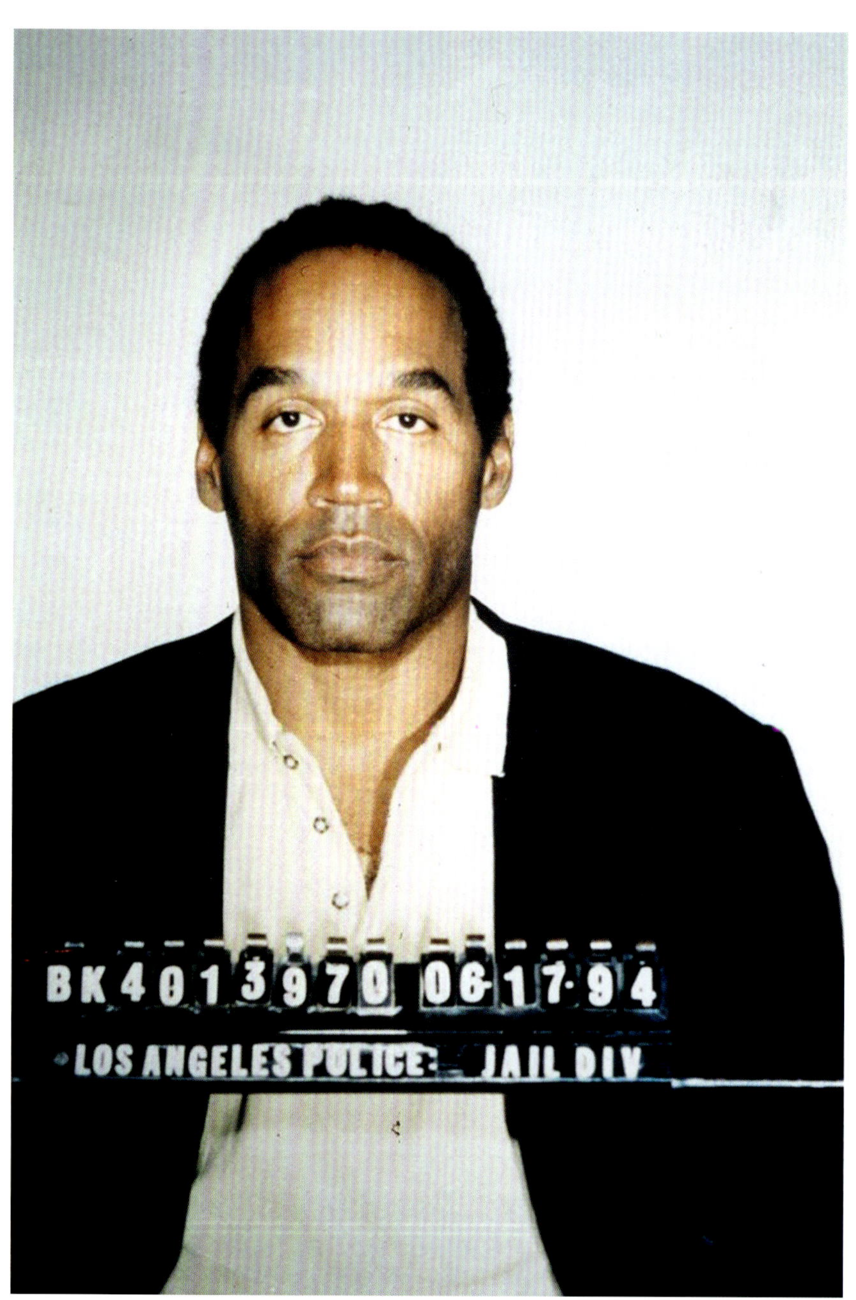
BK4013970 061794
LOS ANGELES POLICE: JAIL DIV

Police mugshot of OJ Simpson (1994)

This is a mugshot of the American footballer OJ Simpson, taken by the Los Angeles Police on Simpson's arrest in 1994 for the murder of his ex-wife, Nicole Brown Simpson and another man, Ronald Goldman. It was used in several publications reporting on the murder, including on the cover of *Time* magazine, for its 27 June 1994 edition.

Although, here, the flash seems to have made make his skin lighter (the light has also bleached the line between the white collar and his shirt), Simpson's skin appeared much darker in the version that found its way onto *Time*'s cover. It becomes clear when the cover is viewed beside the original police photograph that *Time* considerably darkened Simpson's skin and vignetted the photograph for more dramatic effect. The arrest and subsequent trial, from which he was acquitted, were loaded with racial tension, and *Time*'s treatment of the image on the cover caused an outcry. The editor of the magazine claimed 'no racial implication was intended, by *Time* or by the artist.'

It is hard to imagine the importance and reach of magazines 25 years ago. In an era before the mass-publication of photographs on the internet, their covers carried a great deal of cultural importance, and were seen by a wide audience. The misrepresentation of Simpson's skin colour was criticised for, as many believed, linking black skin with a propensity for violence. What the article inside said has become somewhat insignificant in comparison with the photograph. Although magazines still get into trouble for controversial editorial decisions around their cover images, often around issues of race (recently *Grazia*'s decision to airbrush Lupita Nyong'o's hairstyle on the cover of its 13 November 2017 issue; and the apparent darkening of Gigi Hadid's appearance on the May 2018 cover of *Vogue Italia* prompted accusations of simulating blackface), the power and presence they once wielded is hard to imagine now.

Kohei Yoshiyuki (born 1946)
***The Park* (1973)**

The Japanese photographer Kohei Yoshiyuki took this unusual series of photographs in Tokyo's Shinjuku, Yoyogi and Aoyama parks in the early 1970s, using an infrared flash during his night-time forays. At night, the parks became notorious gathering places for people to have sex, and also attracted spectators, who would watch the acts at often very close quarters, with hunter-style behaviour.

Hidden in the bushes Yoshiyuki spied on the spies, making the voyeurs, rather than the couples, the subject of his gaze. His audience, in turn, is invited to have the last look. In inviting the viewer in, however, the photographer also keeps them frustratingly removed from what everyone in the photographs is looking at. There may be a glimpse of underwear or a pulled-up shirt, but the viewer never fully sees what everyone else in the photograph does. The result is images that are a strange combination of the tender and the crude, the weird and the sexy.

Following a tradition of erotic art in Japan, most notably with woodcuts known as Shunga that were produced from the 16th century through to the 19th century, the charge of these photographs does not lie in the graphic nature of pornography but instead in voyeurism. At play here are unspoken rules of consent. One presumes that the photographer didn't ask the watchers for theirs, and it's unclear if the participants are completely complicit in being watched, or are performing or oblivious. Given this, there is something rather self-consciously creepy about the photographer's behaviour. Although he does make everyone anonymous, his motives and intentions are never quite clear.

The photographs, exhibited as a group in 1979 and published in book form in 1980, are puzzling documents illustrating significant issues in photography that are now more relevant than ever – such as privacy, voyeurism and surveillance. Moreover, they turn these issues on their heads. Who wants privacy and who doesn't, and where should the line between surveillance and voyeurism be drawn?

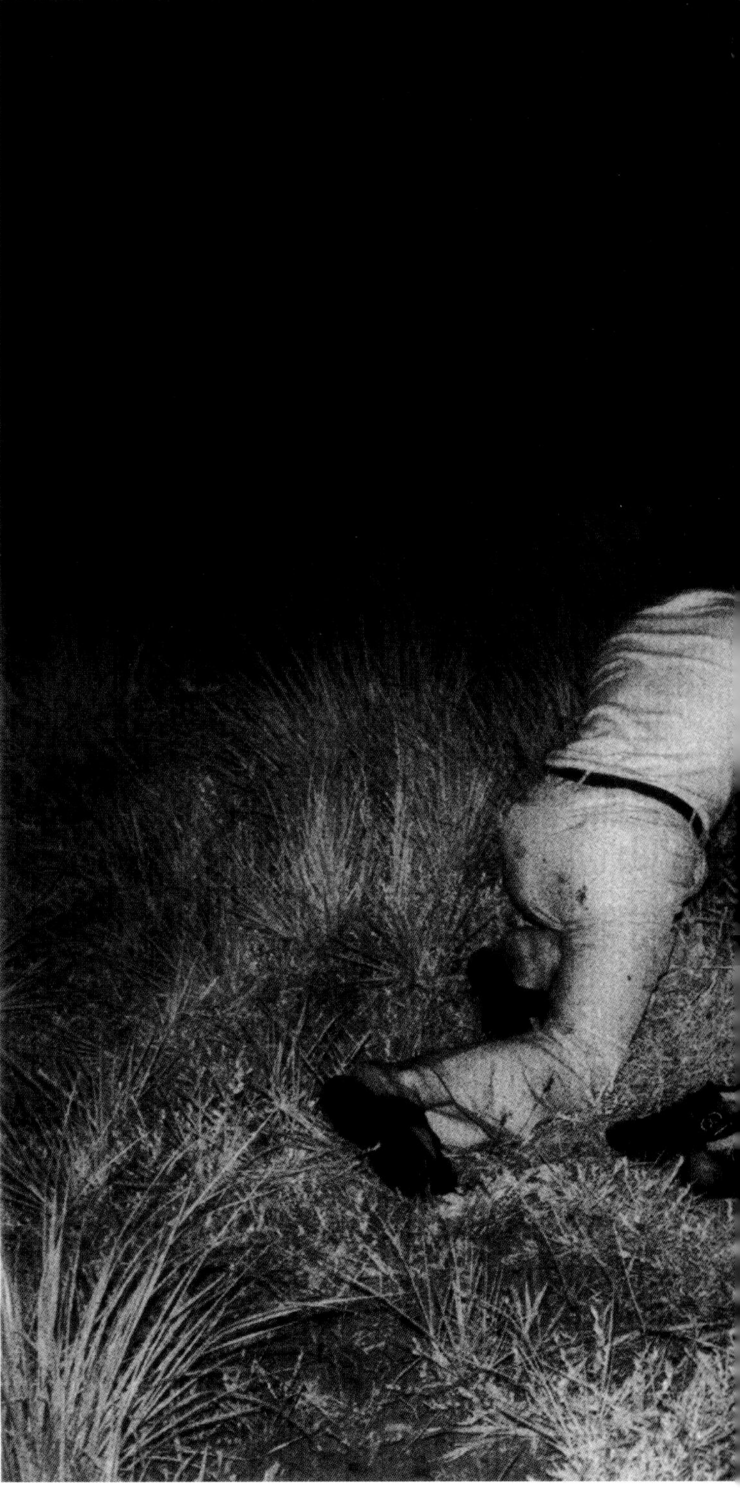

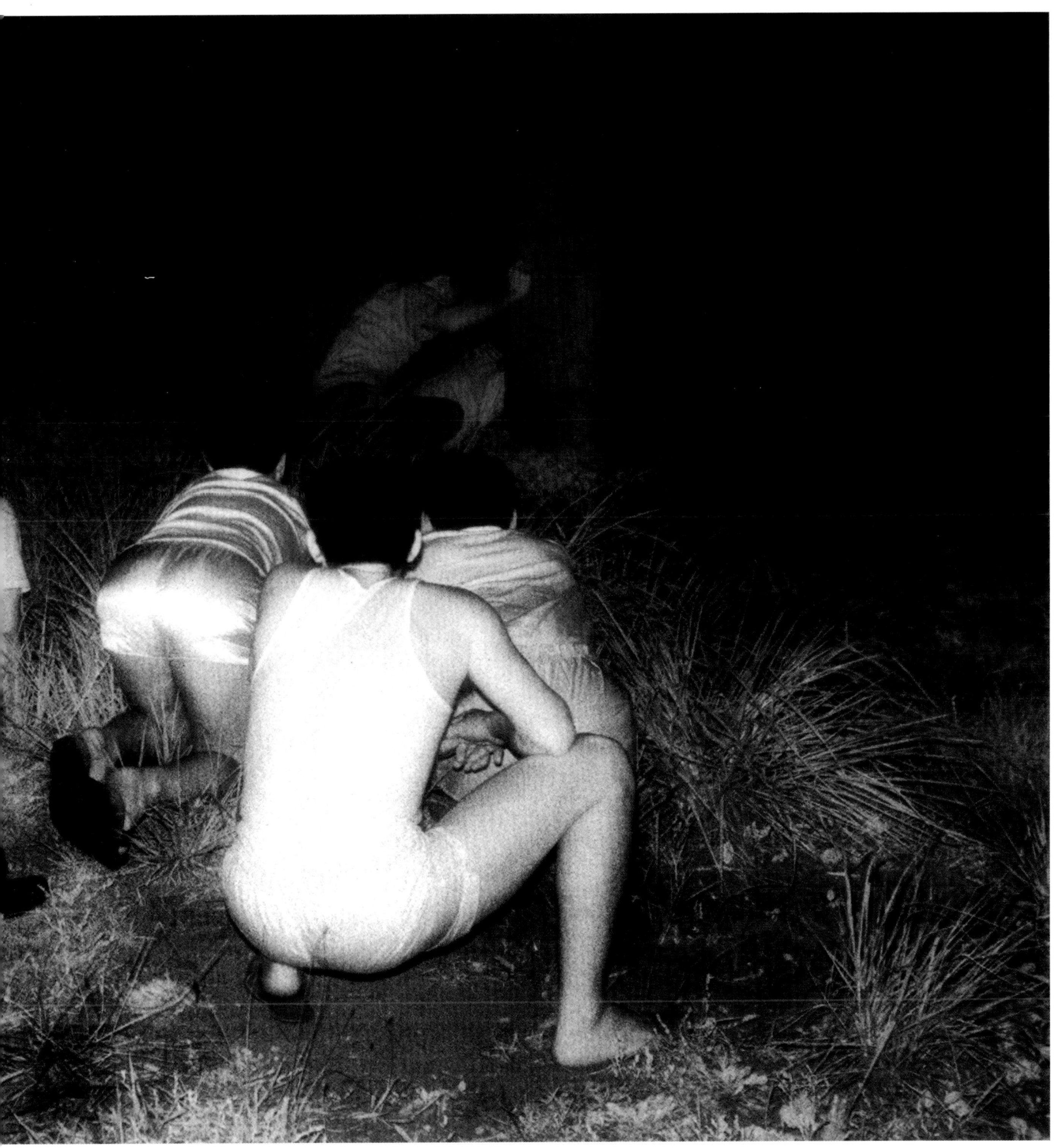

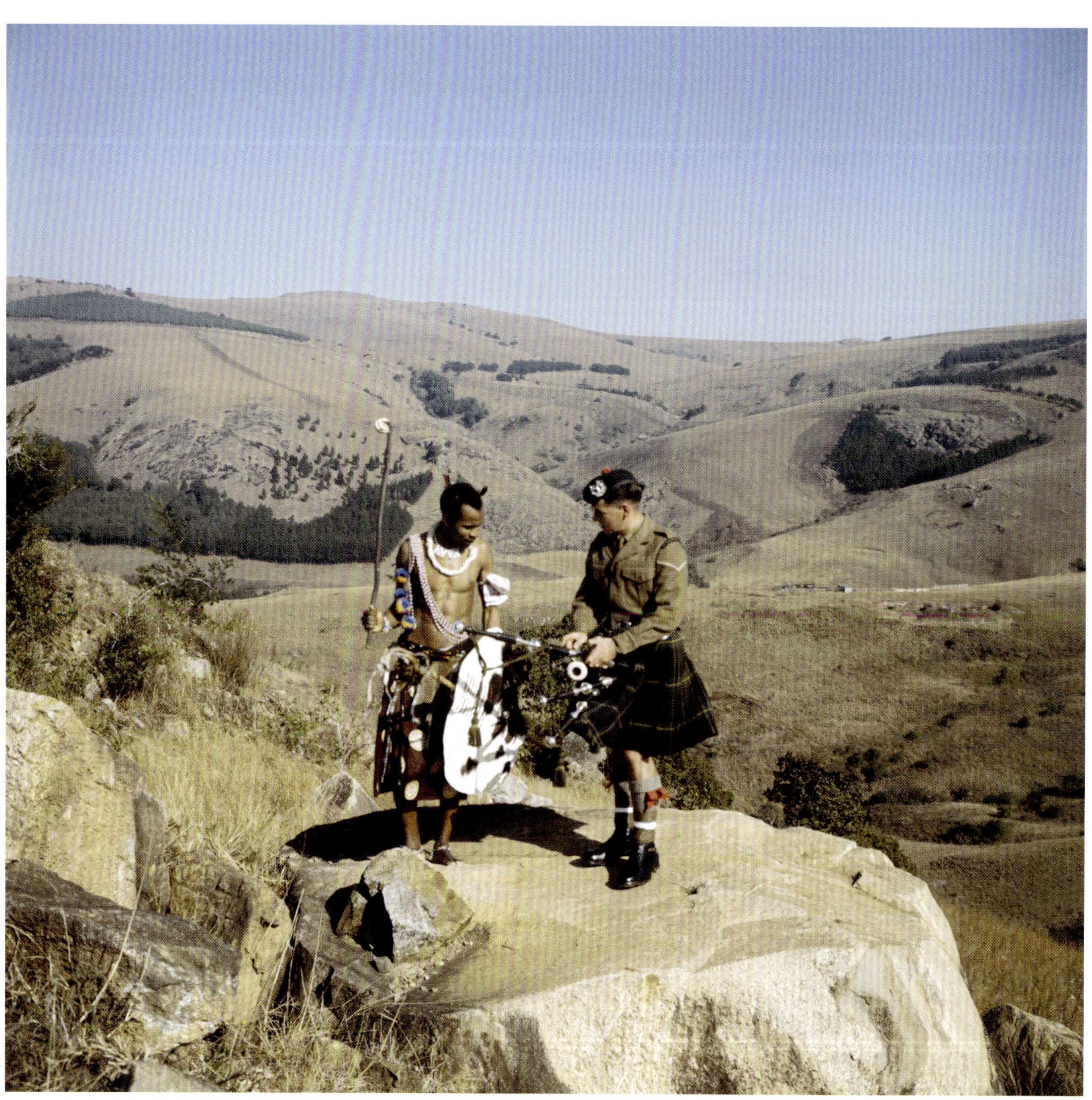

Unknown photographer
'A piper of the 1st Battalion Gordon Highlanders, meeting a warrior in full battle dress in East Africa, 1963' from *The British Empire in Colour* (2002)

This image, originally shot in 1963, appears in a book by Stewart Binns that accompanied a three-part television series about the British Empire, using original colour archive film. Unfortunately, it is not credited nor is any context given. The only information the viewer has is the caption, as given in the title above, which is incomplete in that it gives information only about the Scottish man and not the place or the tribe that the African man belongs to. It is left to the viewer to piece together the image based purely on what it represents and the context of it used in a book to represent the British Empire on television. The use of colour film and photography has a curious effect on the viewer who, at least until recently, was accustomed to seeing much of early and mid-20th-century history, such as the two world wars, in black and white. The effect of using colour is complex. It can perhaps appear to be more nostalgic, or perhaps even lessen the prejudice, discrimination and violence that often occurred. On the other hand it could be said that colour makes the world portrayed seem more like ours and so bring it closer.

This picture here – showing two warriors each elaborately dressed in the clothes of their respective clans – is a posed picture with a purposely upbeat feel presenting the two men as equals, however much we know this not to be true in the imperial gaze behind the camera. It is taken with a photojournalist's instinct for drama, here achieved by placing both men on what looks like a cliff edge and in front of a spectacular view. It is highly crafted (colour photography has not always been an easy process) with a careful eye for muted tones, turning a complex relation into an pretty, idealised image.

Post-colonial theory is an attempt to look at the wider and lasting issues of imperialism, and has done much to push thinking about representation forward, especially where stories have previously been told only from one side. How do you get the political and social complexities of nations, such as the violence of the Mau Mau Uprising (1952–84) in British-ruled Kenya, across in photographs alone? One can ask whether it is even possible.

Weegee (Arthur Fellig) (1899–1968)
***Life Saving* (1940)**

Weegee was quite a character. Bold and brazen, he was a self-taught photographer of a kind that no longer exists. As a freelance news photographer active in the Lower East Side of Manhattan, New York, he was aware that he had to be the first to arrive 'on the scene'. This is why he slept in his clothes next to his portable police-band shortwave radio, ready to jump into his car – which was equipped with a self-built darkroom – as soon as a report of a murder, manslaughter or fire came through. Sometimes Weegee was there even before the police arrived. The story goes that he would then not hesitate to rearrange a corpse if doing so resulted in a better picture.

Weegee took this photo on Coney Island, New York City's summer pleasure grounds. A young man has drowned and has been taken out of the water by the rescue brigade. He is given oxygen and a doctor is with him, wearing a stethoscope to detect a heartbeat, but it does not look good. Weegee has already pushed himself forward through a crowd of bystanders as he wants to shoot the best possible picture. How did he get the attention of the distressed girl who is kneeling by her drowned boyfriend? The only explanation for her strange, automatic smile is that Weegee has called something like 'Smile for the camera!' This would certainly explain the furious looks of the crowd behind her.

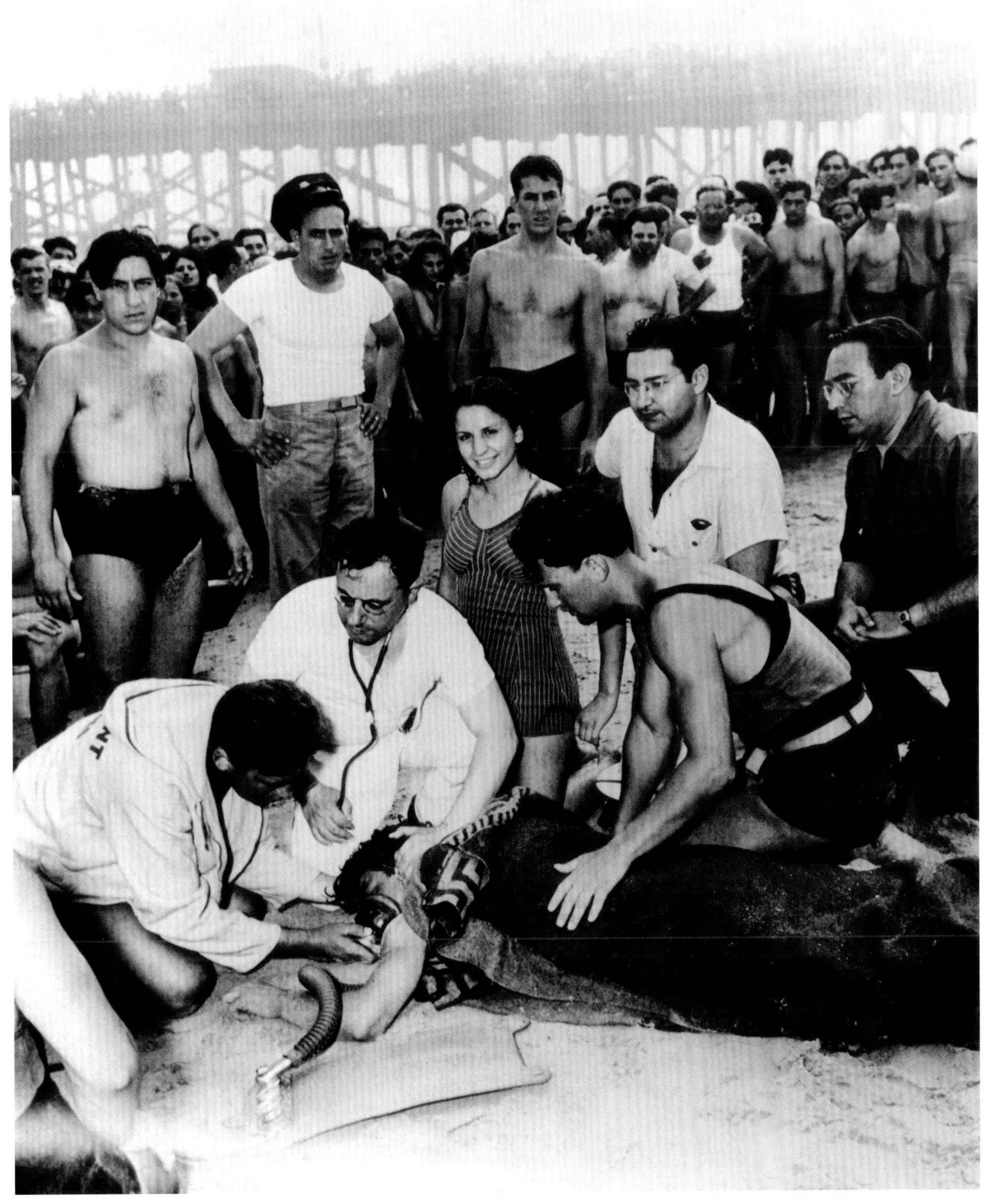

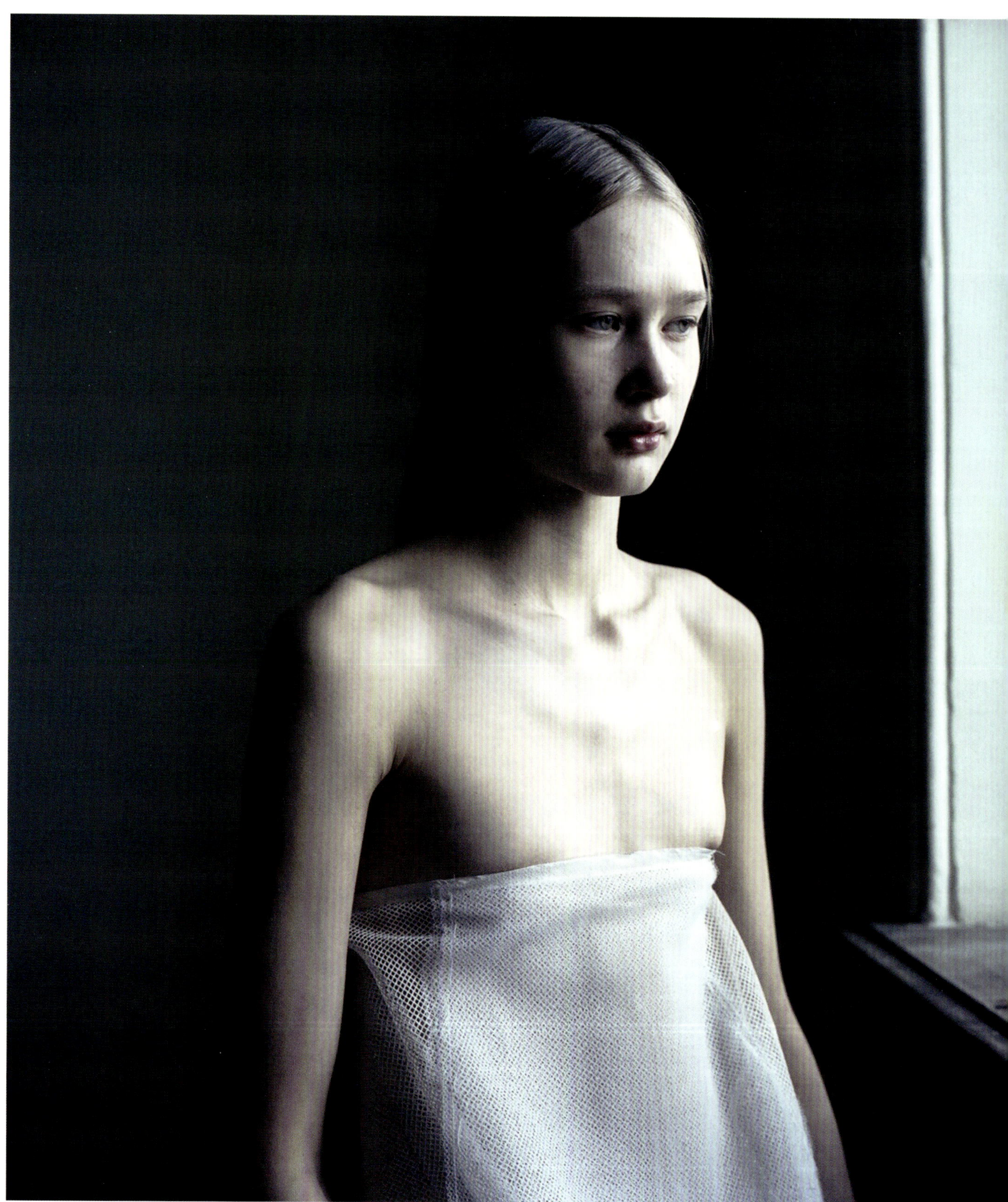

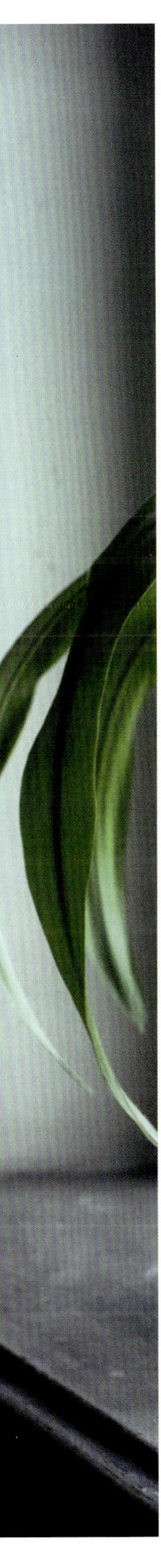

Hellen van Meene (born 1972)
***Untitled (#365)* (2010)**

Sometimes we come across a photograph and we do not know what to think of it. These are often intriguing images which encourage us as viewers to think a little harder. Doubt can be an important part of the intellectual process of looking. If you do not know what to think of this picture, first try to imagine that you are being asked by a photographer to pose like this. How would that make you feel?

Within the context of this chapter, many works from the Dutch artist Hellen van Meene's oeuvre could have been selected. She has made children and adolescents one of the most important subject areas in her work and in doing so she ventures into contentious territory. After all, an adult (usually and at least superficially) has some choice whether or not she or he wants to be photographed, and over what the end result might be; an adult can also indicate limits. Children do not always know how they are expected to act in a picture, and tend to follow the instructions or wishes of the photographer, especially when that photographer radiates authority inspired by their status as a professional or celebrated artist.

Van Meene finds her young models both within her family circle and out on the street. How special must these children feel to be picked out of a crowd and photographed by a distinguished photographer? Of course, the photo will be successful aesthetically and resonate widely only if the sitter cooperates. Van Meene aims to capture an awkward phase between childhood and adolescence. But does she encourage a child to exceed her limits? And to what degree is she responsible for how we look at her images?

Volker Krämer (c.1943–1999)
***Three tiny people working on a funfair in Hassloch, Western Germany* (1977)**

Fortunately, the times when fairground folk earned their money by selling tickets to people who wanted to peek behind a curtain to see a bearded woman, an 'Elephant Man' or an 'exotic' black woman are over. People with restricted growth, however, can still be seen today in a specially designed theme park in China, and until the mid-1980s they were a fixture in West Germany, where this photograph was taken by the German photographer Volker Krämer. Until he was shot and killed in Kosovo in 1999, Krämer worked for *Stern* magazine (for whom this image was shot) for decades, often capturing ironic situations.

In this photograph, Krämer shows spectators at a funfair scrambling in front of a window to get a look at three neatly dressed people with dwarfism in their living quarters. Grandfathers, mothers, fathers and children press themselves against the window. Only the woman in the middle shows any discomfort in being looked at from two sides at the same time. Of course, it is impossible to know what people are thinking in photographs; it's always a matter of conjecture.

The photograph confronts us with ourselves, however: as a viewer, we stand in the place of the photographer, which is an uncomfortable position to be in. The eye contact we make with the three people who are on display, and with the child outside, makes us complicit. Who should feel shame? The people with dwarfism because they do not belong to a majority, or the viewers?

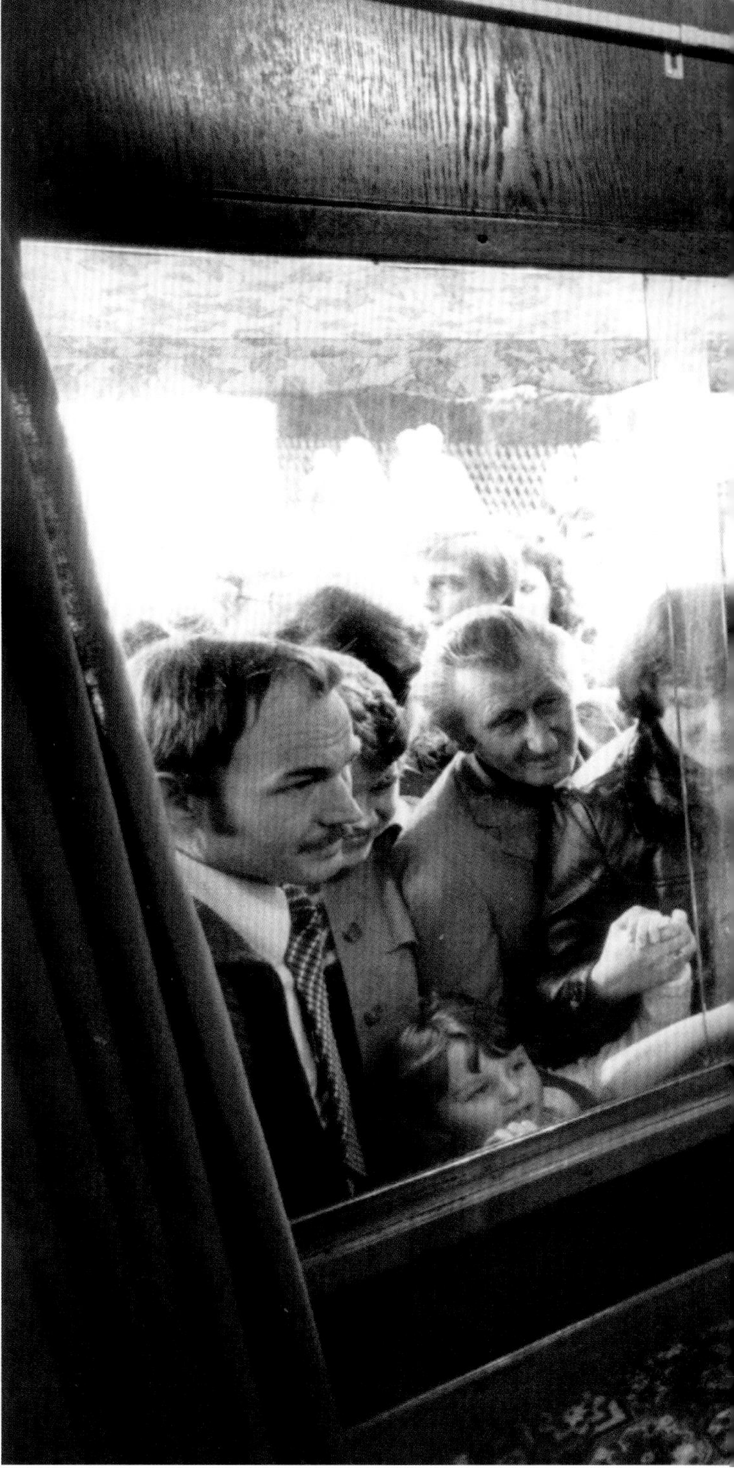

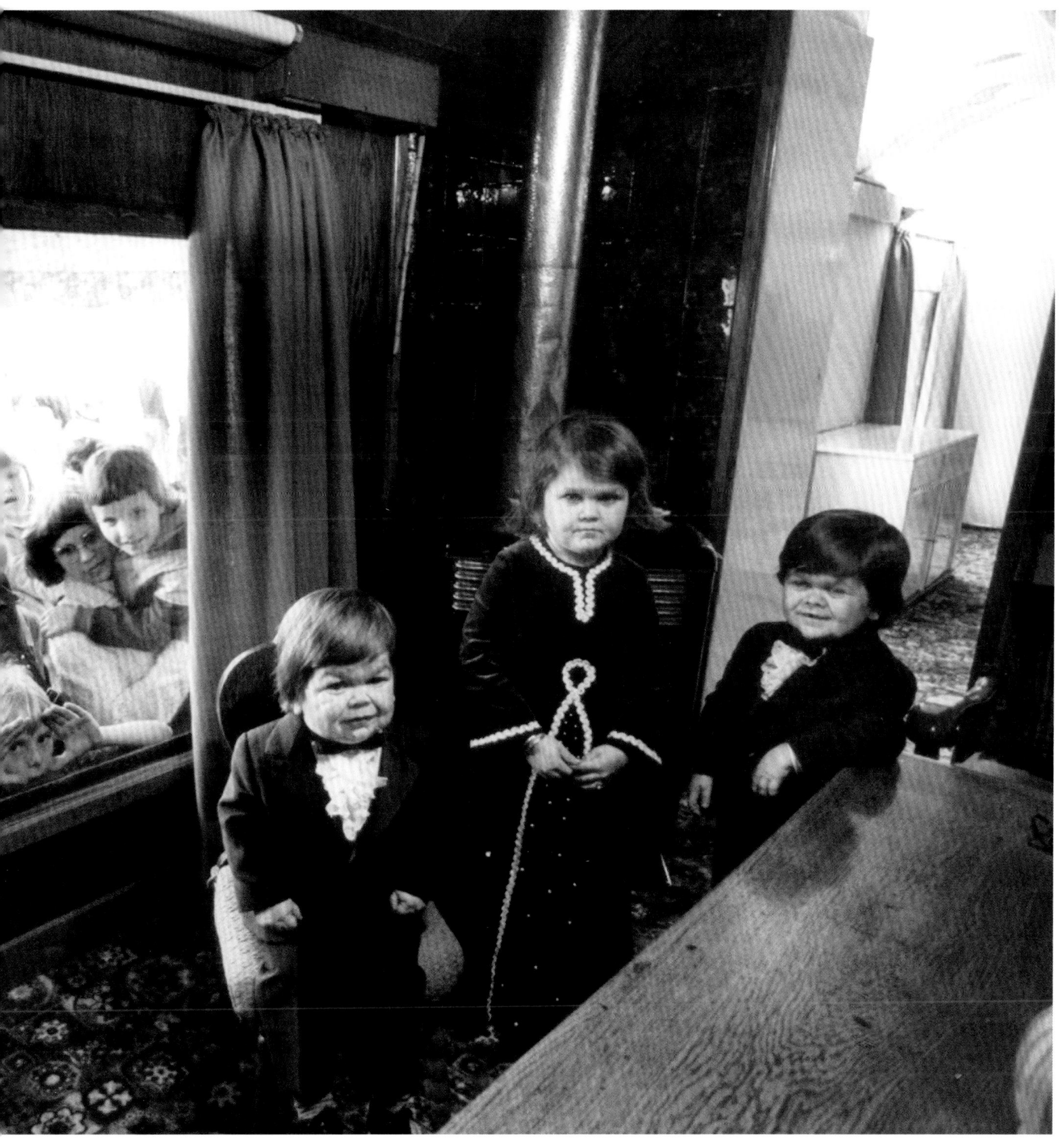

Who do you
think you are?
**Who do you
think you are?**
Who do you
think you are?
Who do you
think you are?
Who do you
think you are?
Who do you
think you are?
Who do you
think you are?

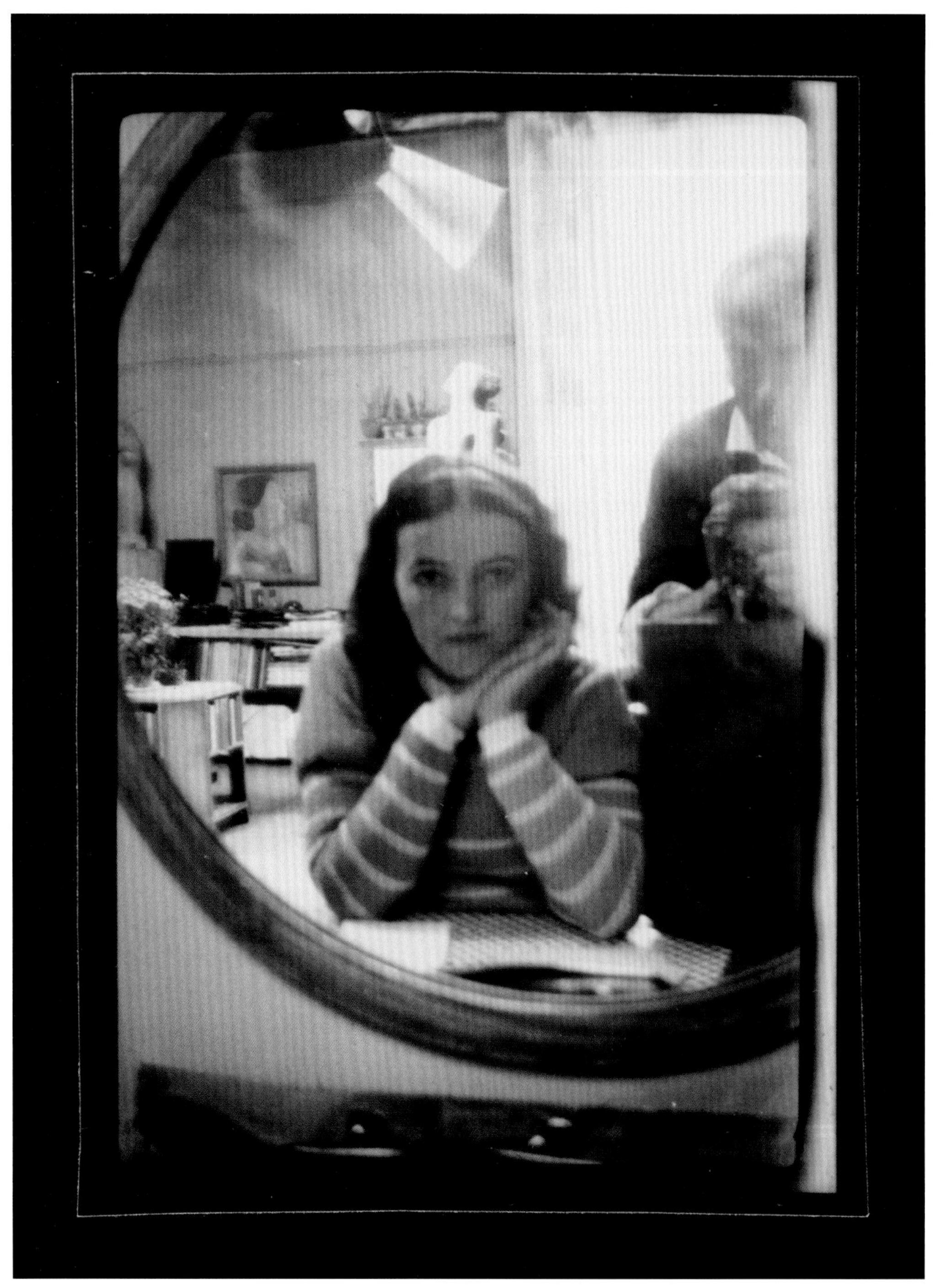

Ben Nicholson, *Ben Nicholson taking a photograph of Barbara Hepworth* (c.1932)

In today's culture, photographing oneself or being photographed has become almost as common as eating and sleeping. Social media timelines flow like visual autobiographies, sharing and commenting on a life lived. We perceive our online life on Snapchat, Instagram and Facebook as nearly-real-time visual accounts of what we are doing and what we look like on that day. Although what we post might be carefully chosen, filtered and performed, our online identity is more commonly seen as an outward gesture of our personality and identity and of how we wish to present ourselves in the wider world.

In this picture (left), the British painter Ben Nicholson (1894–1982) is photographing the sculptor Barbara Hepworth. With Nicholson just in view at the right-hand side of the frame, the photograph could also be read as a self-portrait with his wife-to-be. He is already in Hepworth's life, but not entirely. The mirror is a common strategy for self-portraiture – but can it tell us anything more about ourselves than how we actually look at that moment? Mirrors and windows as metaphors litter the history of photographic self-portraiture, supposedly reflecting, and giving access to, key elements of our identity onto the paper.

Today, the mirror has become ubiquitous in 'selfie culture'. While the selfie is a relatively new form in terms of photographic genres, the inclusion of the mirror in the frame is part of photographic self-portraiture and its history, which is commonly understood to have, to a certain extent, a 'truth-telling' or testimonial function. When considering the selfie as it is today, cultural trends and preoccupations must also be considered – such as the rise of the personal blog and with this the ability (and intention) to record and distribute personal information to a potentially large audience.

It is the element of dissemination and response that differentiates the selfie from the traditional self-portrait, the latter typically made by artists for use by a gallery, and less commonly for the personal album. What sets selfies so dramatically apart from earlier analogue snapshots (self-portraits or not) is the reliance of the online community upon a communal understanding of norms and conventions. This codifies and crystallises selfie culture as a very specific movement in contemporary photographic culture. The use of hashtags, tagging and emoticons/emojis, and extended multivocal commentary, is completely new to photography, allowing photographs to be experienced in a fluid dynamic with an emphasis on grouping, categories and taxonomies.

How we see ourselves does not necessarily come from who we really are but from how we believe other people see us. This idea comes from the American sociologist Charles Horton Cooley, who developed the 'looking-glass self' theory – the cornerstone of the theory of socialisation – which states that we shape our self-concept based on our understanding of how others see and evaluate us. This concept cuts to the core of the selfie, where affirmation is a key expectation. As long as we interact with others, we are vulnerable to our own self-image being damaged or inflated. Contemporary studies show that we are not shaped just by how others see us, but also by the creation of a collective social identity that contrasts us against relevant others. A selfie thus also shows your network that you are one of 'them', a peer, which helps establish confidence.

These ideas are tested out in the 1994 series *Scarred for Life* by Australian artist Tracey Moffatt (born 1960). The text for the image from the series entitled *Useless, 1974* (opposite, top) reads, 'Her father's nickname for her was "useless".' When looking at the picture, we have to speculate. We cannot know what she is thinking, but we can see she does not look particularly useless. She is working and her gaze is strong. This is not straightforward documentation – Moffatt casts actors and sets her photographs in the past, dismantling photography's affiliation with truth-telling, which traditionally has been at the heart of many explorations of identity in art or literature. Neither can the viewer be sure whether Moffatt is making autobiographical references or intending a more general work, dealing with the politics of identity, be that through race or gender. Moffatt's works often question established norms and positions of power using a wide range of photographic techniques and methods of presentation.

Questions of self and identity have long concerned artists, and are intensified as digital lives become ubiquitous and an aspect of performance becomes the norm in terms of modes of behaviour. Identity can be explored through the body or through portraiture, as we discussed above, but also through the use of objects or landscape. The identity being explored does not necessarily have to be personal; it can also be cultural, political or national.

Photographers often try to avoid archetypes, stereotypes and exclusivity. So why does British artist Keith Arnatt (1930–2008) pigeonhole people in his series *Gardeners* (1978–9; right, bottom)? We can ask what gives these people the identity of 'gardener' – the title that designates them as such, or their location and signifiying props? Would they still be gardeners if they were not photographed in their gardens? Their photographic performance (and the 'stage') is key. Some photographers such as August Sander and Irving Penn have set out to capture trade identities – is that what Arnatt is doing here? In reality, very few people are professional gardeners, and the man here does not look like he makes his living in this way. So here the identity is not a professional one, but a mixture of self-identification and the photographer's projection.

Arnatt's series explores sociological and national aspects of a particularly British cross-section of society while simultaneously raising questions about photography's role in shaping or making that collective identity. Examples like these highlight the close relationship photography has always had with dealing with issues of identity – from those of the famous who manipulate it and try to control the way they are seen to those who take matters into their own hands through photo sharing and social networking sites.

Many contemporary artists focus on the fluidity of identity in a world where both the mass media and social media are omnipresent. As our culture comes to rely on photographs more and more, how we present ourselves through those pictures comes as a stand-in for our 'true' self. This in turn becomes more informed by the way those photographs are received. As our connections to the world and the daily choices we make define us, our identity is a complex affair that is in constant flux – a never-ending efflorescence of layers, experiences and images.

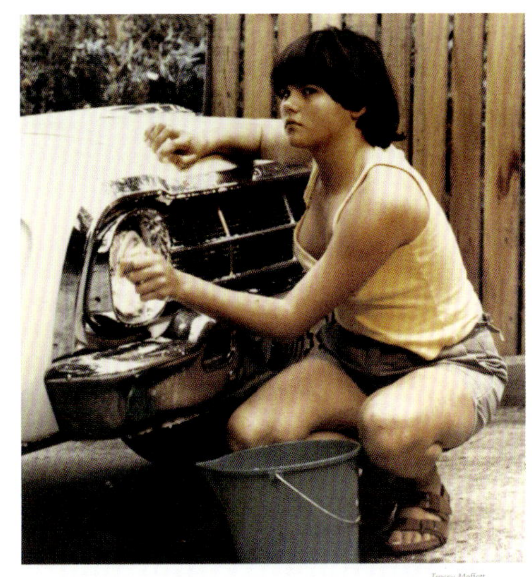

Tracey Moffatt, *Useless, 1974* (1994)

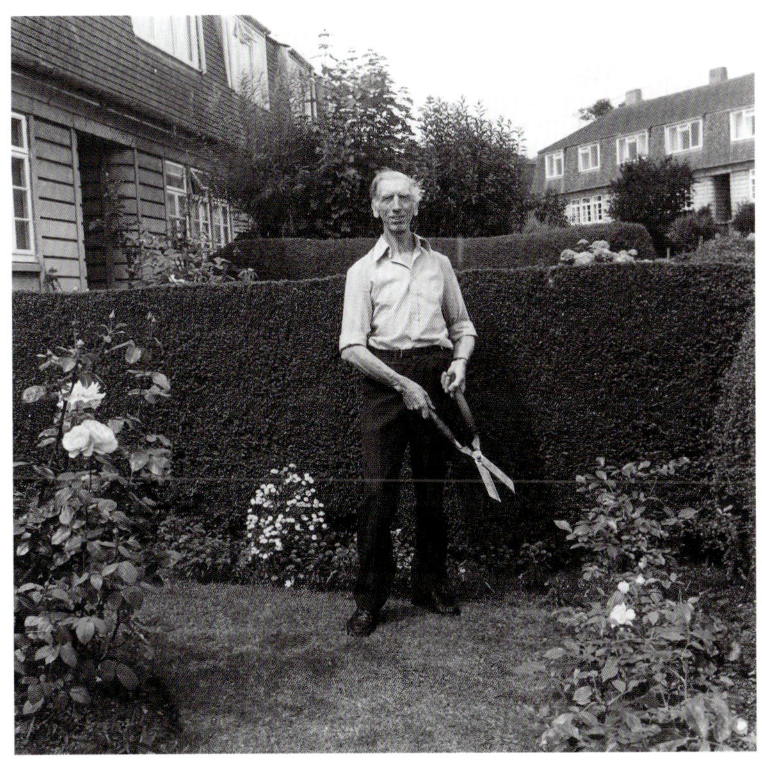

Keith Arnatt, from *Gardeners* (1978–9)

Tracey Emin (born 1963)
***Outside Myself (Monument Valley)* (1995–1997)**

Tracey Emin works across a range of media, often incorporating several within a single artwork. For example, the artwork here can be said to comprise the performance of reading, the book she has written, and the chair she has embroidered and sits on, as well as the photograph that contains the other three. It was taken on a road trip in the USA. Driving from San Francisco to New York, Emin would stop and read from her book *Exploration of the Soul* (1994). Her boyfriend, who was accompanying her on the trip, photographed her. The book, written in ten days, is an intense autobiographical reflection on her life.

Is this picture a self-portrait or a portrait of Emin? Issues of authorship often arise with self-portraits. In many instances it does not matter who pressed the button, as it is the artist who has conceived the idea, and to whom credit must thus be given. Here, Emin is presenting a persona: she is performing being an artist while simultaneously being an artist. This raises questions about what the 'self' is in a self-portrait, and where it is located. When artists conflate their lives with their art, they might exaggerate their experiences for the sake of making better art, just as someone writing a memoir might emphasise certain details and omit others in order to make a better story. In art, a self-portrait has traditionally been understood as an outward expression of inward emotion, but with the advent of post-modernism it is hard to look at a picture such as this and see Emin's inner existential being. That is not the point of the work here – instead it is a mixture of self-regard, self-memorial – a marker of being near the iconic mesas in the background – and self-revelation all created for the camera.

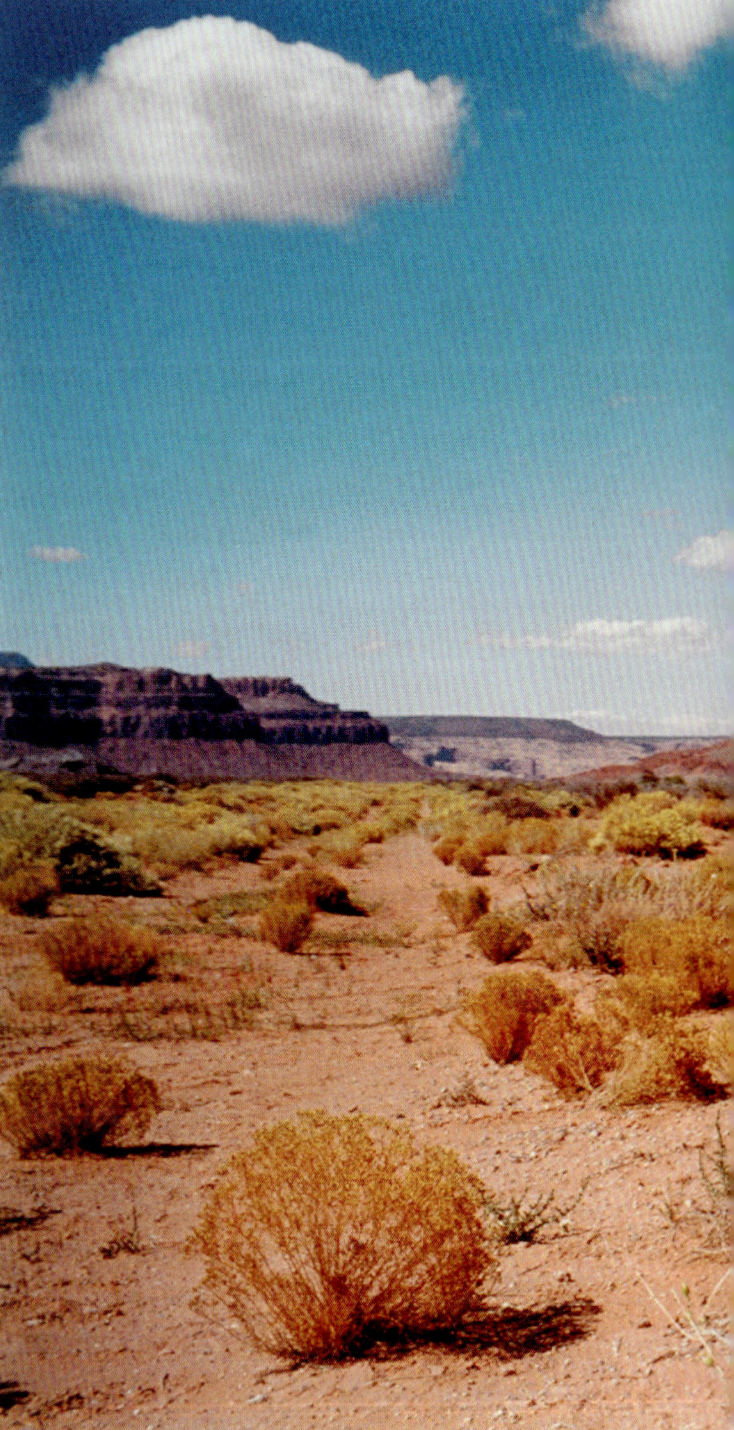

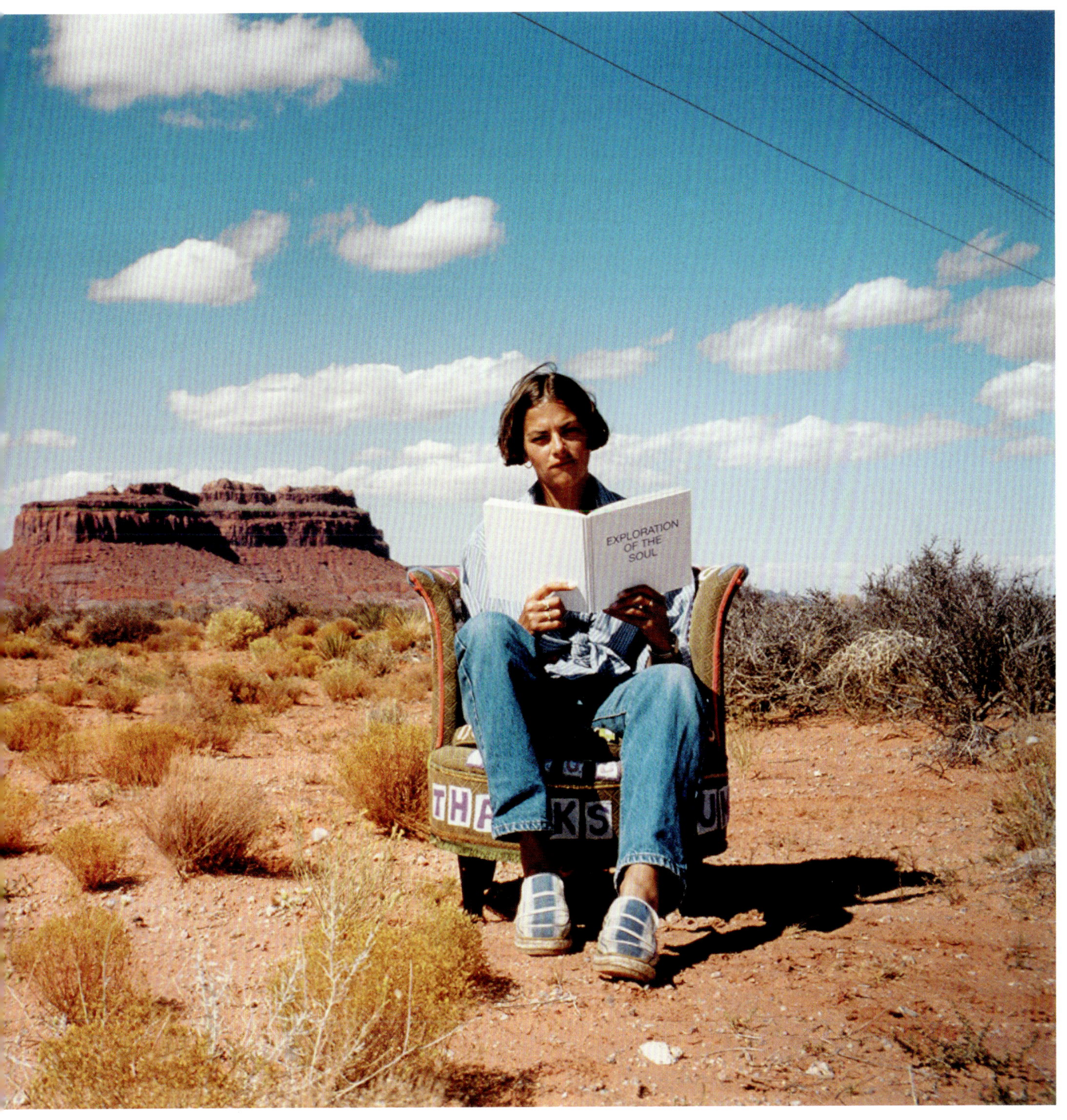
EXPLORATION
OF THE
SOUL

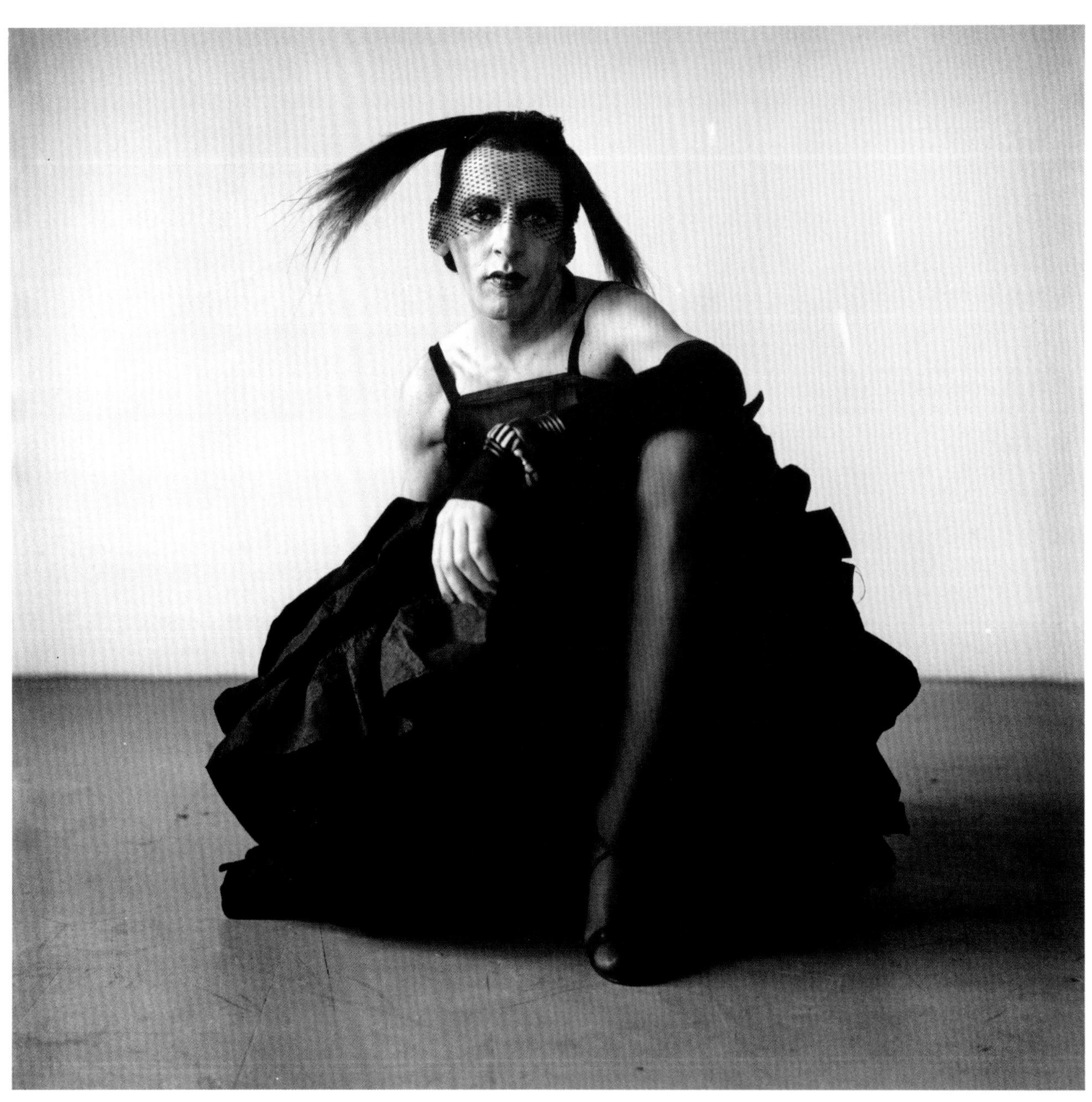

Peter Hujar (1934–1987)
***John Heys in Lana Turner's Gown (II)* (1979)**

Peter Hujar was a crucial figure in photographing New York City's gay subculture during the 1970s and 1980s. However, he is best known for his portraits of the people of the downtown art scene, including Susan Sontag, William Burroughs, Fran Leibowitz, Andy Warhol and John Waters. He captured his subjects in tender black and white and his prints are sumptuous in their exquisite quality of texture and tone. This approach deeply influenced the slightly younger Robert Mapplethorpe, who became considerably more well-known and successful.

Because many of Hujar's portraits were of friends, there is an intimacy to them and a feeling that the subjects could be whoever they wanted. There is no superficiality to these pictures, and they were not made for commercial or narcissistic purposes. The real attraction and authenticity of feeling between sitter and artist gives a depth and connection that can be felt by those witnessing the intensity of the photographs. This is especially so in this portrait of the film director John Heys wearing the actress Lana Turner's gown. The knowledge that the gown once belonged to one of Hollywood's most glamorous and notorious actresses adds a sense of melancholy to the scene. But the drama that followed her is not held mimetically in her dress, and her history is not translated to the film director when he wears her clothes. Heys does not 'act the part'. Instead, he is entirely himself and absolutely in the moment of having his portrait taken.

Relatively unsung as an artist during his lifetime, Hujar was overshadowed by his more provocative artistic peers such as Mapplethorpe and Nan Goldin, who gained popularity during the politically heightened time of the AIDS crisis that they documented. Hujar's more erotic work was not shown or collected regularly, and although artists such as Diane Arbus had exhibited images of men in drag, it was in the context of otherness rather than with the tenderness and inclusivity that we see here.

Martin Parr (born 1952)
Sand Bay, England **(1997)**

This photograph comes from a series about Britain titled *Common Sense*. This title suggests a rather satirical comment on the famous British pragmatism – a value much vaunted by traditionalist sectors of the country. Martin Parr taps into this and works with stereotypes. A simple cup of tea is never just a picture of a cup of tea; it is a lightning rod that says something about a nation. He revels in cliché – fish and chips and tea represent British culture and values, just as hamburgers and coke are shorthand for America. We get this instantly, with both a smile of recognition and a sigh of frustration at this perpetuation of stereotypes.

The tea here is not only about literal taste but also cultural and personal and class taste (Parr is rumoured to have two jars of tea bags in his studio – one labelled 'posh' the other 'peasant'). No other photographer understands the intricacies and subtleties of class and aspiration like Parr. It is telling that he chose to have his tea in a Willow pattern cup and saucer, a Chinese-inspired design that first became popular at the end of the 18th century and has connotations of a lost empire, rather than in a mug. The effect is one of prissiness or perceived conformism even though the tea is served with milk, which has rather more workaday connotations in comparison with the elevated way tea is served in the East. The red-and-white gingham tablecloth on which the tea is served is also significant: those who can read the signs and signifiers know instantly that this tea is being served at a village fête or café, and not in the home.

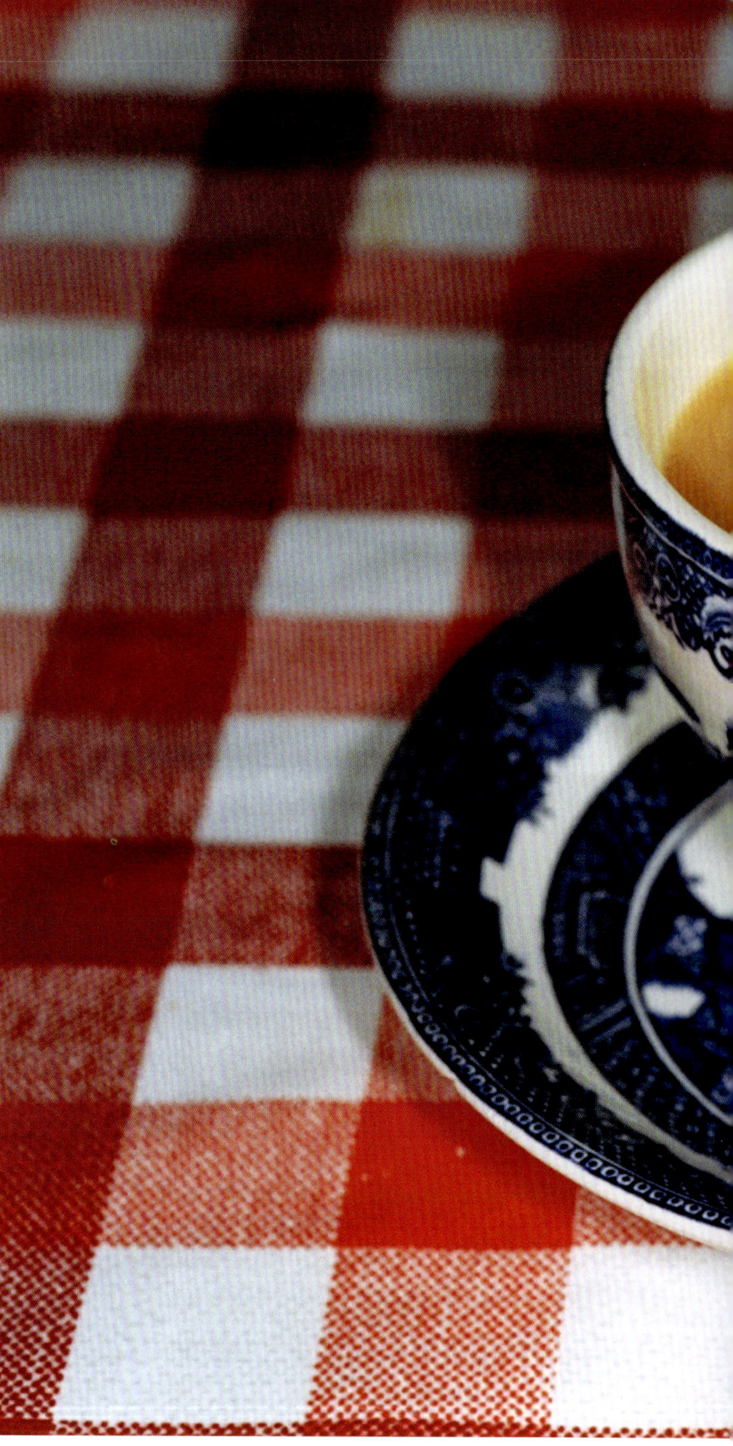

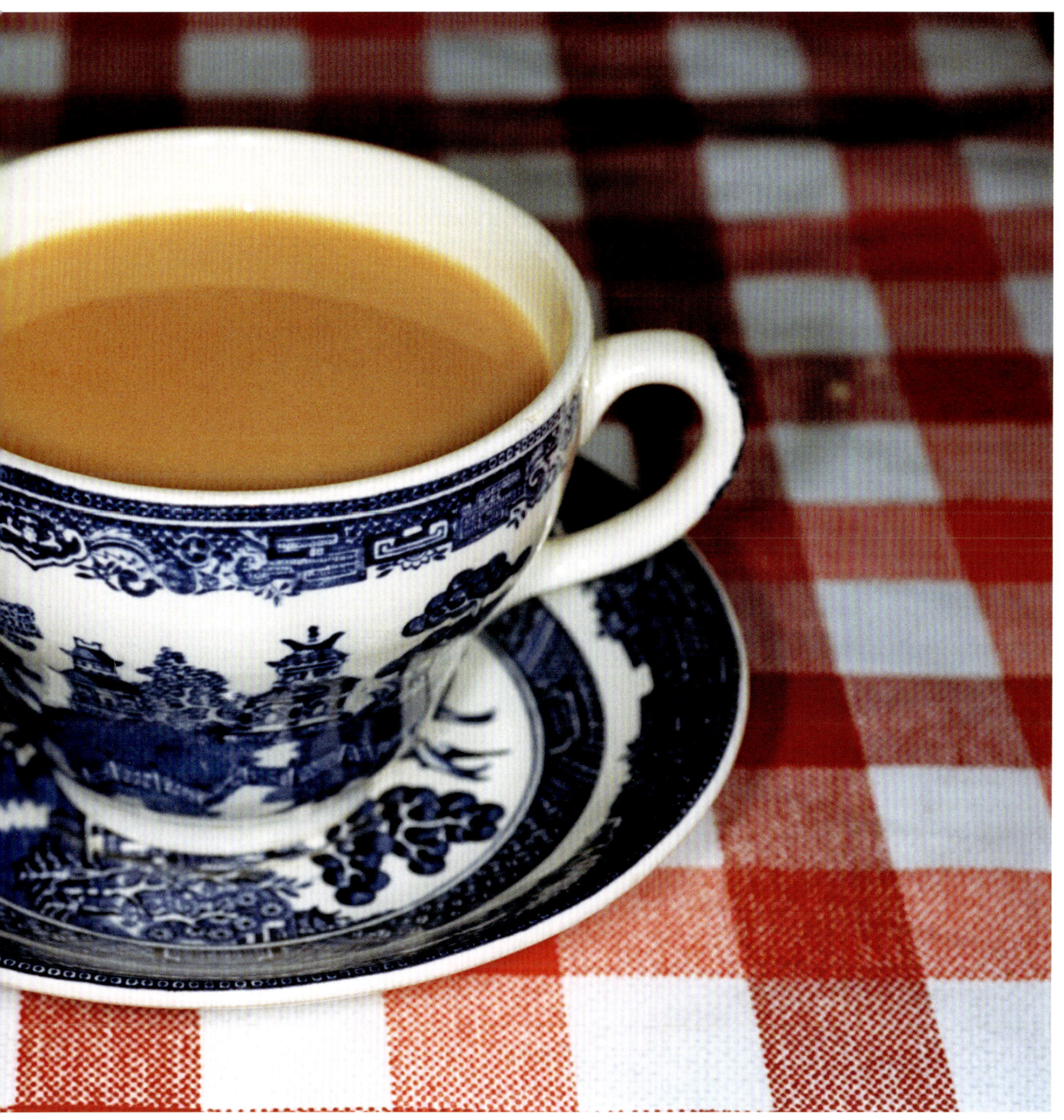

Don McCullin (born 1935)
***Shell-shocked US Marine, The Battle of Hue* (1968)**

Photography for the British photographer Don McCullin is feeling rather than looking, as he has said several times: 'If you can't feel what you're looking at, then you're never going to get others to feel anything when they look at your pictures.' This desire to empathise and identify with the subjects in front of his lens made him depict this US Marine not only as a soldier fighting in the Vietnam War, but above all as a victim: His hands are clasped around the barrel of his weapon, not so much in belligerence but because this is the only thing he can cling to. His staring eyes, gazing into nothing, are a hallmark of shell shock, a form of war trauma. The sitter's identity as a soldier is at once asserted and undermined by his closeness to the frame – he is up front and in our face, but humanised as well.

McCullin's experiences as a veteran war photographer – one who narrowly avoided being struck by a bullet when it hit his camera instead – traumatised him. When printing his negatives, he relived the atrocities he had witnessed over and over again. In an attempt to restore peace to his life, he decided to photograph landscapes for a while. In 2012, however, at the age of 77, and sick of witless news reporting and images of celebrities in the media, McCullin travelled to Syria to record the unfolding war.

McCullin has received many awards and has been knighted, but the greatest recognition of the power of his work perhaps came when the British Government successfully tried to keep him away from the 1982 Falklands War, by telling him that he could not travel to the islands because the warship was already full.

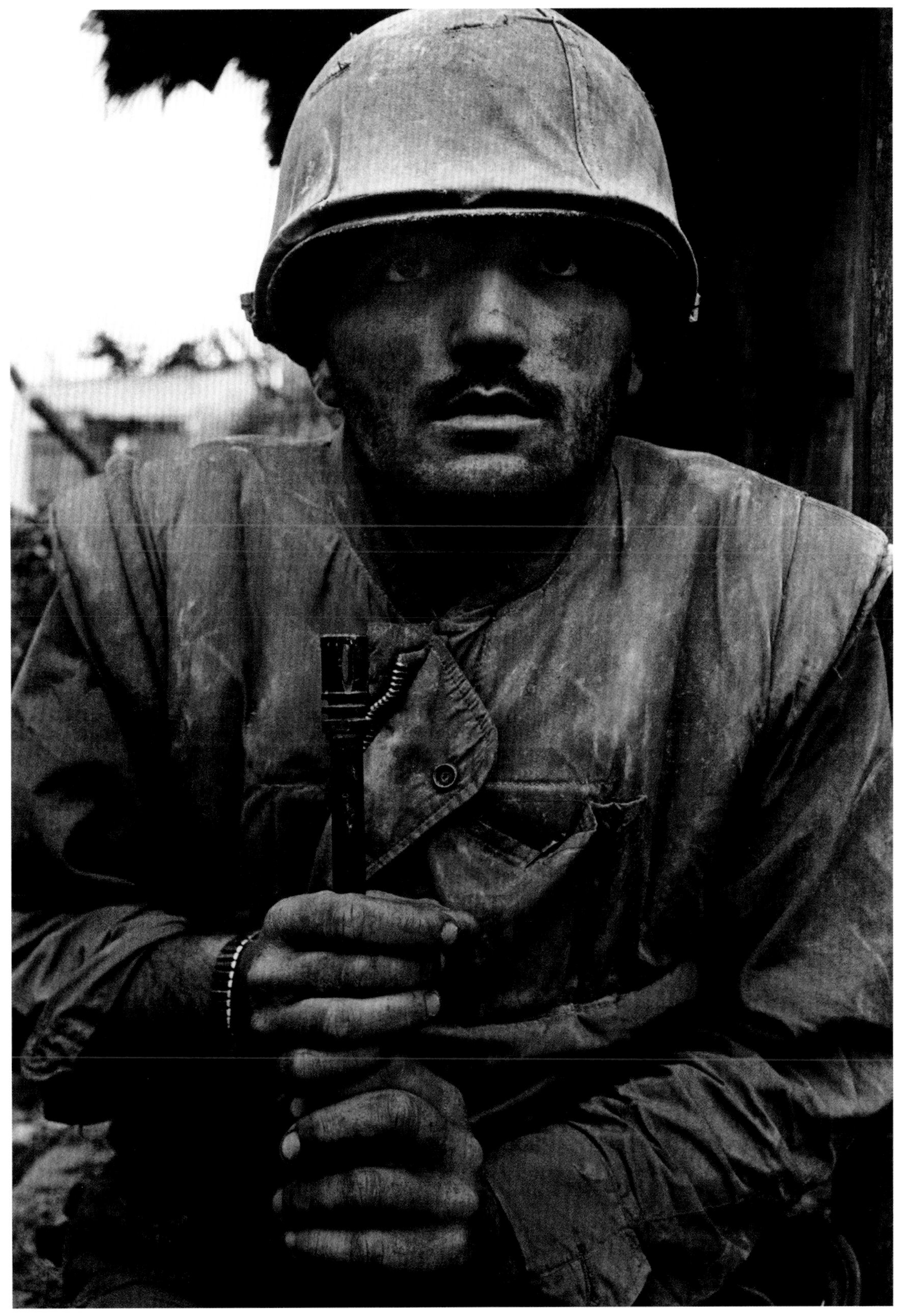

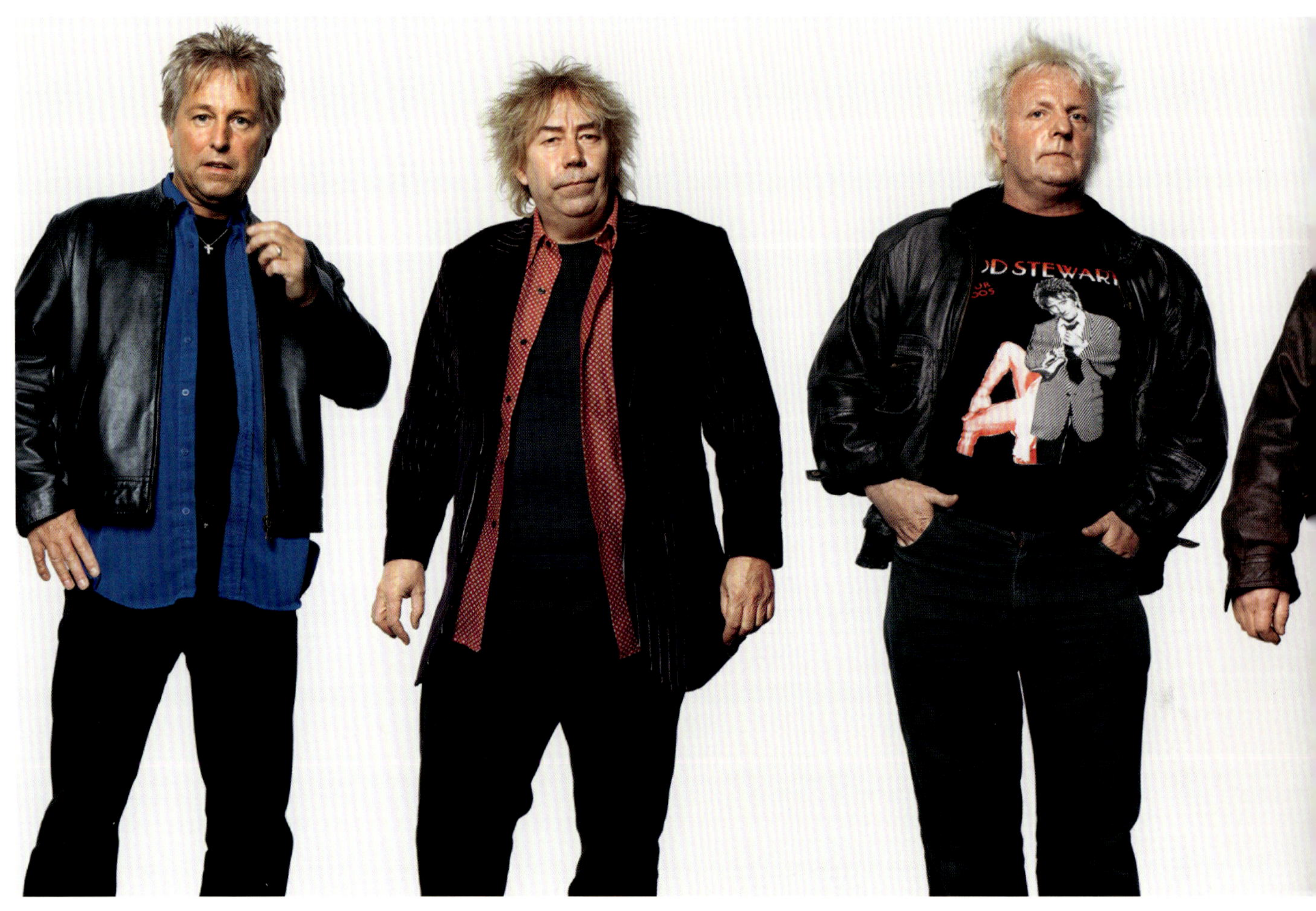

James Mollison (born 1973)
***Rod Stewart – Earls Court, London, 20th December 2005* (2005)**

Finding our tribe is vital to forming our identity: being among like-minded people, with certain norms of dress and appearance to adhere to, gives us the criteria by which we can measure ourselves. Over a period of three years, James Mollison attended concerts around the world photographing fans outside venues for his *Disciples* series. For these panoramic views he stitched together the fans as if to make a 'family', highlighting how fans copy their hero's/heroes' identity to make it their own. The photographs capture people as they relive their youth, both celebrating and gently sending up their efforts, revealing how individuals like to see themselves and the gap between that self-image and how the world might see them.

With the Rod Stewart fans, Mollison shows the struggle of the individual between his own identity and that of his idol. These men all have bleached hair that has been carefully blow-dried to give the right wild, rock-and-roll look. However, they are no playboys with fashion-model girlfriends, but British blokes in badly fitting jackets, who look like they've just returned from a holiday in the sun or perhaps just a drink down the pub. This group portrait might make you chuckle, but Mollison has made sure that he gives the men their dignity. By using a low camera angle, he elevates them from average guys to heroes. They look down on us proudly – half themselves, half Rod.

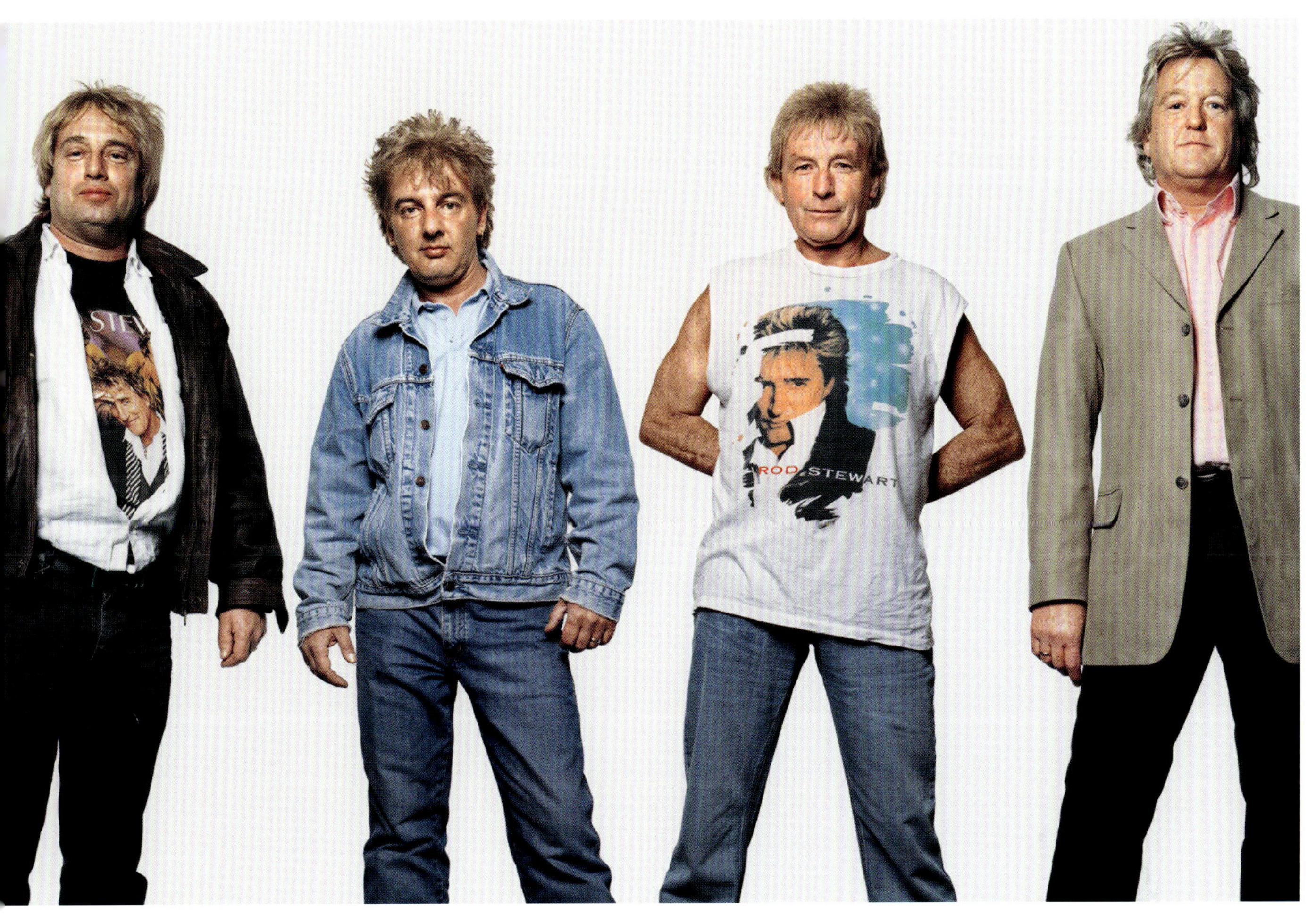
ROD STEWART

Seydou Keita (1921–2001)
***Family with Two Guitars and Amplifiers Outside the Studio* (c.1960)**

The inclusion of props is a long-used device in the history of Western portrait painting and photography. If we see an 18th-century painting with a man holding a violin, we know he was a musician; a woman with a palette must be a painter. The props in this photograph might be thought to have a clear significance, then, but are things so clear cut? Are the family, or at least the man and woman, members of a band? We assume (perhaps incorrectly) that the guitars and the amplifiers belong to the man, because he holds one so protectively. However, the photographer, the Malian Seydou Keita, kept many props in his studio – accessories such as hats and glasses, which were signs of modernity for a newly decolonised Mali – so the guitars might feasibly have belonged to another sitter or indeed to Keita, and have nothing to do with this family.

Keita's photographs represent a new, young nation, and they are full of hope and exuberance. He made studio photography that was particular to Mali, free from the Western canon and the traditions of colonial photography. His subjects are not represented for the curiosity of Western eyes, but have a great sense of freedom and personality. His studio, which he operated in Bamako, the Malian capital, between 1948 and 1962, was enormously popular, and he took as many as 40 portraits a day, both inside the studio using traditional Malian cloth as backdrops, or outside, as we see here, to make the most of the bright natural light. His sitters' obvious enjoyment of having their picture taken is a theme that runs throughout his work, and there is a wonderful humanity and joyousness in his portraits.

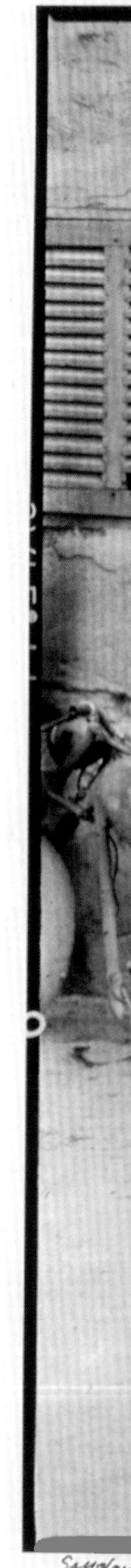

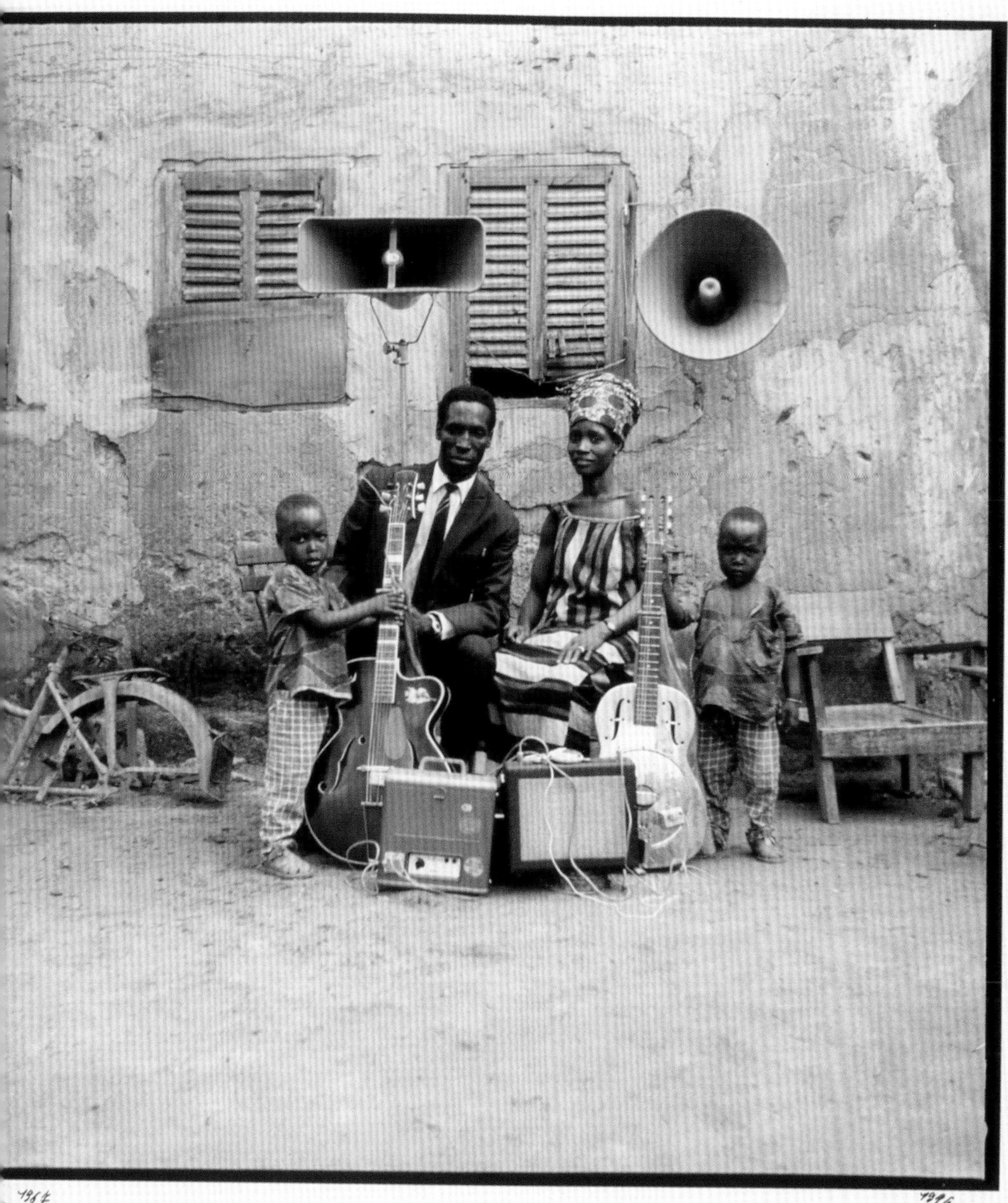

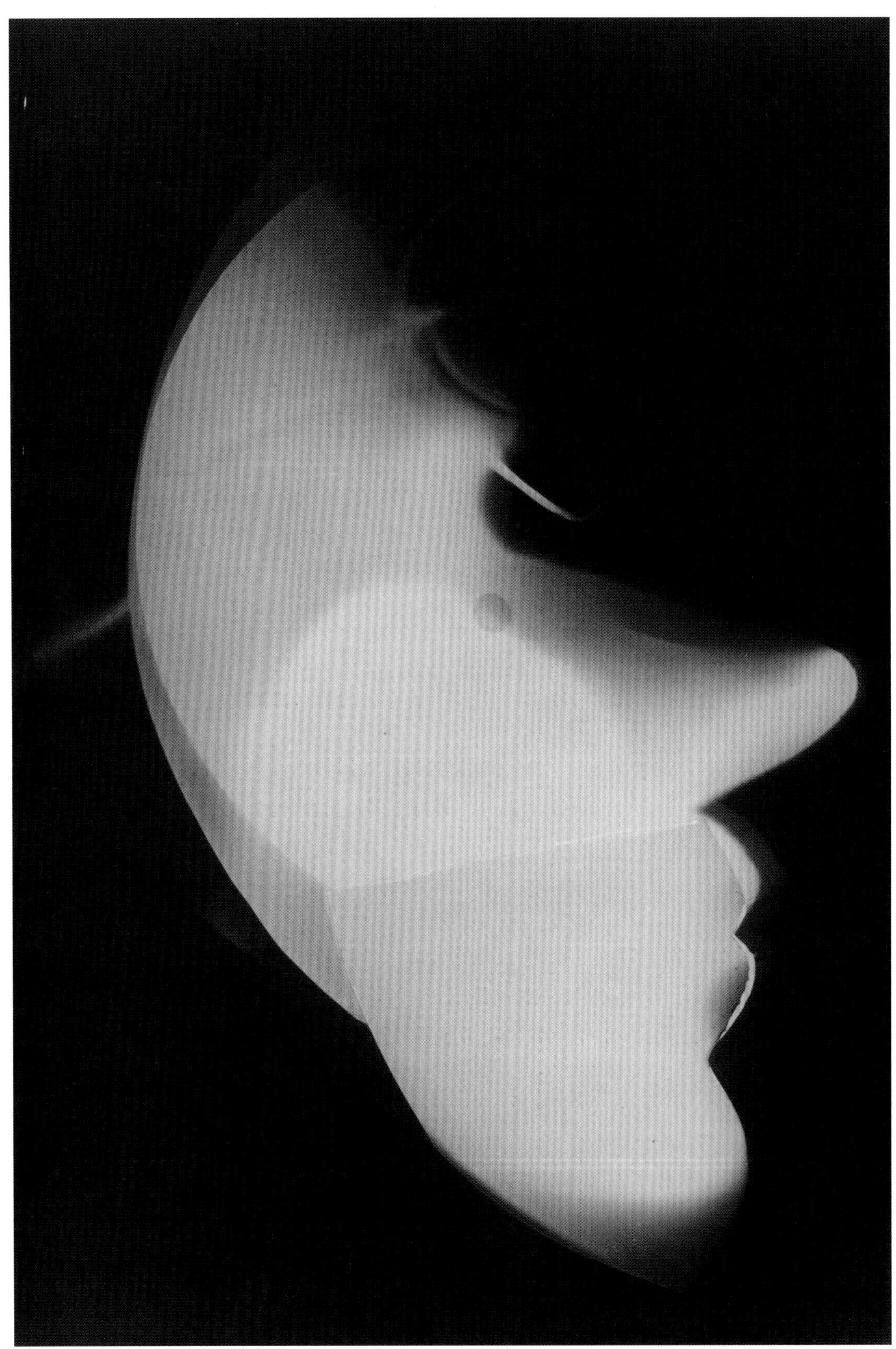

László Moholy-Nagy (1895–1946)
***Untitled (Self Portrait)* (1926)**

One of the great photographers and thinkers on photography of the 20th century, the Hungarian artist and Bauhaus professor László Moholy-Nagy, claimed: 'The enemy of photography is convention, the fixed rules of "how to do". The salvation of photography comes from experiment.' As the work of many interwar artists shows, experiments in photography were rife, and it was a time of great technical, theoretical and artistic development.

In this image, Moholy-Nagy has created an image of such abstraction that we might question whether it is really a self-portrait at all. However, it is titled as such, and a faint outline of the artist's trademark glasses can be seen, so the viewer must trust what the artist tells them, and consider only what he means to say about himself. He has used a camera-less photographic process that involves exposing objects on light-sensitive paper to create what he dubbed 'photograms'. In this instance, he may have used objects that stood in for his face or even somehow wrapped the photographic paper around his face. Perhaps, in offering the viewer such an abstract, X-ray image of himself, he is suggesting an interior, hidden world. Or, more realistically, he is attempting an impossible image – as one can never see oneself as others do. The self here then could be seen as both self and other (both literally and figuratively).

As many other photographs in this book indicate, objects can stand in for identity. An object can become freighted with the identity of a person, or a place, as is the role of souvenirs. All these strategies of abstraction, objects and experiment are investigations into the dismantling of an authentic, unitary self that had gone before theories of postmodernism, which instead introduced ideas of multiple selves. Photography is ripe for such explorations, as it is not so tied to traditional art genres and their associated symbolism.

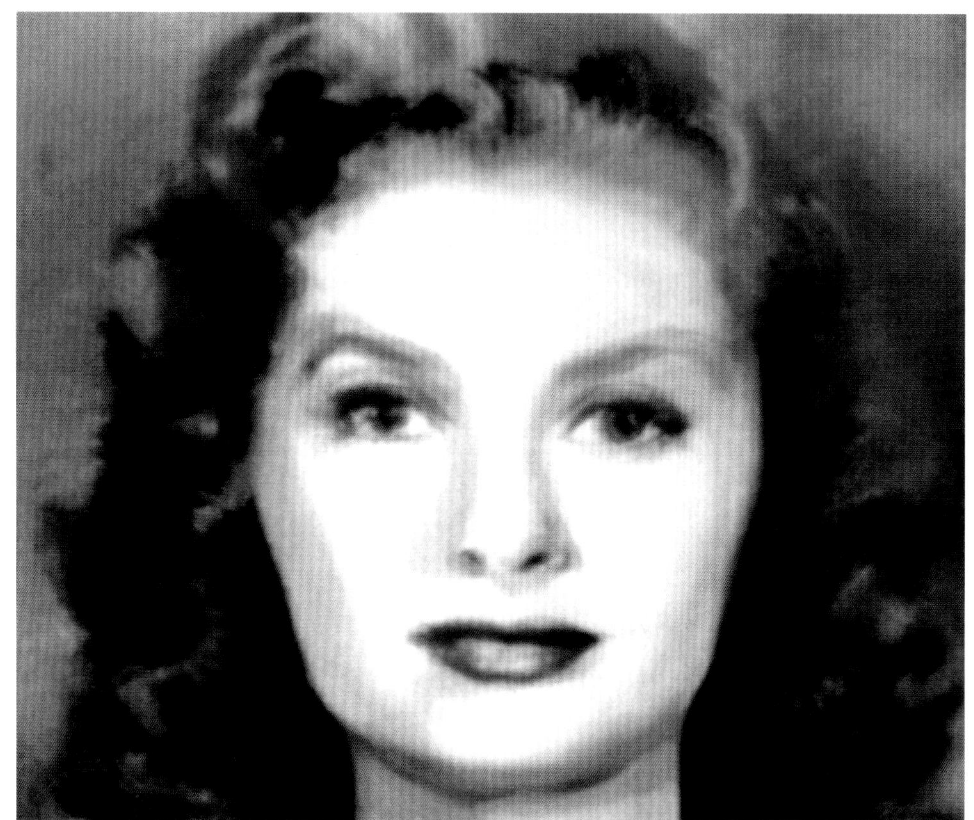

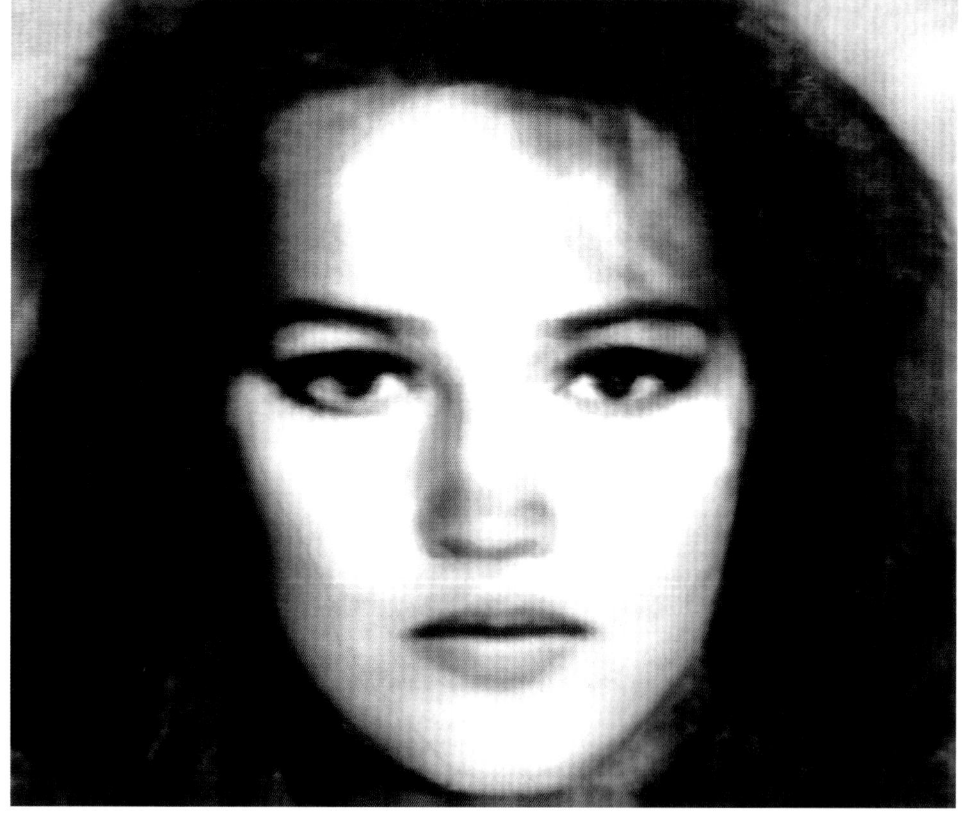

Nancy Burson (born 1948)
***First and Second Beauty Composites* (1982)**

It is said that time heals all wounds, and sometimes this applies to photography, too. Anyone who has trouble with the outward signs of ageing can find solace in photography: a photograph that at the time of its taking startled you by mercilessly confronting you with your age can, ten years later, amaze you by revealing how young you actually looked.

The apps that now instantly transform your portraits into younger versions of yourself would probably not exist without the pioneering work of American artist Nancy Burson. In the 1980s she developed technology that made it possible to picture how children's faces age, resulting in portraits that helped the FBI find children that had been missing for years. She also did the opposite: she reversed the ageing process and created sham baby portraits of Marilyn Monroe and Elvis Presley.

In the series *Composites*, which she worked on from 1982, she morphed together existing portraits of other famous people, world leaders or, in the work *Androgyny* (1982), men and women. In the examples shown here, she combined the faces of Bette Davis, Audrey Hepburn, Grace Kelly, Sophia Loren and Marilyn Monroe (top), and the faces of Jane Fonda, Jacqueline Bisset, Diane Keaton, Brooke Shields and Meryl Streep (bottom). By combining the faces of female movie stars from the 1950s and the 1970s, respectively, she shows how our ideals of beauty are shaped and change over decades. The lack of actresses of colour in the composites is striking, but equally telling. For her work *The Human Race Machine* (2000), she used race morphing technology in an interactive tool for the resolution of the world's racial issues, suggesting that the notion of race is social rather than genetic.

Nick Hedges (born 1943)
***Irish Immigrants Recently Moved to Moss Side* (1969)**

Almost every society in the world includes groups of people who are overlooked and almost invisible to the majority of its citizens. These people tend to be society's poorest: the homeless, and those living in precarious economic situations. In 1968, Nick Hedges was commissioned by the UK housing charity Shelter to document the living conditions of the poor in the UK. Over a period of four years, Hedges photographed people in slums in major British cities such as London, Birmingham, Liverpool and Glasgow. While criss-crossing the UK, he also captured street scenes and the countryside. This makes Hedges's Shelter archive not just a series showing the misery and squalor found in housing estates around that time, but also an eminent social document, comparable to the photography programme of the Farm Security Administration in the United States (see page 96). Apart from showing decay and disconnection, as well as beauty, Hedges's poignant work records a momentous part of Britain's past (and present), and it gives a face to those who are so frequently ignored.

The fact that we see the face of the father in this photograph is rare, and the absent mother is significant. Many fathers declined to be photographed as they felt responsible and ashamed for their families having to live under such conditions. The wallpaper is partially peeling off the walls, owing to mould and damp, and on it are pasted torn-out pages from magazines and calendars, showing pictures of boxing heroes and pin-up models. The son is an echo of his father in the way he poses in his chair, unsmiling. His younger sister, who stands between them, looks into Hedges's lens with a tilted head and her chin down. She seems to practise her budding identity by copying the pose and look of the pin-up girl behind her on the wall.

Fifty years on, Hedges's Shelter archive is a major, yet still relatively unsung part of the Great Britain's history and national identity.

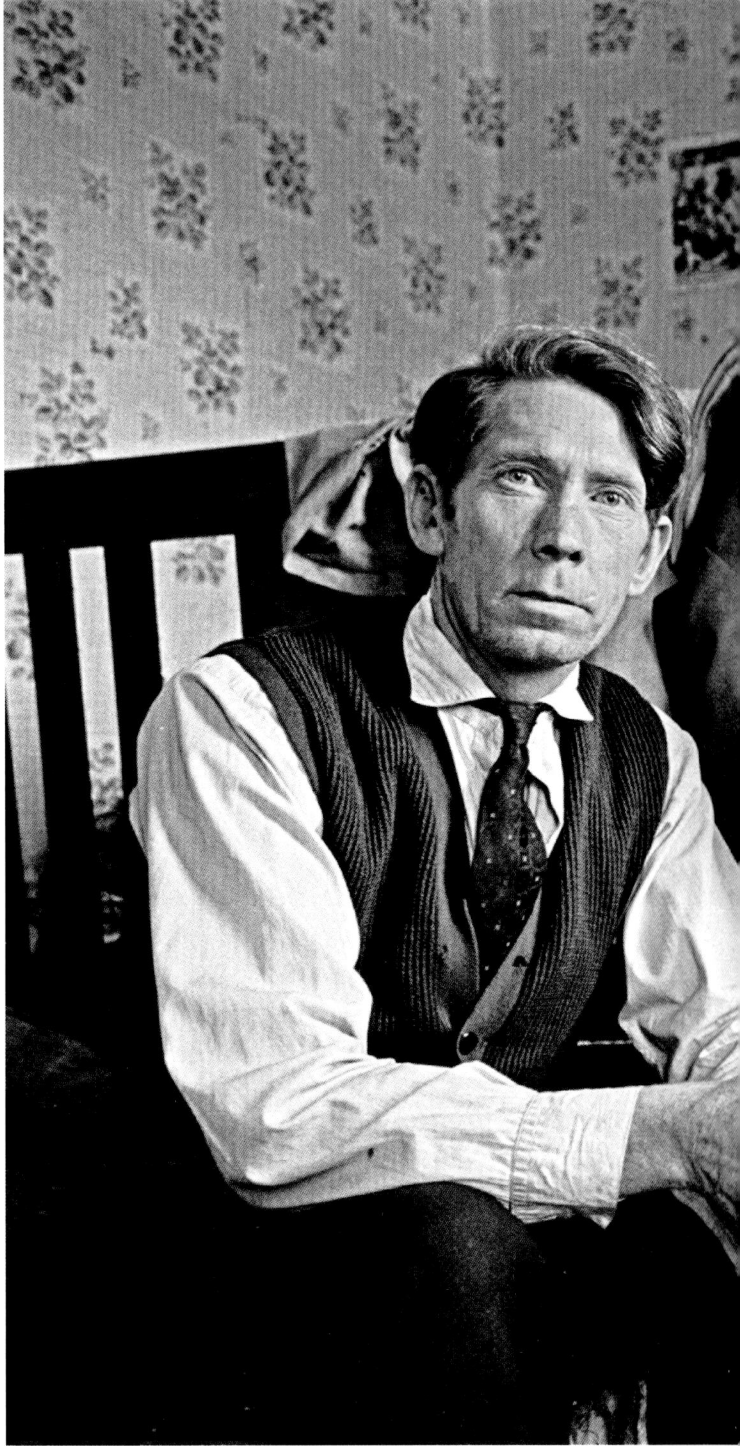

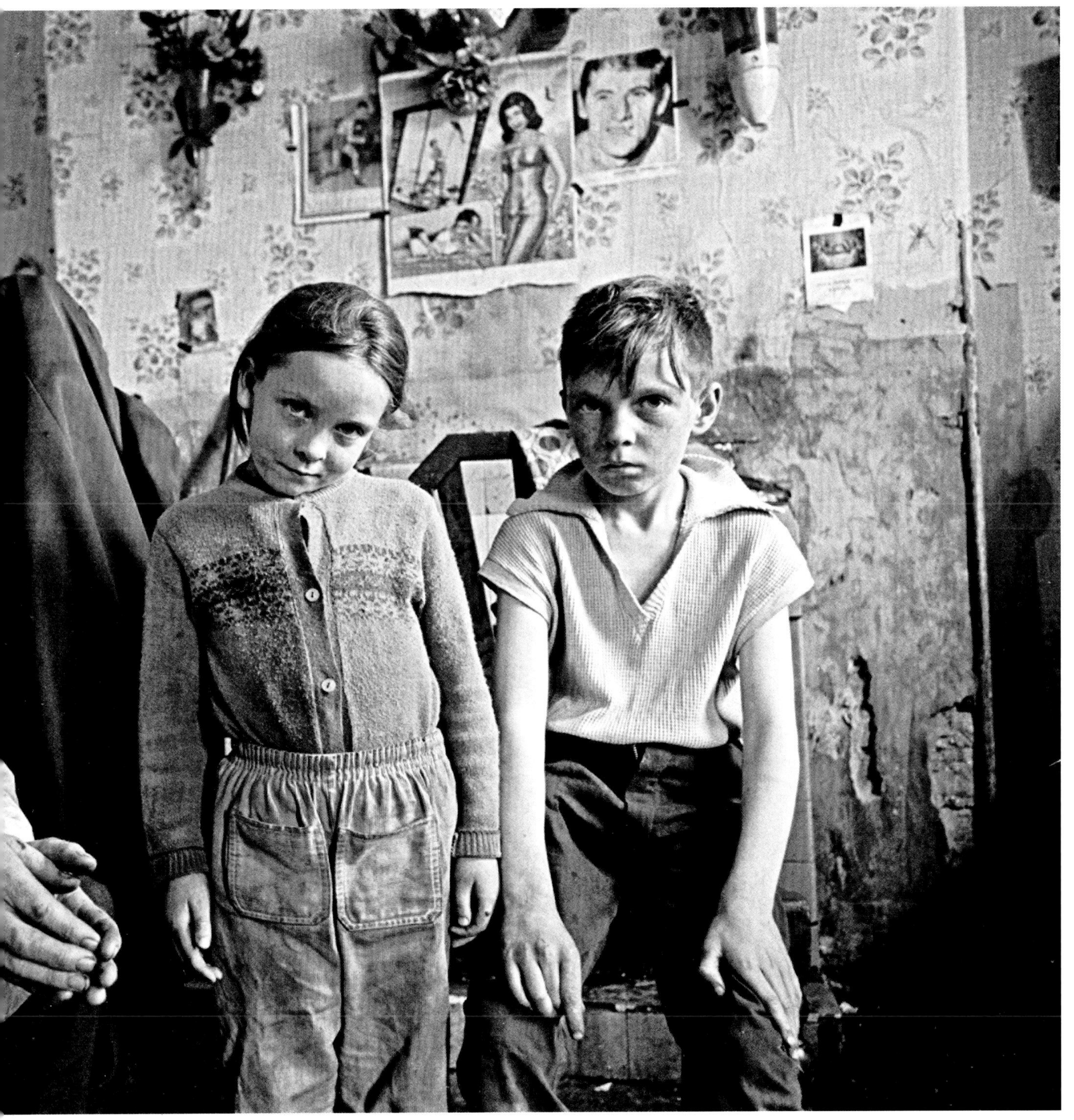

Stealing or
borrowing?
Stealing or
borrowing?
Stealing or
borrowing?
Stealing or
borrowing?
Stealing or
borrowing?
Stealing or
borrowing?
Stealing or
borrowing?

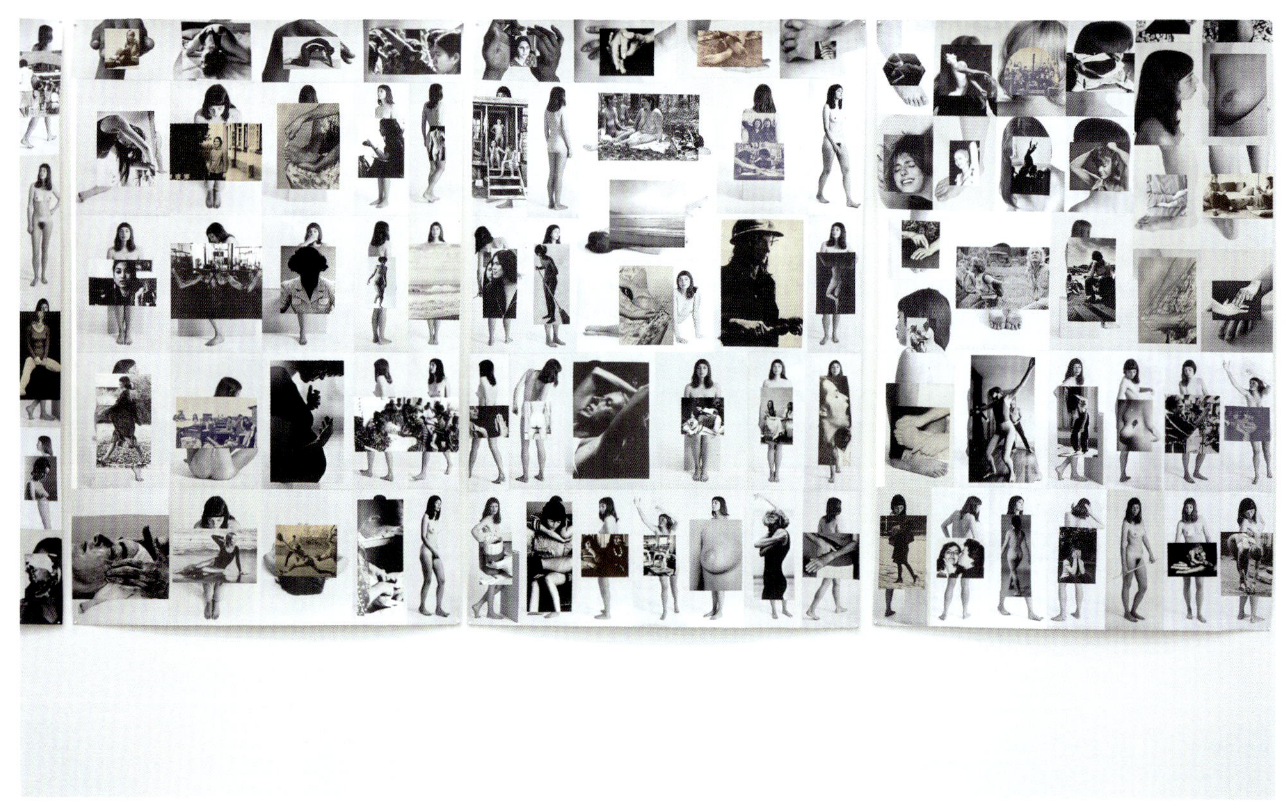

Carmen Winant, *Body/Index* (2018)

If someone took a photograph you shot and posted to your social network, and then posted it on their own blog or profile page without crediting, mentioning or tagging you, would you call that stealing? Users of YouTube, Facebook, WhatsApp and Instagram manoeuvre through a virtual world where issues involving intellectual property are complicated. Even the judicial system regulating attribution and appropriation grapples with providing clarity on the matter.

Give credit where credit is due. In theory, we know this. In practice, nearly everyone clicks 'agree' when signing up to the latest social media site without realising that, in doing so, they may be handing over the rights to their material – assuming it is their material in the first place. Ethically speaking, sharing someone else's photograph as your own can be viewed as an act of fraud. Artistically, issues around appropriation are more complex.

'Appropriation' means borrowing ideas, sounds, objects and images from others to create art. Would we be able to listen to songs by Amy Winehouse if jazz music hadn't existed? The ancient Greeks could claim the intellectual property of the design of their columns when these elements reappeared in the 17th-century Palace of Versailles, if they weren't long perished by then. Both are clear cases of appropriation, yet deemed acceptable. It is impossible to create new styles in music, architecture and visual arts from a void, or without incorporating components from previous artworks and styles.

The concept of appropriation in 20th-century visual arts began with the cubists – the artists Georges Braque and Pablo Picasso who, from around 1912, were incorporating newspapers into their collages. French artist Marcel Duchamp took this further with his 'readymades' including *Fountain* (1917), the famous urinal, signed and presented as a work of art, and labelled 'the most influential modern artwork of all time' by 500 British art experts in 2004. Appropriation was also a characteristic of the dada movement, of which Duchamp was a member, in which artists such as Kurt Schwitters and Hannah Höch used everyday materials like newspaper scraps and photographs in their works. In the 1950s, artists such as Eduardo Paolozzi, Richard Hamilton, Robert Rauschenberg and Jasper Johns widely used borrowed photographs and objects in their art. All four became known as early artists within the pop art movement.

Pop art was attracted to photography not because of its artistic abilities, but due to its lowly everyday status. Just as dada and cubism had before, pop art presented a challenge to the traditional visual arts in terms of high and low culture, and photography was a perfect medium for this. Pop art incorporates imagery from popular culture, such as comic strips and news and advertising images, often removed from the original context or combined with unrelated elements.

In a vast collage of 'found photographs', American artist Carmen Winant's 2018 installation *Body/Index* (opposite) consists of an array of images of women, taken from a series of posing reference guides for photographers. Freed from their context, meanings slide from view and the oddity of many of the photographs is brought to the fore. One is left wondering what Winant is attempting to show about women, what they are 'indexing' and why. The term 'found photography' suggests an element of chance, but in fact these images have been actively sought. In addition to the indexing of women, some images are also collaged together, making strange unrelated visual riddles in a site-specific installation.

Winant (born 1983) works with a quantity of vernacular images. She has commented on how the narratives of women's lives are often ignored in the history of art, and has explored subjects that have traditionally been seen exclusively as female experiences, such as birth, cooking and childcare, all in a similar process to that of *Body/Index*. The mass of archival photographs illustrates who is photographed and who is not. Attracted to the politics of the second-wave feminism of the 1970s, and also the photography of the same decade, Winant highlights the lack of diversity in the photographs of the time, especially in the representation of women of colour. With this ellipsis in mind, we are forced to ask what we think these photographs show us, and also what they do not or cannot.

Using images that are printed matter, and not taken from the internet, the histories that existed before the installation can be considered. These photographs have been touched and studied, and have physically moved through people's lives. This adds a particularly tactile element to the work, and knowing that these are the very same images that circulated with the intention of sharing a certain knowledge or idea about women gives them a charge and agency – a metamorphosis occurs when they are reproduced in this new, very different context.

In the 1980s, artists such as Barbara Kruger, Richard Prince and Sherrie Levine also engaged in appropriation; Levine (born 1947) explicitly copied the work of famed male artists, as can be seen in *After Walker Evans: 4* (opposite, bottom). Here she has directly re-photographed somebody else's work (the titular Walker Evans), creating a photograph of a photograph. She did the same with famous paintings, criticising how, in her view, female artists in art history were traditionally regarded as second-rate. She even copied Duchamp's idea and made a bronze urinal sculpture entitled *Fountain* in 1991. By making reproductions, these photographers raise questions about what art is. Is it about authenticity? Originality? Or is it about choices and ideas? By copying artworks, photographs and advertisements, what they managed to do was create a completely new meaning, context and set of conceptual associations.

Technology has increased the number of techniques that can be used to create art – and also to appropriate. The ease with which images can now be reproduced, scanned, copied and shared has led to a situation where it is hard to find a museum or gallery anywhere in the world that does not show any photographs or artworks incorporating or alluding to previously made photographs, fine-art masterpieces, games, ads, Hollywood films, or objects from everyday life, let alone anything that can be ripped off the internet. Today's appropriation artists can combine conventional techniques such as painting with modern techniques like scanning and photo manipulation to transform found imagery into authentic works.

An example of this is the work of American artist Daniel Gordon (born 1980), such as *Pineapple and Shadow* (opposite, top). Typically, Gordon uses images he finds on the internet to create a 'sculpture', which he then photographs. He also often references art history traditions and the symbolism of the still life. Gordon mimics reality but also adds obvious Photoshop techniques. He is appropriating, sampling, quoting, re-editing and recombining images and media. It can be questioned whether such strategies continue to challenge notions of originality and to test traditional definitions of an authentic work. Is it just accepted that contemporary art takes from everywhere – and who cares? As everything is available for anyone thanks to Google, the epigone's work itself can subsequently be reappropriated and spread for all eternity.

While appropriation is now a key element in contemporary culture, and copyright law has failed so far to provide watertight guidelines, judges may permit borrowing if the artist can prove that it is a case of 'fair use' – that is, where he or she has transformed the original art work with the objective to satirise, to criticise, or otherwise generally comment on it. Nevertheless, this tactic does not always work, and artists such as Andy Warhol and Robert Rauschenberg have occasionally had to pay licensing fees. In more recent years, Richard Prince has been sued several times for using other artists' photographs. In one case, he had screengrabbed and enlarged selfies from the web.

Any artist who is thinking about appropriating what isn't theirs can ask themselves whether they are respecting other people's property rights. Work can only be used in ways that the owners permit. If asking for permission is not possible, artists could ask themselves how they would want their own imagery to be used. If the ownership itself is unclear, one could ask what kind of damage using other people's material might bring about and whether one feels this is warranted. Or appropriate a loo like Duchamp and Levine did – preferably one that's not copyrighted.

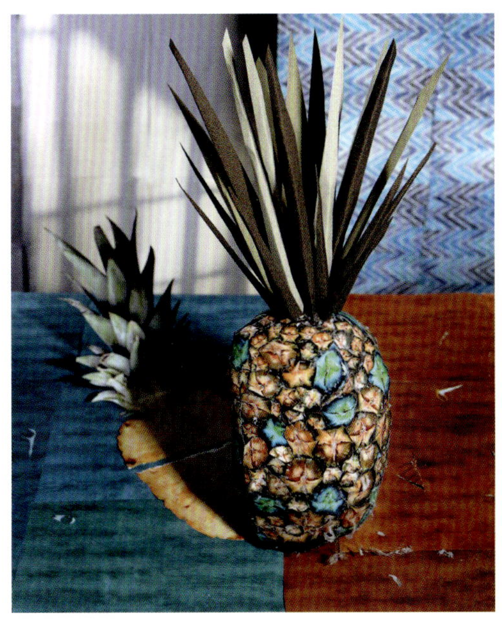

Daniel Gordon, *Pineapple and Shadow* (2011)

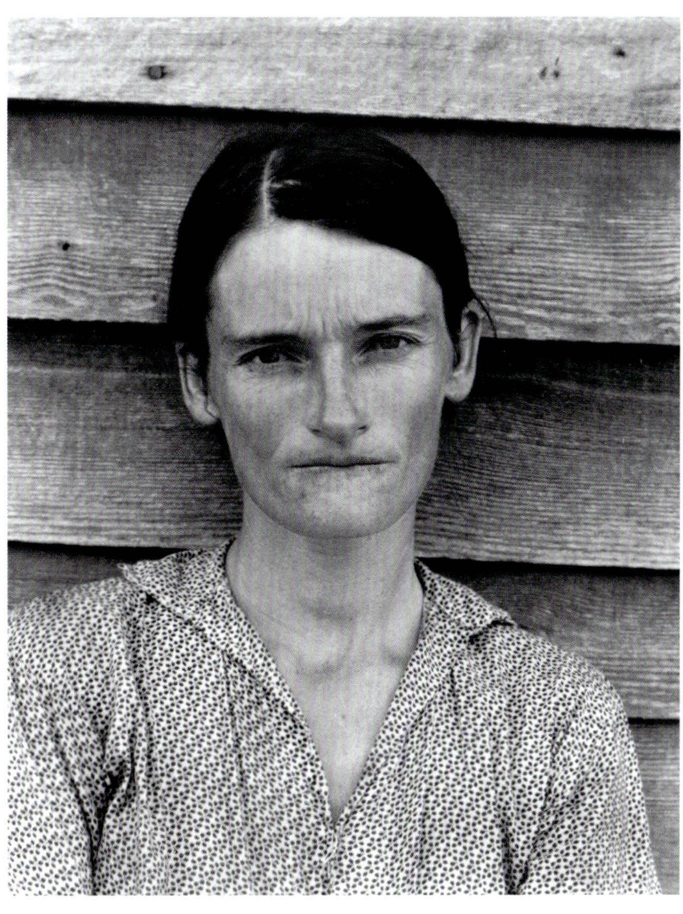

Sherrie Levine, *After Walker Evans: 4* (1981)

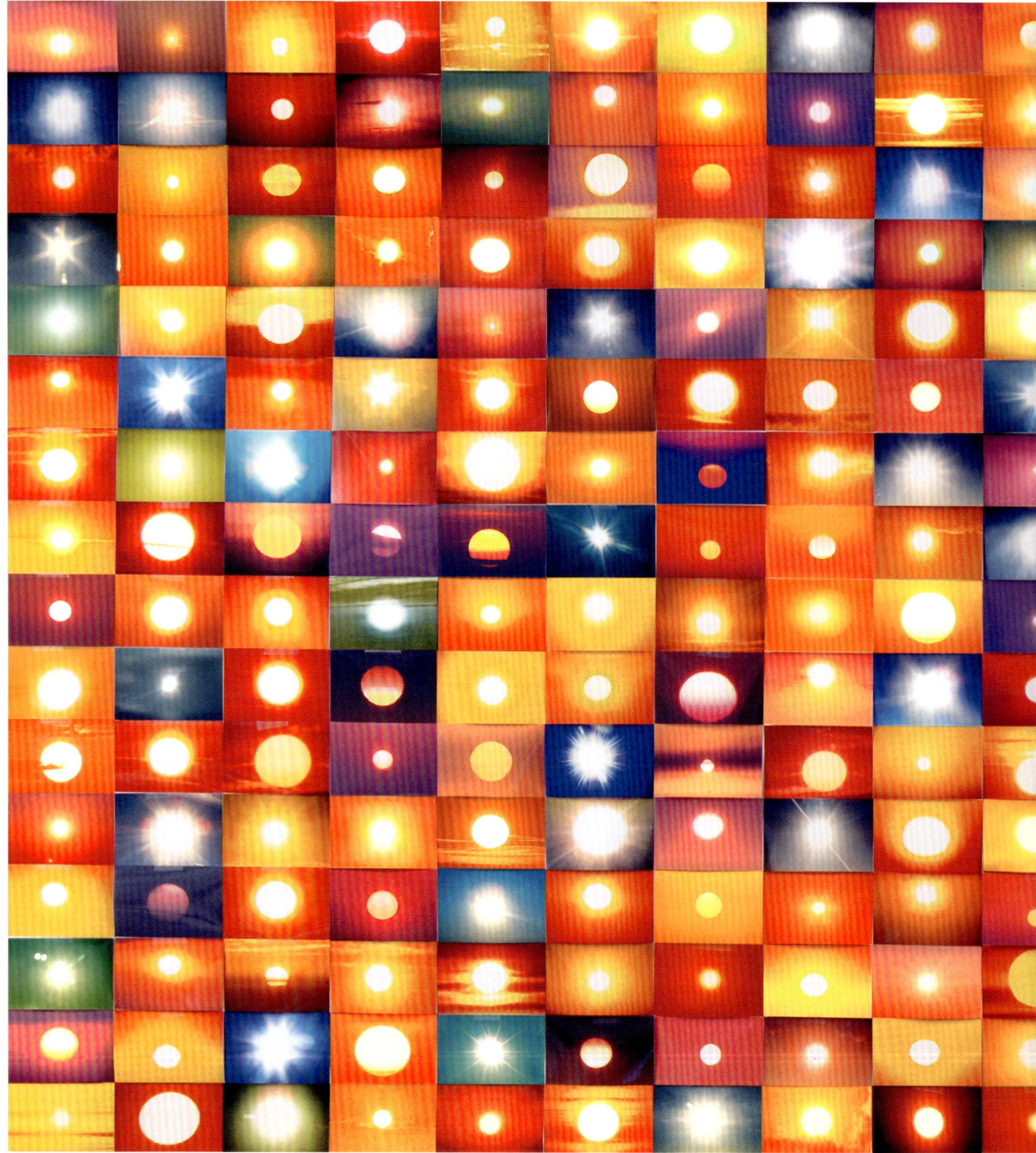

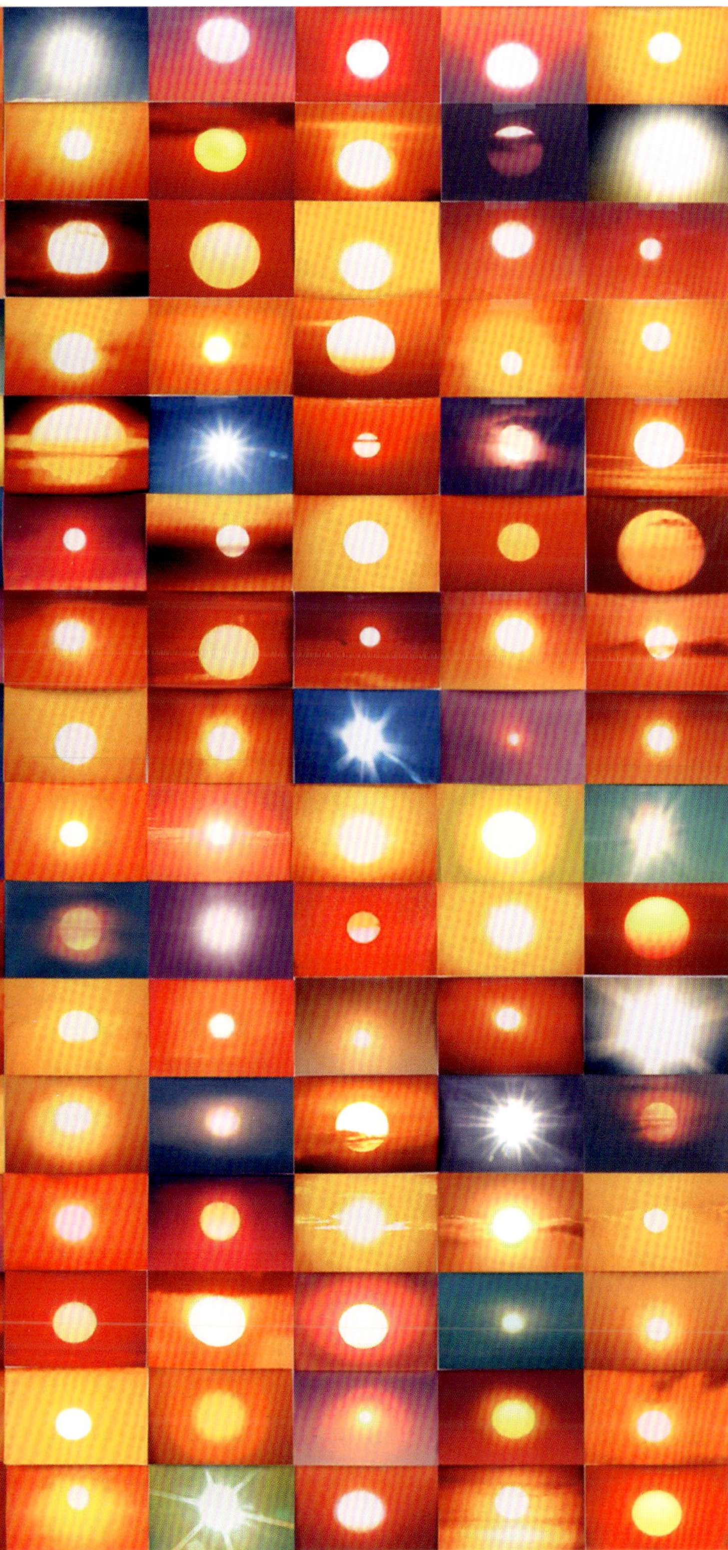

Penelope Umbrico (born 1957)
541,795 Suns from Sunsets from Flickr, (Partial) 01/23/06 **(2006–ongoing)**

What do you think is the most uploaded subject on image-sharing sites? Selfies? Food? Porn? Penelope Umbrico, an American artist who works primarily with found imagery, started this project while asking herself the same question. Looking for the most photographed subject matter uploaded onto Flickr on a certain day in 2006, she discovered that the answer – at least on this platform and this day – was sunsets.

Umbrico's art takes the form of site-specific installations, each created for the museum or gallery space that commissioned them, and varying according to the result of the number of hits she gets when she types in 'sunsets' to the search function on Flickr on a particular day. She carefully crops each of the photographs so that the sun is in the middle, and then prints it out on cheap photographic paper. Each picture is then combined together into a single large collage. The sun belongs to us all, but is it OK to take somebody else's picture of it, manipulate it and make it your own? The ownership of the constituent pictures is perhaps questionable after they have been cropped, printed and combined with others.

In Umbrico's first project from 2006, shown here, she received 541,795 hits for 'sunsets'. An installation created in 2011 was titled *8,730,221 Suns from Flickr (Partial) 02/20/11* and in 2016 she produced *30,240,577 Suns (from Sunsets) from Flickr (Partial) 03/04/16.* The increasing number of suns in the titles through successive installations is a clear indication of the ever-rising use of photo-sharing platforms and of the increasing access people have to them. It also illustrates that subject matter is becoming ever more pre-scripted on image-sharing sites, and that individuality and creative flair are often not the point.

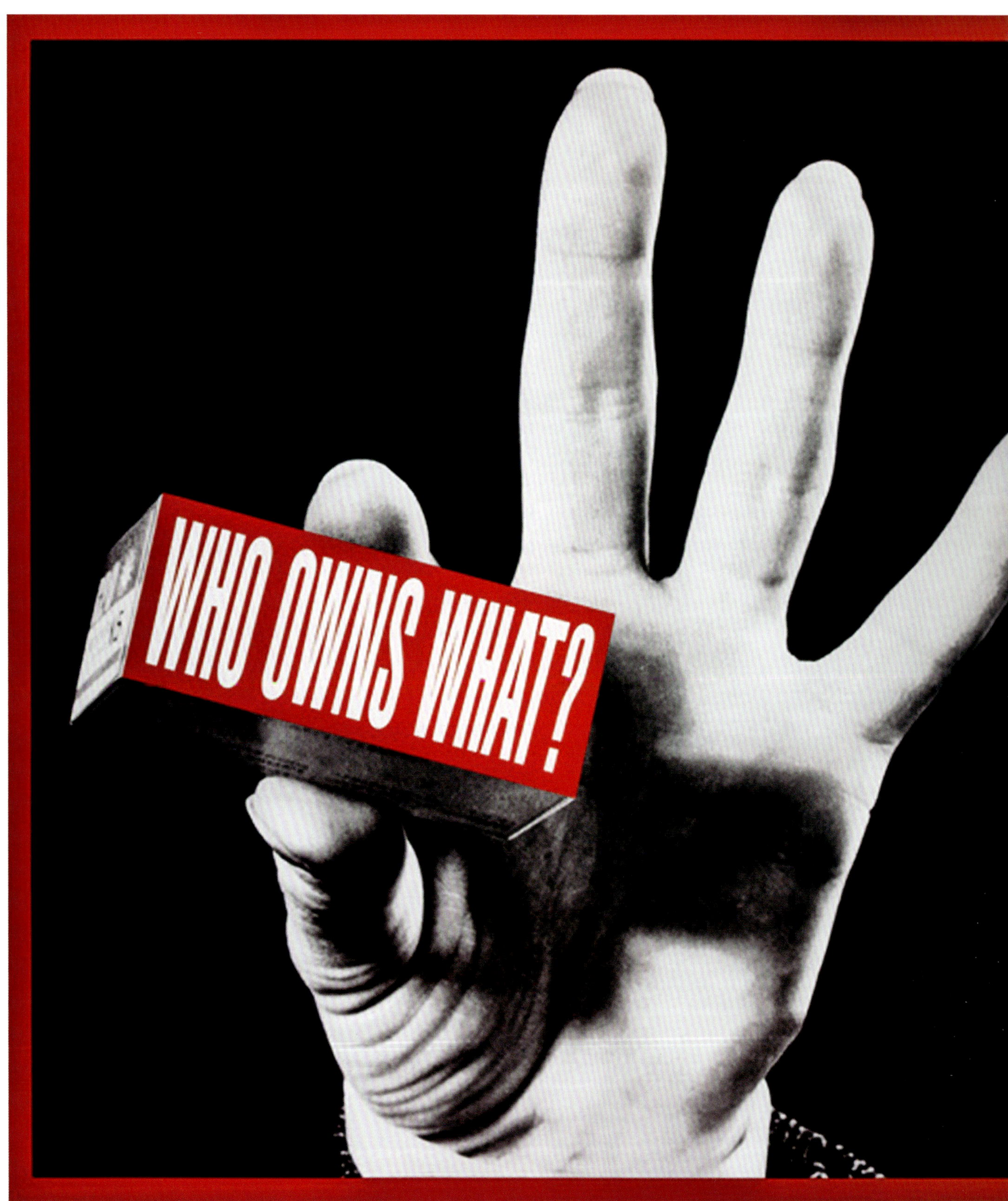
WHO OWNS WHAT?

Barbara Kruger (born 1945)
***Untitled (Who Owns What?)* (1991/2012)**

This picture aptly addresses the issues examined in this chapter. Although the question 'Who owns what?' speaks to larger issues of ownership and control (be that of wealth, bodies or power), it is also self-referential. Who does this picture belong to? Barbara Kruger, the American artist who created it, or the unknown photographer who took the shot she is using?

Kruger frequently uses found photography in her work, and can be understood as an artist of the postmodern generation of the 1970s and 1980s that used appropriation as a deliberate gesture or strategy in their work. On top of these images, Kruger adds text in a characteristic white-on-red font. The statements made and questions asked by her works are direct and provocative, their power due not only to the simplicity of the language but also to the graphic use of type, colour and imagery – features typically associated with advertising.

Because she uses commercial photography from some time ago, the original contexts of the photographs Kruger's works are based on have been lost, and the photographer, in any case, would often not have been credited in the first place. Thus, questions of appropriation are not so much about the ownership of legal rights of the image, but more about the moral rights. Kruger herself denies that such issues come into play: when used in a new context, the photographs are transformed, are given new meanings, and they are instantly recognisable as hers.

They also seem not to date. Many of the slogans Kruger adopted during her early career are just as relevant and powerful today – rather than feeling as though they belong to a certain era, as some of her postmodern contemporaries' artworks do.

Harold Edgerton (1903–1990)
***Milk Drop Coronet* (1957)**

Advert for Nixon headphones (2009)

Everyone takes from everyone else. This we know. Original ideas and genius artists are rare, if not mythical. Influences come from everywhere and feed into, and off, various and varied parts of culture and society. The commercial/art crossover is an area that is particularly fertile. Once seen as polar opposites in terms of hierarchy and acceptability, the worlds of art and commerce cross-pollinate regularly – stealing and borrowing from each other constantly to produce the best works they can in their own contexts.

This phenomenon can especially be seen in contemporary art, where deconstruction, collage and appropriation of commercial imagery are regularly turned to, and advertising often uses tropes from classical and iconic artworks, and other well-known images. An example of a scientific photograph (albeit one with aesthetic qualities) clearly inspiring a commercial imitator is *Milk Drop Coronet* (opposite) by the American engineer and photographer Harold Edgerton, and an advertisement for Nixon headphones (below).

The famous milk drop was an example of Edgerton's groundbreaking use of stop-motion photography, which, like the pioneering work of Eadweard Muybridge (see page 104), showed actions that could not be seen by the human eye. Can you claim the right to the concept of an image? Once a photograph is out in the world, it is liable to be copied and referenced; its communicative power allows it to become part of the vocabulary and grammar of photography, and it can be rephrased or rewritten to become something else.

Here, the advert wants to convey that the arrival of the headphones has the same impact as Edgerton's now-iconic photo had. It is not literal imagery (headphones can't work when wet) but instead suggests modernity and dynamism; the impact the headphones will make. It aspires to the same wonder – the very technical ingenuity that the headphone brand hopes to radiate – as the first photograph to capture a drop of milk.

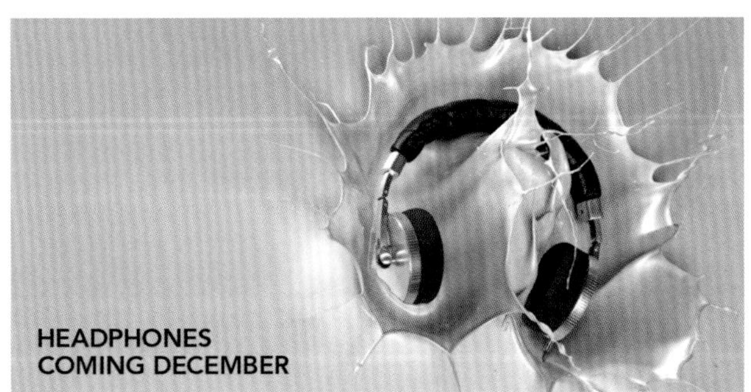

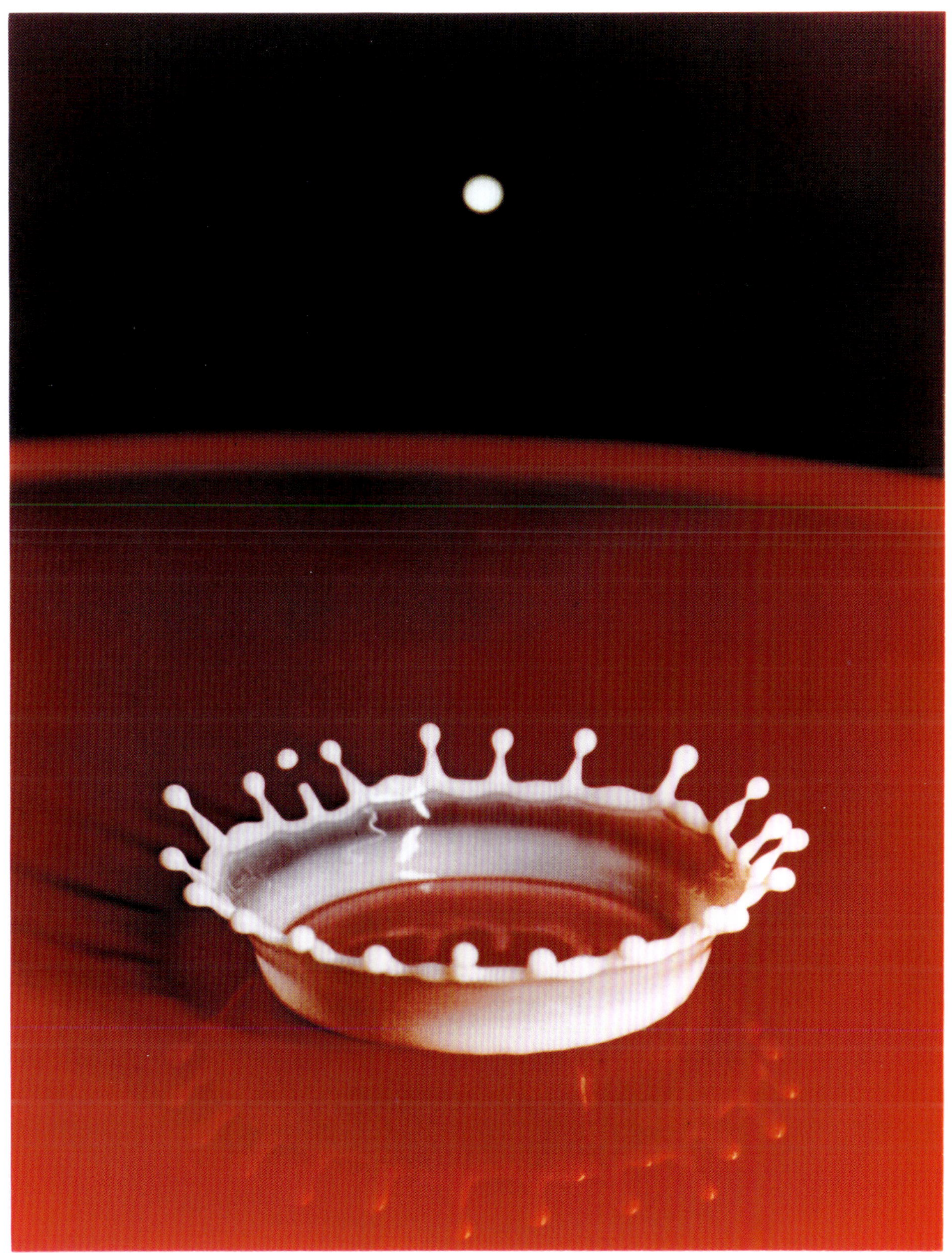

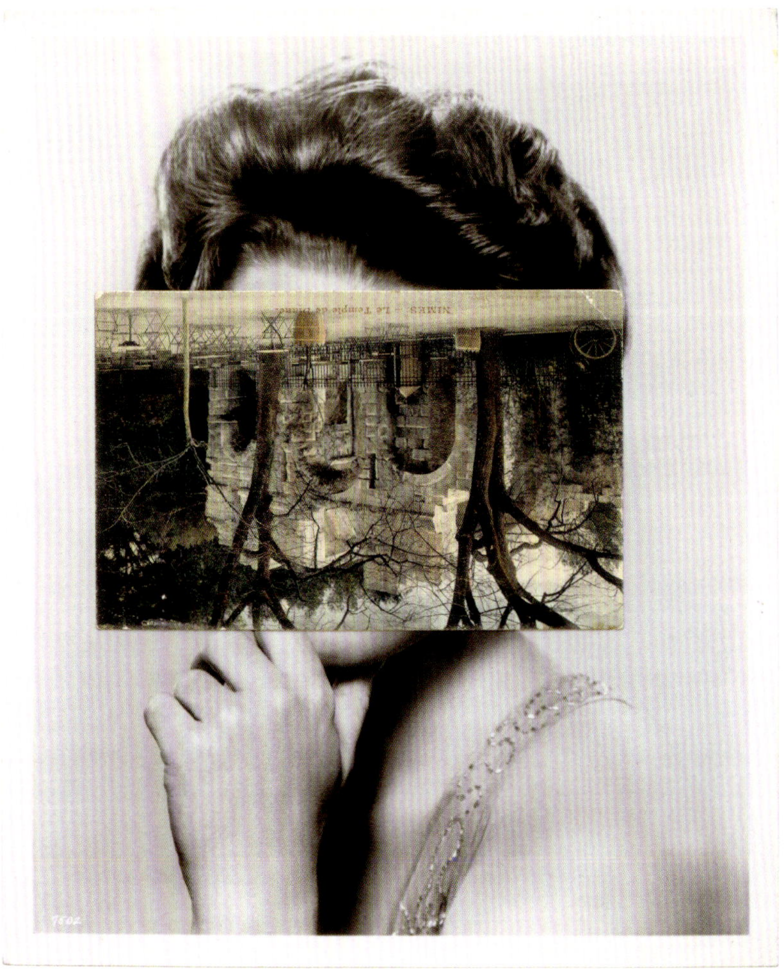

John Stezaker (born 1948)
***Mask XIII* (2006)**

The *Mask* series by the British conceptual artist John Stezaker is an example of using 'found' materials to create something original. What is intriguing about these images is that they look contemporary even though there is nothing contemporary about the imagery they are comprised of. Stezaker took publicity stills of actors from the 1940s and 1950s and overlaid them with photographs or postcards of landscapes, masking the face. He chose the landscapes meticulously, to give the appearance of faces (or, more accurately, skulls) when superimposed in this way; their crevices, cracks and crannies becoming the features of the face.

The technique of using obsolete imagery to contemporary effect was adopted by the surrealist artists of the 1920s and 1930s, such as Man Ray and Marcel Duchamp, by whom Stezaker is obviously influenced. The surrealists took up many of the psychoanalytical theories of Sigmund Freud, among them his notion of the 'death drive' – the urge towards death and self-destruction buried in the human psyche. It is an idea that Stezaker also finds intriguing and which underpins his *Mask* series. The image here uncannily evokes death, not only through the skull effect, but also by the obliteration of the beautiful young starlet's face. The image acts as a memento mori, but there is also something sadistic about it – he has disfigured a woman's face. He is violently appropriating not only the photograph but also the woman's face and identity.

By using the techniques of a well-known artistic movement, as well as the impulses that drove many of those artists, Stezaker shows that appropriation can restore something – ideas as well as images – obsolete to relevance, so that it becomes new, and even original, once more, in its contemporary setting.

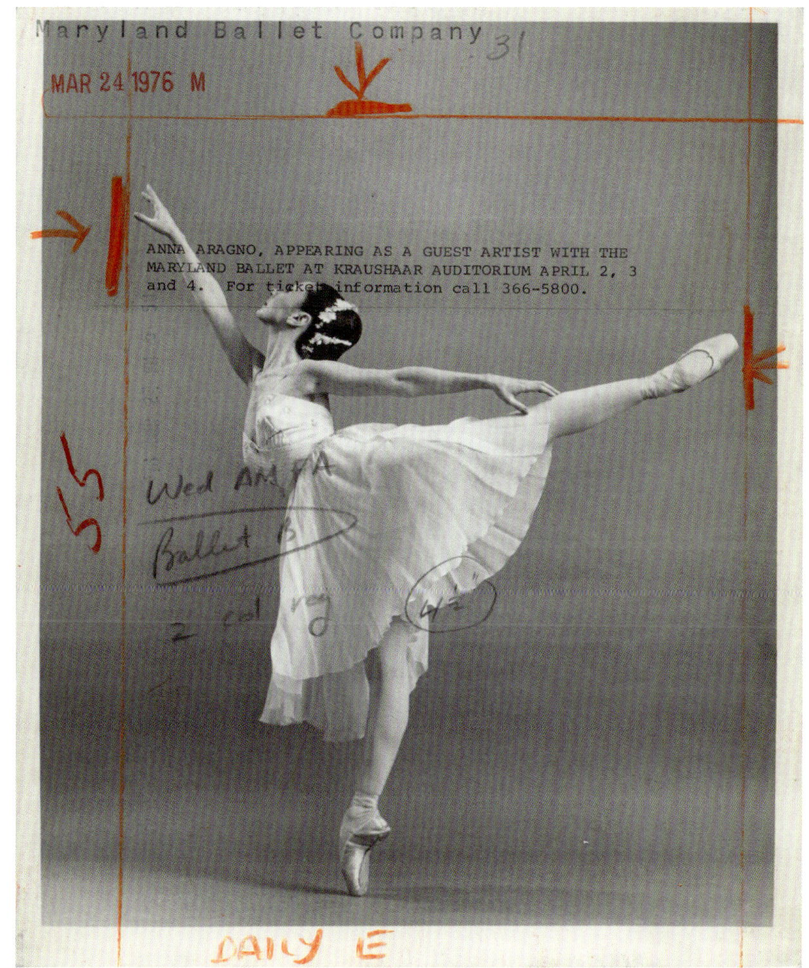

Thomas Ruff (born 1958)
***press++30.47* (2016)**

For his *press++* series, the German photographer Thomas Ruff bought American press photos dating from the 1920s to the 1970s via eBay and scanned the fronts and the backs. He put the two sides together in Photoshop, including the cropping lines, comments, stamps and smudges, and subsequently created one enlarged image.

Ruff's work has been described as 'typically German': distant and humourless. In relation to *press++*, the latter can be disputed: not only does he mock the commercialisation of art, which values single authorship and the one-off masterpiece, but also the practice of appropriation itself. After all, there can be no misunderstanding the previous authorship: the makers and copyright holders are now prominently stamped on the front of the work. Ruff also shows that one needs to look carefully: this photograph is not titled in a way that reveals the artist's intentions. As with most images, the viewer can make their own associations and give substance to the work.

More importantly, however, Ruff is actually making another statement. While he searched out the most interesting pictures from the thousands of existing press photographs, time passed and the 'sea level' of images rose higher and higher. Instead of providing the world with even more new content, Ruff relocated images from the genre of press photography into art photography. With this act of photographic recycling, restoring the past to the present, he gave shape to the fact that already forgotten histories keep repeating themselves. Because nothing has really changed between the day the press photographer took his or her picture and the day Ruff presented it as an artwork. Wars are still being waged, and dancers continue to dance.

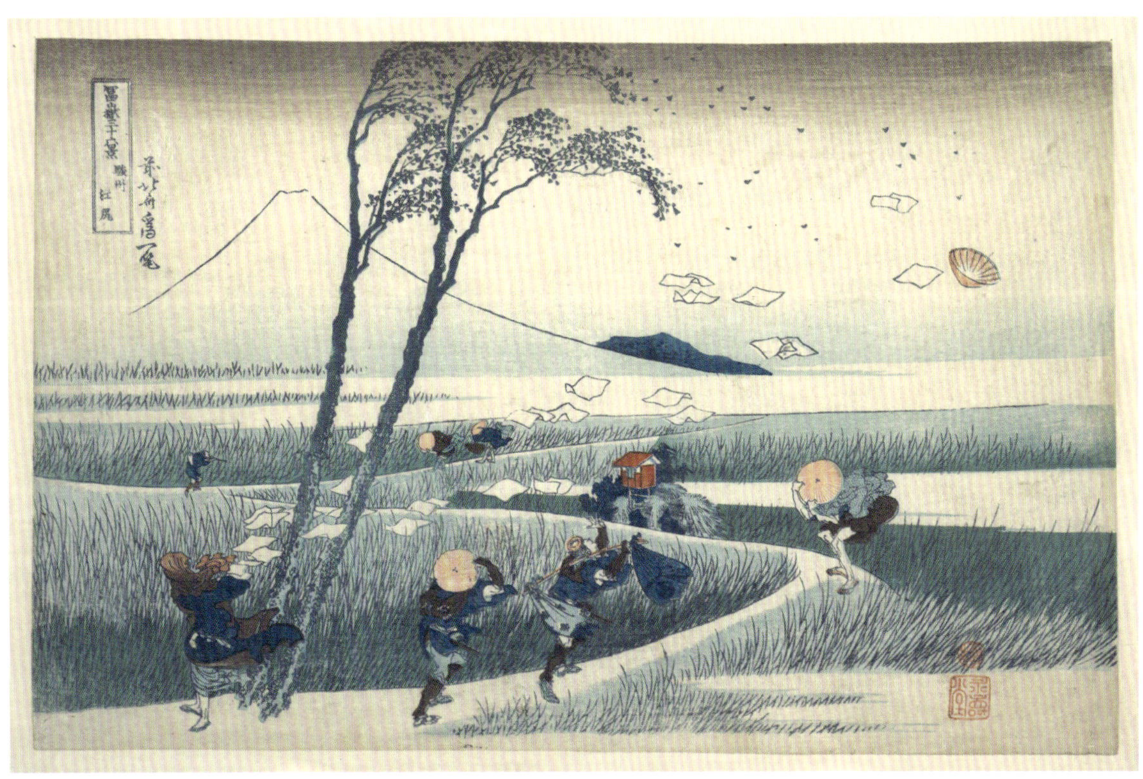
冨嶽三十六景
駿州
江尻

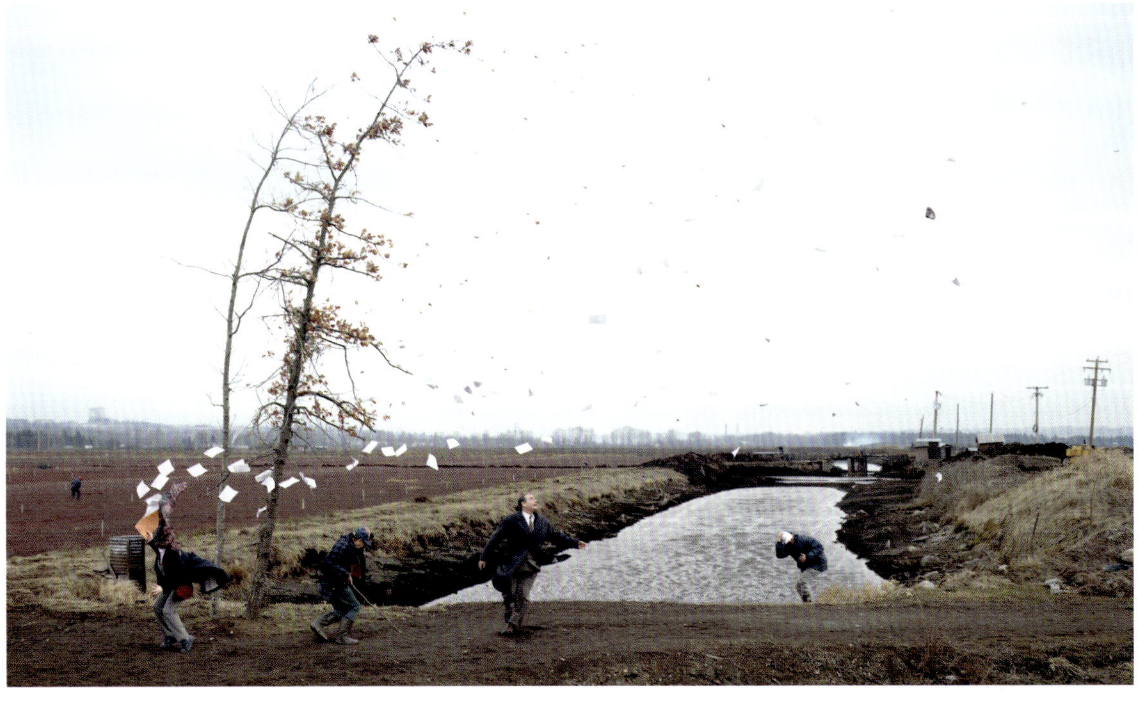

Katsushika Hokusai (1760–1849)
Ejiri in Suruga Province **(1830–1832)**

Jeff Wall (born 1946)
A Sudden Gust of Wind (after Hokusai) **(1993)**

Canadian photographer Jeff Wall's large photographic tableaux have been described as complex, one-frame cinematic productions involving a crew, sets, models and a painstaking production process. The life-size scale fascinates Wall, as the focused photographic image can sharply convey all possible information that he wants to give.

Wall's model here is *Ejiri in Suruga Province* (left, top), a woodblock print by the Japanese artist Katsushika Hokusai. In appropriating the scene, Wall wanted to imitate the dual nature he found present in Hokusai's work. He started by very carefully analysing its composition, drawing lines to discover how Hokusai had used a rectangular grid as the basis for ordering its elements. All the figures, the trees and every sheet of paper turned out to have been placed in specific sections of this rectangle, creating a classical composition which at the same time appears very natural, as if it could be a modern snapshot. Wall wanted his own restaging, too, to hover between two perceptual states: one in which the viewer believes that the scene could be spontaneously unfolding in front of his or her eyes, and the other in which she or he can appreciate it as the product of an elaborate process. To achieve this, he combined more than 100 individual elements in a digital composite (left, bottom).

Is it possible to see that this is an elaborately staged scene? A clue can perhaps be found in the slightly surrealistic details: the man looking up to the sky seems immaculately dressed, as though for an important meeting at the office, yet he wears sturdy outdoor boots that are more suitable for walking the dog on a windy autumn day. The fact that the man thought of wearing his long hair in a bun, and the electricity poles echoing the shape of Japanese characters, are intelligent details that add to the homage.

Public or private?
Public or private?
Public or private?
Public or private?
Public or private?
Public or private?
Public or private?

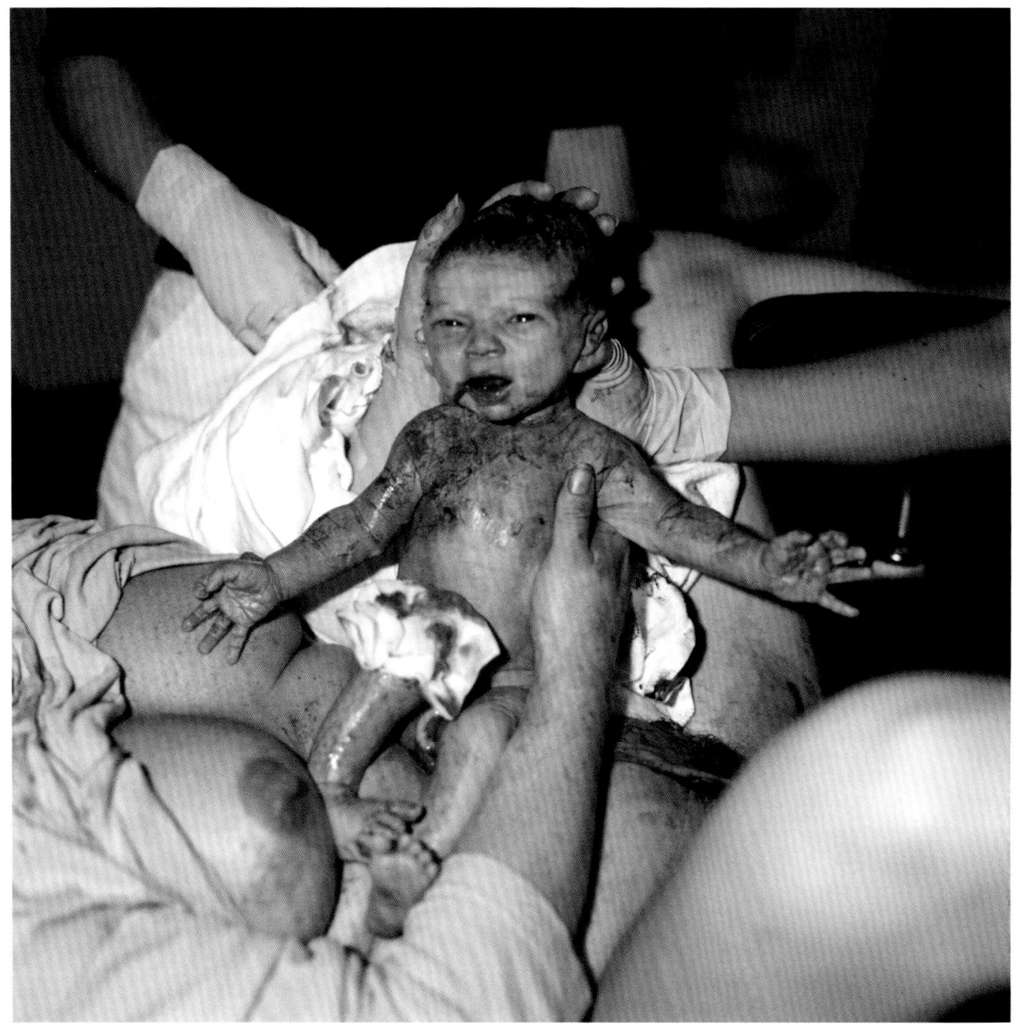

Koos Breukel, *Casper, Alkmaar* (2000)

A photograph shared on social media of a new father cradling his baby with his top off is deemed acceptable, while a mother breastfeeding the same baby is not. The reactions to these images, and the images themselves, reflect how attitudes to intimacy and photography have changed, and how partisan and biased they can be. Historically, pregnancy and the very early months of motherhood were not photographed at all, and, if they were, they were for very private consumption only. Now, however, these experiences are shared as a badge of pride, and even scans of foetuses are widely shared within networks.

It is not just what the photograph shows in terms of content, but also how it is tagged, viewed, liked, geotagged and commented upon which determines how we understand it in terms of its nature as public or private. Photography has always been an excellent medium for making the private public, especially in documentary photography. It has the ability to take a viewer into another world that is not theirs. The more private, distant, different or confrontational this is, generally the more affecting and arresting the work.

Take, for instance, this work (left) by the Dutch photographer Koos Breukel (born 1962). It is rare to see the reality of a baby being born. If we have not given birth ourselves or been witness to a birth, our experience of it is usually a sanitised Hollywood version. A question that a photograph like this might provoke is: Why would anyone else be interested in seeing a picture of the photographer's baby being born? It is a valid question, but it is worth considering that it is not one that is often asked of literature – biographies and autobiographies are big sellers, but personal photography is often seen as self-indulgent.

For Breukel, the ruthlessness of life and death is essential to his work. As a young photographer he took portraits of politicians and pop stars, but the performative aspect of public personas and the portraiture genre made him long for more genuine content. Boiling down human existence to essential components became a major driving force for Breukel, and is indeed an important narrative thread for many photographers. Like personal stories in literature, the best autobiographical photography also taps into something universal that many people can relate to. The sharing of traditionally very private moments seeks a similar set of goals: to record, to reveal, to interpret and, possibly, to influence – perhaps even to change – the social world or at least the viewer's understanding of it.

Another question that arises is what the notions of private and public really mean. Is the distinction dissolving in our media-driven world, when people are filmed constantly in streets, squares and shops, often without realising is happening? Meanwhile, people photograph and film themselves in the most banal situations and put the results online. As photography, social attitudes and technology struggle to keep up with one another, new lines are drawn daily in terms of what is acceptable, to whom and in which cultures.

Recently, the Dutch documentary makers Tim den Besten and Nicolaas Veul conducted research into the effects of being online 24/7 in an experiment called 'Super Stream Me'. They attempted to stream their lives continuously for three weeks. During the study, they experienced the well-documented phenomenon of the performative online identity, in which a version of the self deemed most appropriate for the assumed audience is created. The constraints they imposed upon themselves caused so much stress that they had to end the experiment prematurely. In real life, expectations are different and depend on the platform on which you share your life (for example Facebook, Twitter, Instagram or Snapchat). José van Dijck, author of *The Culture of Connectivity: A Critical History of Social Media*, claims: 'On Instagram, you don't portray yourself; you paint a desirable persona ... so each selfie peculiarly reflects the flair and function of the platform through which it is posted, perhaps even more so than its sender's taste. The medium is a big part of the message.' One can reasonably ask, then, if the act of sharing a photograph today is not 'making the private public', but a denial of the possibility of genuinely private moments, as determined by the platform of your choice.

Aside from the autobiographical narratives so dominant now, there are many other ways in which photographers grapple with what is truly private and how it becomes public. For example, the portraits of Berber Muslim women taken in 1960 by the French photographer Marc Garanger (born 1935) in colonial Algeria give rise to ethical questions of privacy. While working for the French Army in the Algerian War (1954–62) he was commissioned to make identity cards for detained women. This woman (right) stares into the lens with a silent but unmistakable anger. It is part of a series of unveiled women – one of 2,000 portraits taken by the photographer. These portraits have been called images of violation: not only was the women's right to privacy taken from them, but the subsequent display of the images (initially created for administrative purposes) decades later within a gallery context, as well as their inclusion in this book, could be interpreted as further violations. However, when Garanger returned to Algeria in 2004, he met many of the women again, and discovered that in a lot of cases his portraits were the only photographs they had of themselves, and were treasured private documents.

The lines between private and public are complex. Different contexts result in ever-changing attitudes and circumstances. Returning to the theme of birth, imagine, for example, a mother sharing a photo of herself breastfeeding her baby on a social media profile open only to those she has invited. This mother will probably find that commercials for formula milk start to dominate her sidebars shortly after she posted. This is because the platform has effectively sold her private picture to advertisers. So a loving moment shared in good faith with close family members turns out to be not very private after all.

This makes it worth considering, before we post any image, why it seems worth sharing, who might be looking at it and who has access to it. Private moments are sometimes best kept private – especially with photographs of those who are not yet in charge of their digital identity.

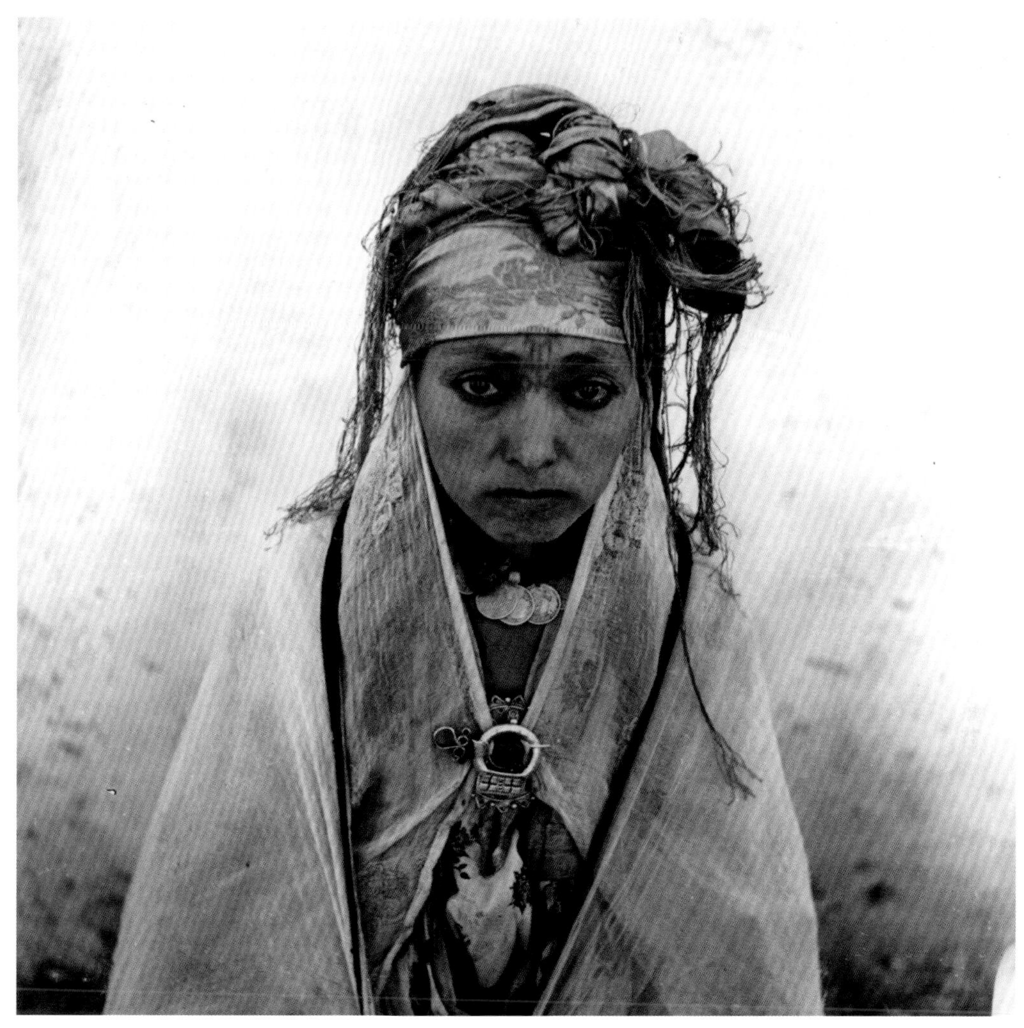

Marc Garanger, from *Algerian Women* (1960)

Susan Meiselas (born 1948)
***Ginger, Carlisle, Pennsylvania* (1975)**

Photographed over a period of three summers during the time of debates around women's liberation, American photographer Susan Meiselas's 1972–75 *Carnival Strippers* series documents backstage moments with women who stripped in itinerant carnivals around the USA. Working with a handheld camera, travelling with the women and enduring the long nights with them, Meiselas was able to gain their trust, leading to them giving her intimate portraits and interviews. Portraits like this one of Ginger were done at the request of the young women, as many did not find the pictures of the actual show to be of any interest.

Working closely and hearing the stories of the women, Meiselas learned that many of the women came from poor backgrounds, but quickly had to shift her assumptions and judgments about them as victims. She has spoken about how she was struck by their ease and self-assuredness with regards to their bodies. The interviews that accompany the portraits give the women a voice and negate any judgments that might occur in reaction to the photographs. In the case of Ginger, she saw her profession as a trade-off, acknowledging that she was being exploited, but only in the service of a larger purpose – to save up for college.

The final project resulted in a book and an installation for an ongoing exhibition consisting of photographs, sound (made from 150 hours of tape) and moving images. The shift from the public shows, where the women are on display, to the more relaxed moments occurring backstage, and these personal portraits, highlights the stark contrast in the ways in which people behave in public and in private, and how everyone is complicit in shaping the difference.

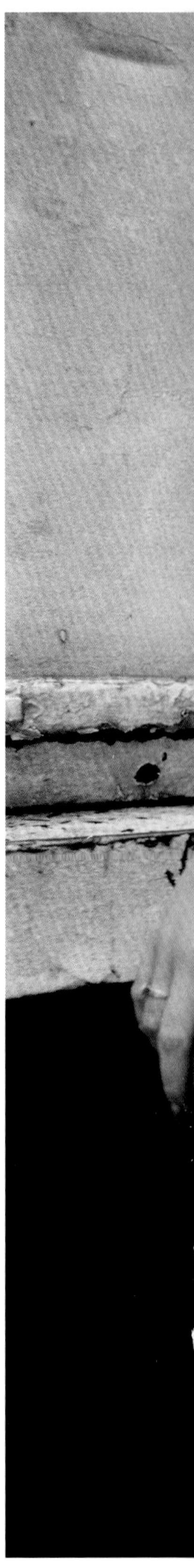

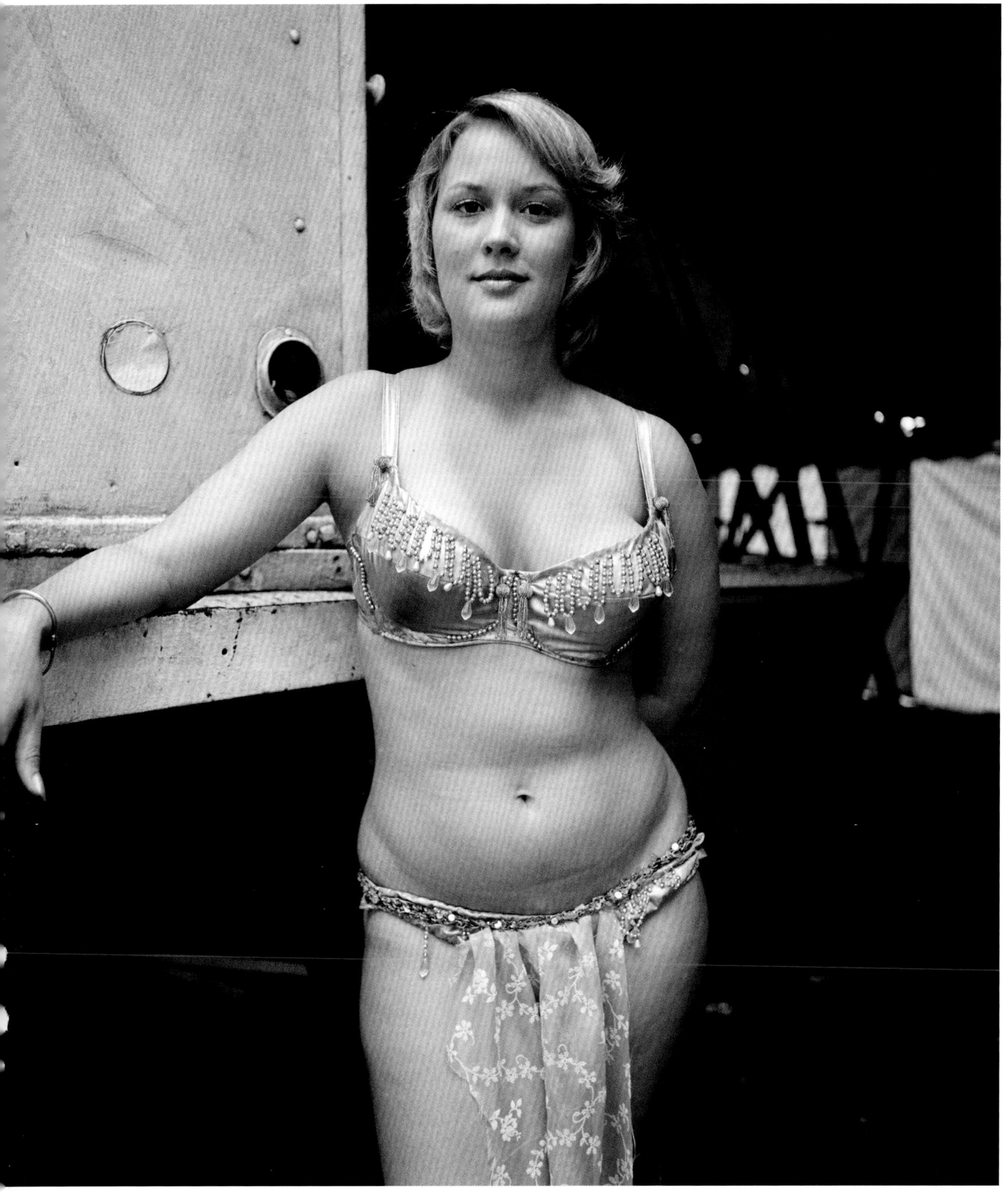

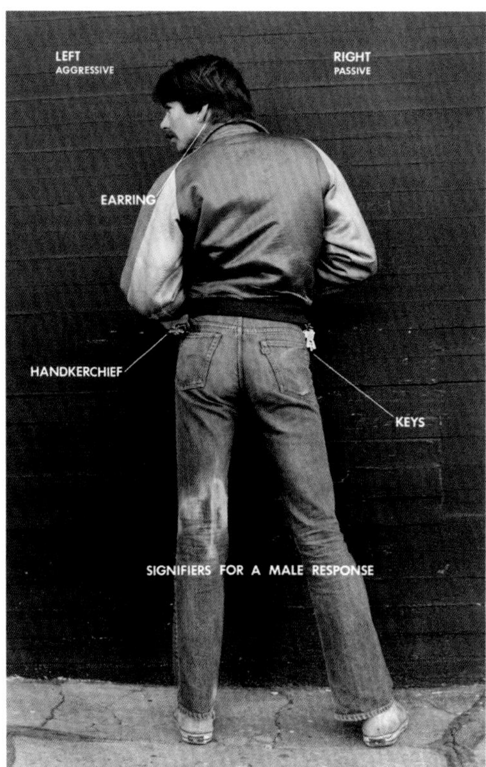

John Wickens (1865–1936)
***Henry Cyril Paget, 5th Marquess of Anglesey* (c.1900)**

Hal Fischer (born 1950)
***Signifiers for a Male Response* (1977)**

Since the invention of photography, the portrait genre developed fast. By the end of the 19th century, everyone who was anyone had had their picture taken. The commercial side of the medium – in the form of *cartes de visite* and, later, postcards – was thriving, and did much to promote the celebrities of the day, giving them national (and international) presence. Those who were formerly known only through visits to the theatre or rare public sightings became public property.

An example of this is provided by this photographic postcard (opposite) of the so called 'Dancing Marquess', so named for his semi-private performances of eroticised 'Butterfly Dances'. Henry Cyril Paget was an eccentric, extravagant and short-lived British aristocrat who frittered away much of the vast family fortune on furs and jewels. Embracing the performative joys of photography to construct his dazzling, transgressive public persona, Paget posed regularly in elaborate costumes that he had made especially for him and his troupe of actors who performed in the converted chapel of his ancestral home.

Photography made Paget a public character that his family would have rather kept private. After his early death at the age of 29 in 1905, his family destroyed all other records of him and sold his belongings. His *Bystander* magazine obituary stated, 'His example will remain one of the strongest arguments against our hereditary system that the most ardent revolutionist would wish for.'

Although his sexuality was never openly discussed, Paget's identity as a gay man was signalled through his clothing. To be able to do so betrays a position of privilege that is not afforded to everyone. Hal Fischer's project *Gay Semiotics*, in which the photo above was published, took this idea and (with tongue in cheek) showed the subtle methods of communication and identification that gay men in the Castro neighbourhood of San Francisco used to signal to others their sexuality. Fischer has said, 'The whole series and my subsequent work in that period, was about me, and my place in time, and the community I was in.' It was about coding sexuality in order to be understood when it was not possible to speak openly about it.

In the culture of apps like Grindr and Scruff, with their own coded queer languages, Paget's and Fischer's examples can both be seen as early methods of making private information public to those who know how to access it.

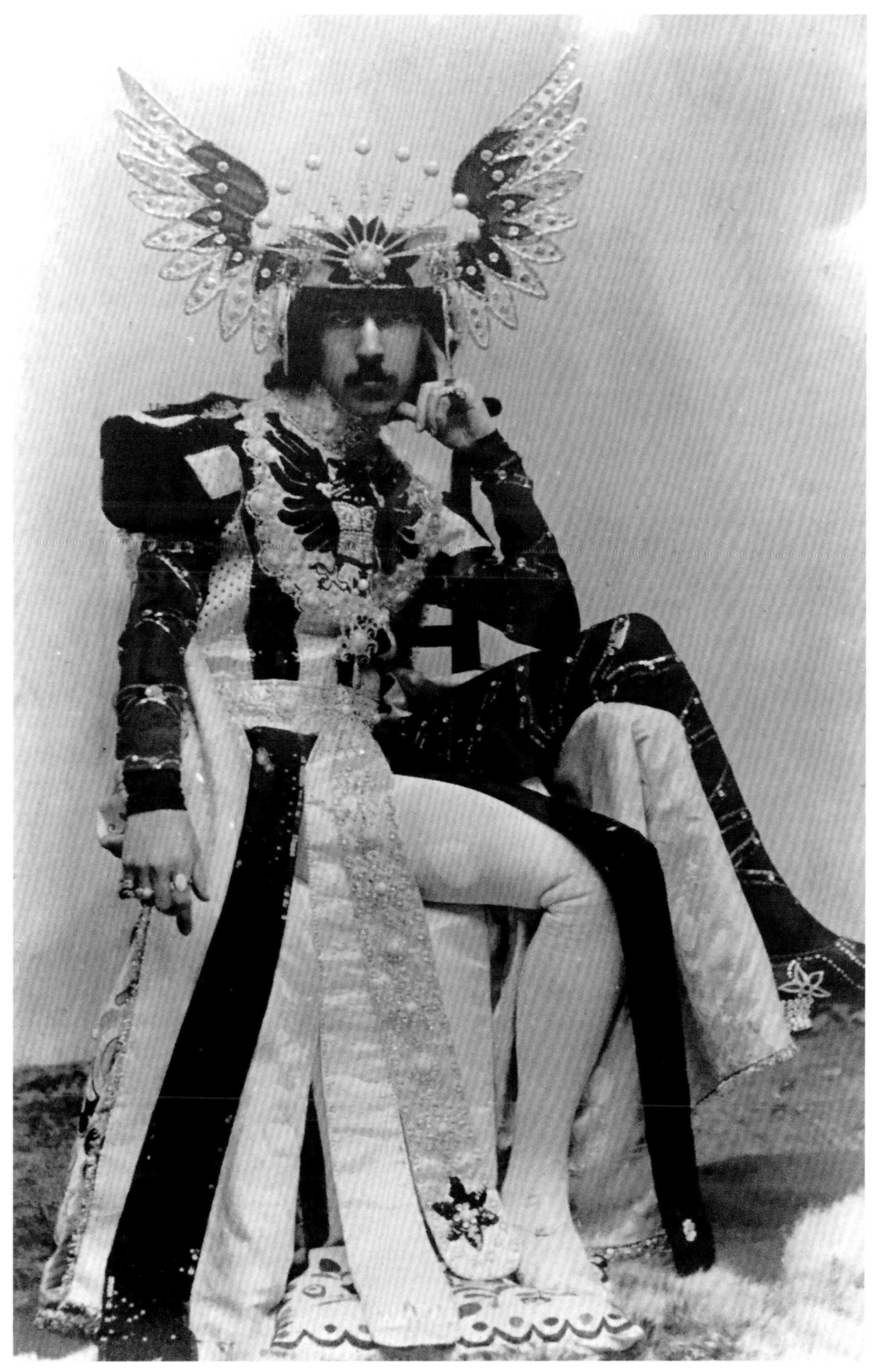

Lady Clementina Hawarden (1822–1865)
***The Return From the Ball* (c.1863)**

This mysterious photograph comes from an album by the Victorian photographer Lady Clementina Hawarden and shows her two daughters, Clementina Maude and Isabella Grace. Like many early pioneers of photography, Lady Hawarden was wealthy and privileged – photography was an expensive and time-consuming pursuit. Little is known about her, but her photographs show remarkable skill and a striking aesthetic. She was a skilful manipulator of natural light, and her photographs often utilise windows, sunshine and shadows to arresting effect.

In Hawarden's scenes, the rooms of her house become a stage on which her daughters pose enigmatically to create mysterious tableaux. One of her characteristic devices is the use of twinning – either by the mirrored shapes formed by the poses of her daughters, or more literally via the use of mirrors. Clementina Maude and Isabella Grace are often dressed in their own clothes, but also sometimes wear elaborate costumes, as was common in aristocratic circles at the time. The photographs are private glimpses into a convivial female world from another era. They are dreamy and atmospheric – an effect that is exaggerated by the albumen process used to develop them, which over time has washed the photographic paper with a yellowish glow due to the egg white used in the emulsion.

Making these photographs would have been a slow and painstaking process, and the fact that so many of Hawarden's photographs have survived is a testament to the shared commitment of the women in the family to creating this intimate photographic world. At the time of their creation, the images were pasted into albums to be enjoyed privately, but they became public in 1939 when Hawarden's granddaughter Lady Clementina Tottenham donated 775 photographs to the Victoria and Albert Museum in London. They have become an important marker in the history of photography, and have since influenced many contemporary artists using the medium.

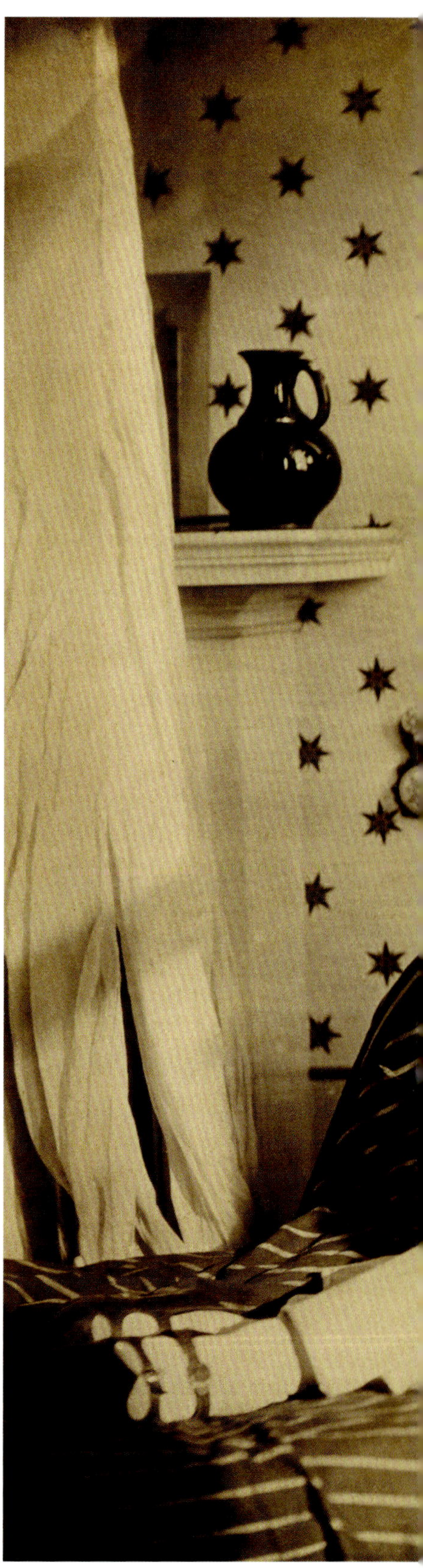

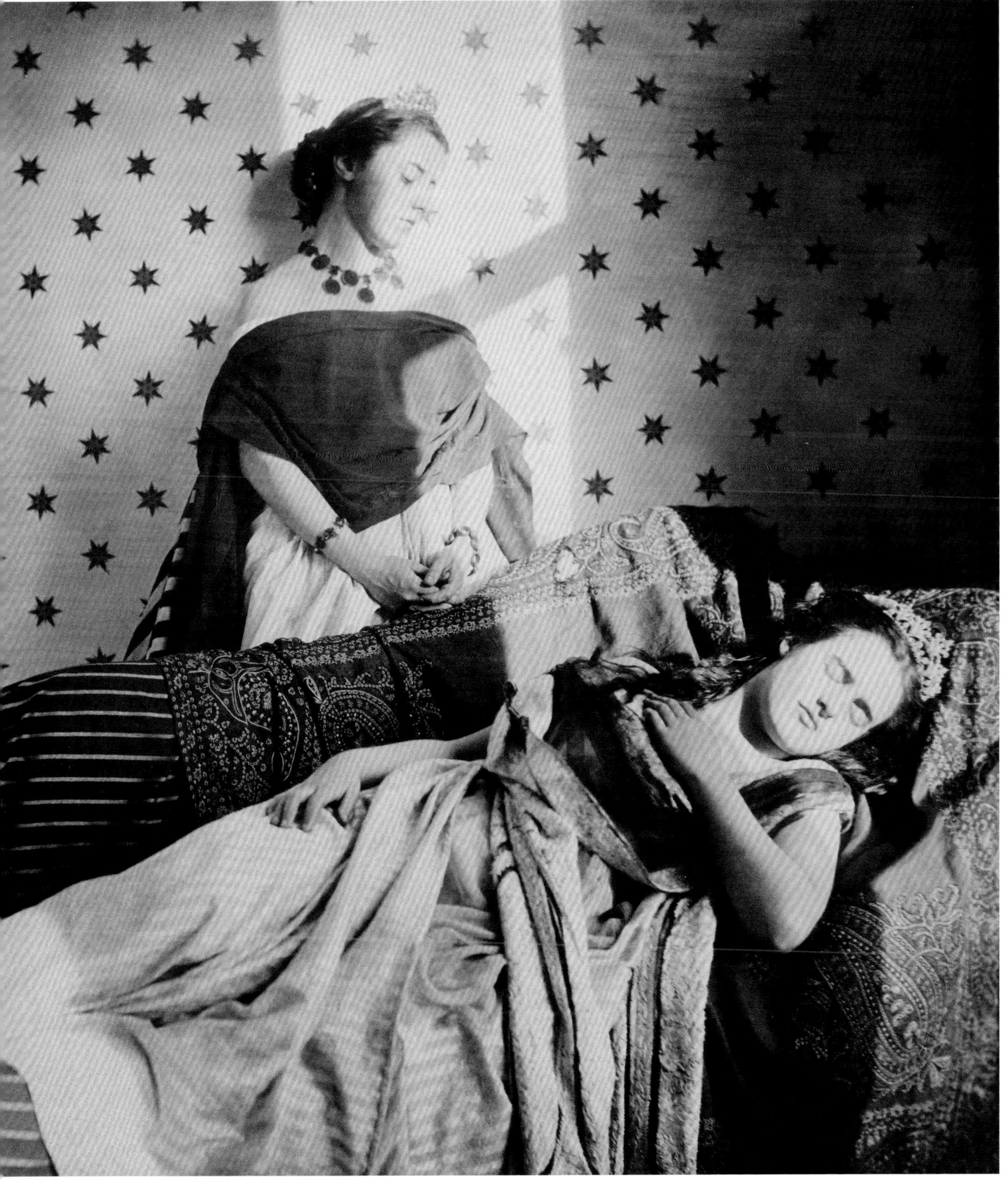

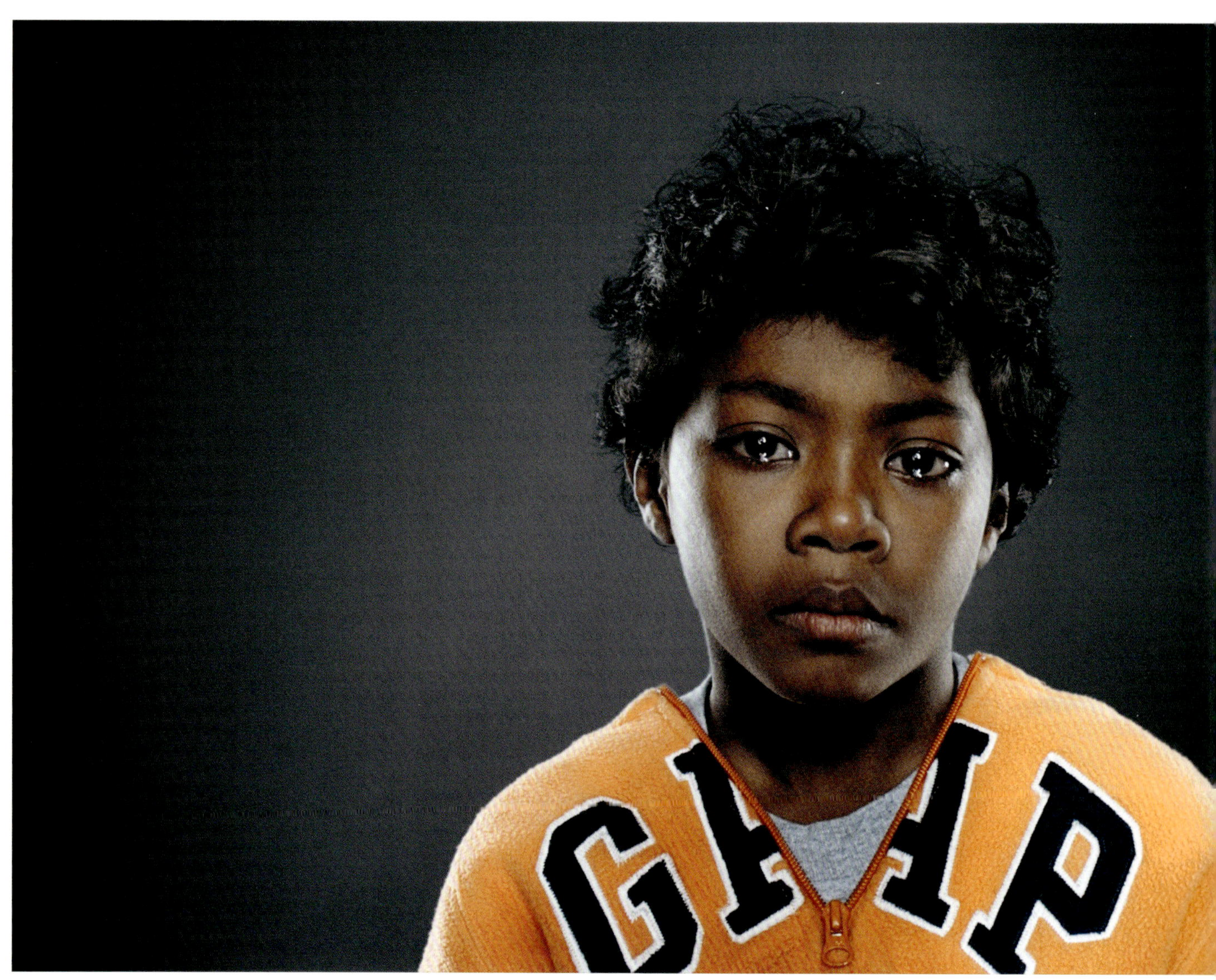
GAP

Robbie Cooper (born 1969)
Drew Hugh, 7, Playing 'Hulk', New York, USA, 2008
from *Immersion* (2008)

Amazed by the amount of time children spend in front of the screen, British artist Robbie Cooper filmed a cross-section of society as they watched a cartoon or horror film, or while they played a game. Because of their engrossment in the film or a virtual world, the children forgot that they were being filmed. Cooper applied a technique whereby the children appear to be looking directly at the camera, thus producing a voyeuristic sensation in the viewer: one is face to face with the children's undisguised emotions. The hatred, joy and fear – and also the apathy – is alarming.

The children are so absorbed in their games that they uninhibitedly talk to the screen – Cooper captured this on video. They seem to address the viewer as they snarl: 'Come back here, let me stab you', 'Let me kill you' and 'You'll get knifed'. The sound of machine guns does not evoke horror, but makes them grin instead. But here, Drew Hugh has tears in his eyes, lending this image the quality of a modern-day version of Bragolin's *Crying Boy* painting that was mass-produced during the 1950s.

Cooper's stills and videos play to concerns about the anti-social consequences of lengthy screen time and the children's supposed social isolation, as cut off from the real world. Once, similar questions were asked of reading and writing. Socrates argued that writing weakened the memory because one had to remember less, and in the 19th century, there was concern because the accessibility of books was said to have a damaging effect on society. The criticism failed to inhibit a further spread – just as daily lengthy screen time has now become normalised.

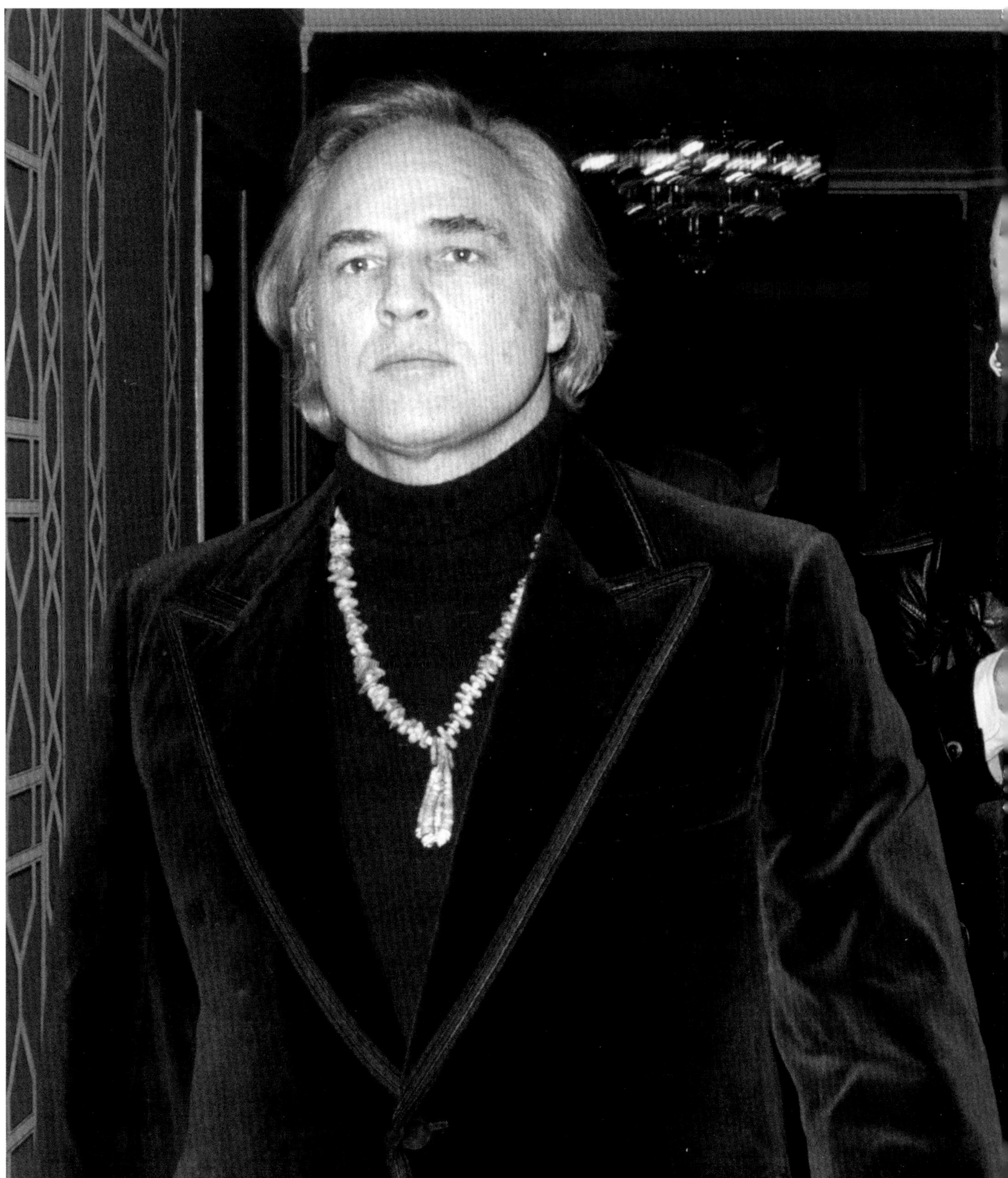

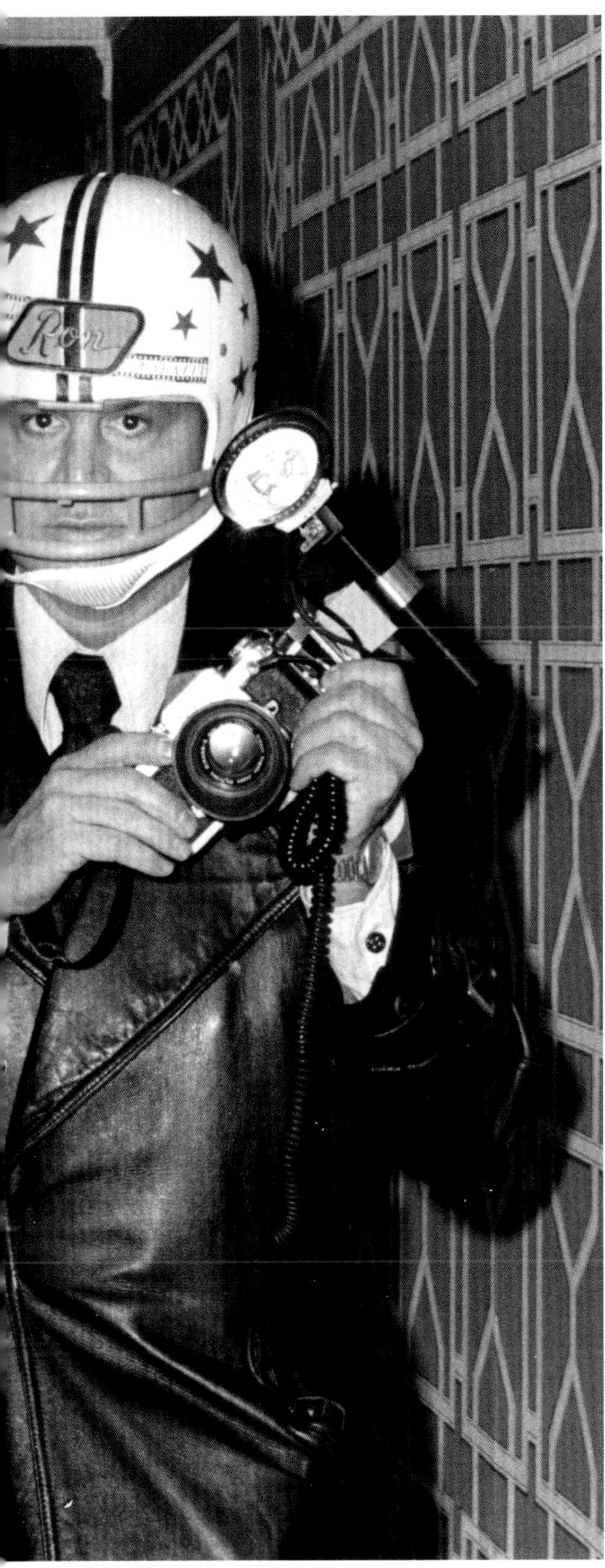

Ron Galella (born 1931)
Marlon Brando and Ron Galella at the Waldorf Hotel, 26 November 1973 **(1973)**

The paparazzi genre raises questions about the cult of celebrity, the celebrity's right to privacy, and press freedom. 'There is a popular notion that the photographer is by nature a voyeur,' artist Nan Goldin has said. The American Ron Galella, one of the most noted and notorious paparazzi in the history of the profession, claimed that he was just as interested in the private personas of celebrities as he was in their public image, curious as to whether they were as glamorous in real life as on screen. The fact that getting your picture on the cover of a magazine yields a lot of money might also have been a motivation for his chosen career.

In 1973 Galella followed the Hollywood actor Marlon Brando to a New York restaurant. It wasn't the first time the photographer had stalked the actor, but this time, it seems, Marlon lost all self-control – in one single punch knocking five teeth out of Galella's lower jaw. The paparazzo subsequently sued Brando but nonetheless continued his pursuit of the actor. On their next encounter later that year, however, he took the precaution of donning a football helmet with his first name on it, and a fellow photographer, Paul Schmalbach, took a photograph of the encounter.

Galella became known for the retaliative actions taken by his 'victims': Jackie Kennedy Onassis obtained a restraining order to keep him at a distance (the trial became a groundbreaking case in the area of paparazzi photography), Brigitte Bardot had him hosed down and Richard Burton sent people to steal his film and beat him up. Ironically, the Brando incident and the lawsuit that Onassis filed made Galella himself famous, which was his ultimate goal – and he carried his nickname 'paparazzi superstar' with pride. Not all celebrities shunned him, however. Andy Warhol was an advocate for Galella's work, saying: 'My idea of a good picture is one that's in focus and of a famous person doing something infamous.'

Mary Ellen Mark (1940–2015)
***The Damm Family in Their Car, Los Angeles* (1987)**

Sometimes photographs that at first glance look tender and beautiful turn out to be as shocking as a war scene. The American photographer Mary Ellen Mark dedicated many years of her career to a documentary series about the 'unfamous', as she called the most vulnerable people in society – from 11-year-old Indian girls sold by their parents to brothels in Mumbai, to the Damm family in Los Angeles, shown here.

At the time Mark took this photograph, the mother and her children's stepfather were addicted and homeless, living with a six-year-old daughter and four-year-old son as well as a pit bull terrier in a car. *Life* magazine published the photographs of the Damm family in the same year that Mark made them; the story, names and faces of the children were made public. It might be argued that the publication served a worthy purpose: to draw attention to the appalling situation a family can find itself in. Readers showered the Damm family with donations.

When *Life* followed up on the family eight years later, with Mark returning to photograph them, nothing had improved. Just months after the donations had poured in, the money was all gone and the family were homeless again. In addition, it transpired that the stepfather had been sexually abusing the daughter. This was all reported in the same magazine.

We might contrast this series with Nick Hedges's Shelter archive (page 168), which similarly shows families with young children living in unacceptable housing conditions. Apart from the initial use of Hedges's photographs by the charity that had commissioned the assignment, the archive was placed under an embargo for 30 years before it could be made public. The aim was to protect the privacy of the people depicted: after three decades, it was considered, they would be unrecognisable.

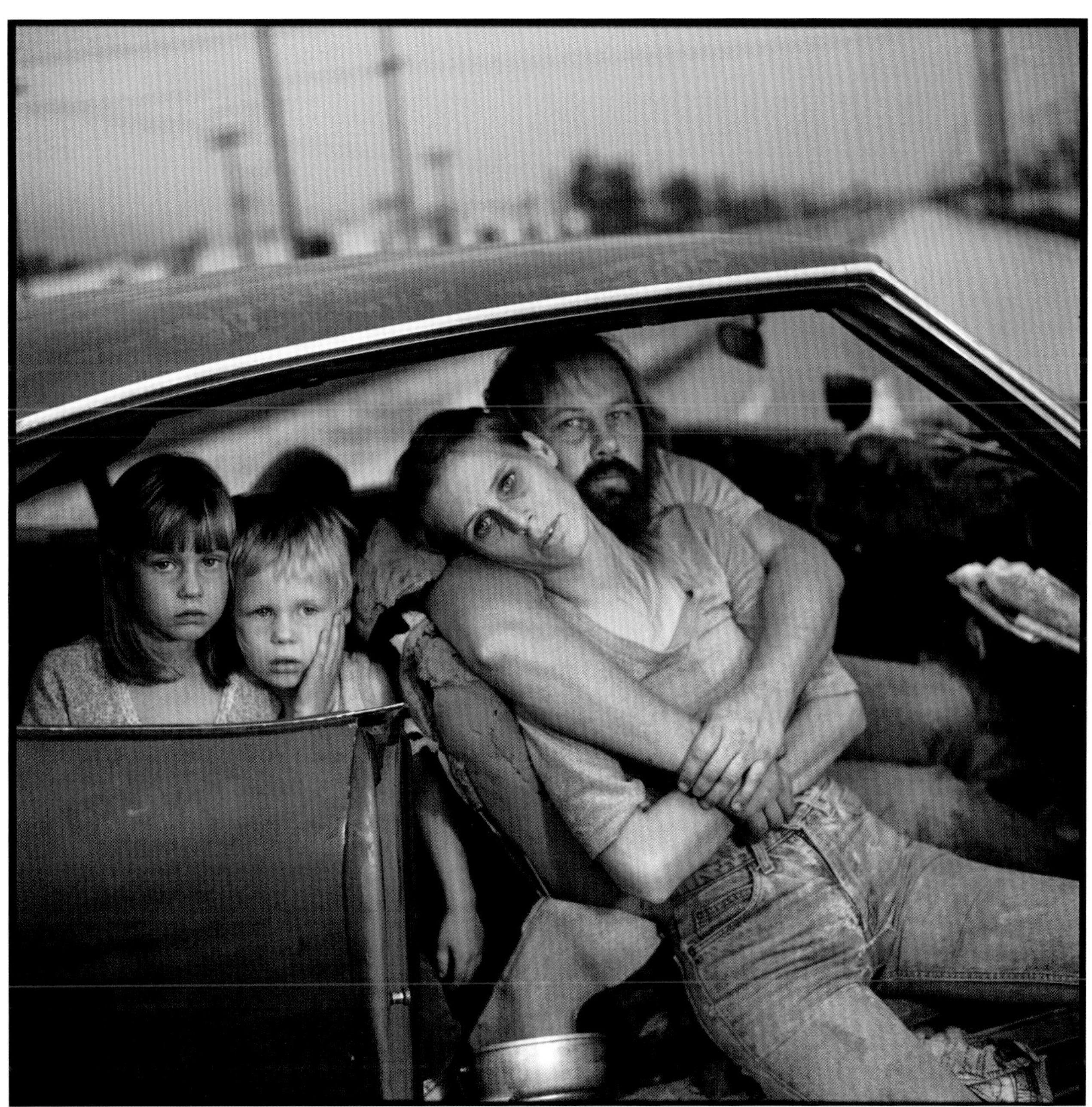

Index

Picture credits

7 © DACS 2019. Courtesy David Zwirner; 8 Historical Picture Archive/Corbis via Getty Images; 13 © Mickalene Thomas/ Artist Rights Society (ARS), New York. Courtesy the artist and Lehmann Maupin, New York, Hong Kong, and Seoul; 16a Collection Société française de photographie; 16b Leo Patrizi/ iStock; 19 © Sophie Calle. ADAGP, Paris and DACS, London 2019. Courtesy Galerie Perrotin; 21 Metropolitan Museum of Art, New York. Gift of John Goldsmith Phillips, 1976. (CC0 1.0); 23 SSPL/Getty Images; 24–25 © Andreas Gursky. Courtesy Sprüth Magers, Berlin and London/DACS 2019; 26–27 Library of Congress, Prints and Photographs Division; 28–29 © Robert Capa/International Center of Photography/Magnum Photos; 30–31 © Joan Fontcuberta; 32 © Viviane Sassen. Courtesy Stevenson gallery, South Africa; 36 © Shimon Attie, DACS 2019. Courtesy Jack Shainman Gallery, New York; 39 Archiv Gerstenberg/ullstein bild via Getty Images; 40 © Tatsumi Orimoto. Courtesy Galerie DNA, Berlin; 41 © Ishiuchi Miyako. Courtesy The Third Gallery Aya, Osaka; 43 Courtesy George Eastman Museum © Nickolas Muray Photo Archives; 44–45 © Nan Goldin; 46–47 Kodak Collection/National Museum of Science & Media/Science & Society Picture Library. All rights reserved; 48–49 PDNB Gallery, Dallas, Texas; 50–51 © Bertien van Manen. Courtesy Robert Morat, Berlin; 52–53 Objects of Study, Studio Shehrazade project, Hashem El Madani collection. Courtesy the Arab Image Foundation; 57 Public Domain via Wikimedia Commons; 58 Welcome to Pine Point (pinepoint.nfb.ca) © 2010 National Film Board of Canada. All rights reserved; 60–61 © Henk Wildschut; 62 photo © Tate, London 2019 © Sebastião Salgado/Amazonas/nbpictures; 64 © Alessandra Sanguinetti/Magnum Photos; 67 © The Estate of Ralph Eugene Meatyard. Courtesy Fraenkel Gallery, San Francisco; 68–69 Courtesy of the George Eastman Museum. With the permission of the Kodak Eastman Company; 70, 71 © Gillian Wearing. Courtesy Maureen Paley, London, Tanya Bonakdar Gallery, New York/Los Angeles, and Regen Projects, Los Angeles; 72–73 © Sarah Lucas. Courtesy Sadie Coles HQ, London; 76 SSPL/Getty Images; 79a Sven Hoppe/dpa/ Alamy Live News; 79b Interfoto/Alamy; 80 © Succession Yves Klein c/o DACS 2019; Photo: Shunk-Kender © J Paul Getty Trust. Getty Research Institute, Los Angeles (2014.R20); 82–83 Alison Jackson, Artist, London. www.alisonjackson.com @ alisonjackson; 84–85 SSPL/Getty Images; 87a TASS/Getty Images; 87b Ria Novosti/AFP via Getty Images; 88 Granger Collection, NYC/TopFoto; 90–91 © Christoph Bangert. Courtesy the artist and Kehrer Verlag, Heidelberg; 94 © Fred Hüning; 96, 97 Library of Congress, Prints and Photographs Division;

98 Courtesy Shady Lane Productions, Berlin and Tanya Bonakdar Gallery, New York/Los Angeles; 99 © Philip-Lorca diCorcia. Courtesy the artist and David Zwirner; 101 © Broomberg & Chanarin. Courtesy Lisson Gallery; 102, 103 © Tate, London 2019 © Mike Mandel and Estate of Larry Sultan; 105 © Royal Photographic Society/National Museum of Science & Media/Science & Society Picture Library. All rights reserved; 107 © Jan Hoek. Image courtesy the artist and Galerie Ron Mandos; 108–109 © Hans-Peter Feldmann, DACS 2019; 112a Pictures From History/Bridgeman Images © Estate of Alberto Korda/ADAGP, Paris and DACS, London 2019; 112b Mauricio Lima/AFP/Getty Images; 115 © Marc Riboud/Magnum Photos; 116–117 Nick Ut/AP/Shutterstock; 118 © Eleanor Macnair; 119 Christie's/Bridgeman © 2019 The Andy Warhol Foundation for the Visual Arts, Inc. Licensed by DACS, London 2019; 121 REX/Shutterstock; 122 © National Science & Media Museum/ Science & Society Picture Library. All rights reserved; 124–5 Kevin Carter/Sygma via Getty Images; 127 © Joel Meyerowitz. Courtesy Howard Greenberg Gallery; 131 The J Paul Getty Museum, Los Angeles. (CC BY 4.0); 132 Unknown. Formerly UPI; 134 Sipa/REX/Shutterstock; 136–37 © Kohei Yoshiyuki. Courtesy Yossi Milo Gallery, New York; 138 IWM/Getty Images; 141 Weegee (Arthur Fellig)/International Center of Photography/ Getty Images; 142 © Hellen van Meene. Courtesy the artist and Yancey Richardson, New York; 144–45 Nationaal Archief/ Collectie Spaarnestad © Estate of Volker Krämer; 148 © Tate; 151a Courtesy the artist and Roslyn Oxley9 Gallery, Sydney; 151b © Keith Arnatt Estate. All rights reserved. DACS/Artimage 2019. Image courtesy Keith Arnatt Estate, London; 152–53 © Tracey Emin. All rights reserved. DACS 2019; 154 © 1987 The Peter Hujar Archive LLC. Courtesy Pace/MacGill Gallery, New York and Fraenkel Gallery, San Francisco; 156–57 © Martin Parr/ Magnum Photos; 159 © Don McCullin/Contact Press Images; 160–61 © James Mollison; 163 © Seydou Keïta/SKPEAC. Courtesy CAAC – The Pigozzi Collection; 164 National Gallery of Australia, Canberra/Bridgeman Images; 166 © Nancy Burson, 1982. Courtesy the artist and ClampArt Gallery, New York; 168–69 © Nick Hedges. Nickhedgesphotography.co.uk; 172 Courtesy Stene Projects, Stockholm. Photo: Carl-Henric Tillberg; 175a © Daniel Gordon. Courtesy the artist and M+B Gallery, Los Angeles; 175b © Sherrie Levine. Courtesy the artist and David Zwirner. The Metropolitan Museum of Art, Gift of the Artist, 1995 © Walker Evans Archive, The Metropolitan Museum of Art; 176–77 © Penelope Umbrico. Courtesy Bruce Silverstein Gallery, New York; 178–79 © Barbara Kruger. Courtesy Mary Boone Gallery, New York; 181 Christie's/Bridgeman Images © Harold Edgerton/MIT, courtesy Palm Press, Inc.; 182 © John Stezaker. Courtesy The Approach, London. Photo: FXP Photography; 183 © DACS 2019. Courtesy Mai 36 Galerie, Zurich; 184a Metropolitan Museum of Art, New York. The Howard Mansfield Collection, Purchase, Rogers Fund, 1936 (CC0 1.0); 184b Courtesy of the artist; 188 © Koos Breukel. Courtesy the artist; 191 © Marc Garanger/Corbis via Getty Images; 192–93 © Susan Meiselas/Magnum Photos; 194 Hal Fischer and Project Native Informant © 2019 Hal Fischer; 195 Public Domain via Wikimedia Commons; 196–97 Historical Picture Archive/Corbis via Getty Images; 198–99 © Robbie Cooper; 200–201 Paul Schmalbach/ Ron Galella/WireImage/Getty images; 203 © Mary Ellen Mark.

With thanks to, Jane Ace, Robert Anderson, Koos Breukel, Ben Gardiner, Giulia Hetherington, Katie Jarvis, Jacky Klein, Rachel Silverlight and Denise Wolff.

In addition, we would like to thank all our students whom we have had the pleasure of teaching, and for everything we learned from them along the way.

Finally, this book is dedicated to our daughters: Mila, Fay and Ruby.

Susan Bright and Hedy van Erp.